Generative Linguistics

ROUTLEDGE HISTORY OF LINGUISTIC THOUGHT SERIES

Consultant Editor: Talbot J. Taylor, College of William and Mary, Williamsburg, Virginia

Generative Linguistics

A historical perspective

Frederick J. Newmeyer

History of Linguistic Thought
Consultant Editor: Talbot J. Taylor

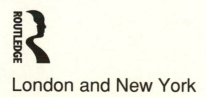

London and New York

First published 1996
by Routledge
11 New Fetter Lane, London EC4P 4EE

Simultaneously published in the USA and Canada
by Routledge
29 West 35th Street, New York, NY 10001

First published in paperback 1997

© 1996 Frederick J. Newmeyer

Typeset in Palatino by LaserScript, Mitcham, Surrey
Printed and bound in Great Britain by
T.J. International Ltd, Padstow, Cornwall

British Library Cataloguing in Publication Data
A catalogue record for this book is available from the British Library

Library of Congress Cataloguing in Publication Data
A catalogue record for this book is available from the Library of Congress

ISBN 0–415–11553–1 (hbk)
ISBN 0–415–17126–1 (pbk)

To Marilyn

Contents

Part III Grammatical theory and second language learning

Note on text

Some of the material in this book has been presented or published before:

Chapter 1 (Original material)

Chapter 2 Never published, but presented at the First Annual Meeting of the North American Association for the History of the Language Sciences, Tulane University, December 1988.

Chapter 3 (1990) in Alice Davison and Penelope Eckert (eds) *The Cornell Lectures: Women in the Linguistics Profession*, Washington: Linguistic Society of America, 43–54.

Chapter 4 (1986) *Language*, 62, 1–19.

Chapter 5 (1989) in Asa Kasher (ed.) *The Chomskyan Turn: Generative Linguistics, Philosophy, Mathematics, and Psychology*, Oxford: Blackwell, 200–30.

Chapter 6 (in press) (co-authored with Stephen R. Anderson, Sandra Chung, and James McCloskey) in A. Crochetière, J. Boulanger and C. Ouellon (eds) *Proceedings of the XVth International Congress of Linguists.*

Chapter 7 (in press) in K. Jankowsky (ed.) *Proceedings of the Sixth International Conference on the History of the Language Sciences*, Philadelphia: John Benjamins.

Chapter 8 (1986) *Linguistic Theory in America: Second Edition*, section 4.2, New York: Academic Press.

Chapter 9 (1986) *Linguistic Theory in America: Second Edition*, sections 5.3–5.5, New York: Academic Press.

Chapter 10 (Original material)

Chapter 11 (1989) *Language*, 65: 2, 395–7.

Chapter 12 (1988) (co-authored with Steven H. Weinberger) in Suzanne Flynn and Wayne O'Neil (eds) *Linguistic Theory in Second Language Acquisition*, Dordrecht: Reidel, 34–46.

Chapter 13 (1987) *Second Language Research* 3:1–19.

Chapter 14 (1990) *Historiographia Linguistica*, 17:1/2, 167–81.

All chapters reprinted with permission.

Note on the paperback edition

The author would like to thank Dr Frits Stuurman (Utrecht Institute of Linguistics OTS) for his valuable help in the preparation of this edition.

Chapter 1

Introduction

This collection assembles all of my papers on the origins and development of generative grammar, as well as a few sections of my book *Linguistic Theory in America* (*LTA*). Several of the papers have never appeared in print before or were published in such obscure locations that this is the first realistic opportunity for interested linguists and historiographers of linguistics to look at them. The essays in this volume were written over a fifteen-year period, from the first edition of *LTA*, which appeared in 1980, to the review of *Ideology and Linguistic Theory: Noam Chomsky and the Deep Structure Debates* by Geoffrey Huck and John Goldsmith, which I prepared expressly for this volume.

I considered two possible organizing schemes for the chapters: chronological or thematic, and opted for the latter. My thinking has developed in various ways, of course, since 1980, but as far as the major issues treated here are concerned – the nature of the Chomskyan revolution, the fights between generative semanticists and interpretivists in the late 1960s and early 1970s, and the recent convergences within generative syntax – I have felt no particular need to re-evaluate profoundly my earlier positions. Hence a thematic organization seems to make the most sense.

The origins and development of generative grammar are now a hot topic, as the amount of recent work devoted to it testifies (Harris 1993a, b; Huck and Goldsmith 1995; R. Lakoff 1989). But when I started to address this question in the late 1970s, I can't say that I received much encouragement, either from the community of historiographers of linguistics or from the community of generative grammarians. The former tended to believe (and, by and large, still do believe) that my training in, and commitment to, the basic foundational principles of generative grammar would distort my perception and thus my analysis of developments in the field. I've never known what to make of such criticism. Would analogous suspicions be forthcoming in any scientific field but linguistics? Would a study of the birth and the early development of relativity theory, for example, be suspect if written by a physicist or historian of physics who believed in its correctness? A 'believer's' view stands in danger of manifesting a certain type of bias, to be sure, but is such bias likely to be more pernicious that than manifested by one who has gone on record as *opposing* the major theoretical pillars of a field? Unfortunately, a sizeable proportion of historiographers of the field fall into the latter category.

The reaction of generative grammarians to my decision to chronicle and analyse the history of the field was more complex. On the one hand, they feared that I would become tarred with the brush of being an 'historian of linguistics', who, to many generativists, occupy a status level even lower than that of 'semiotician'. This attitude results from the belief that most people who write on the history of the field have only the most minimal training in modern linguistics and devote their careers to attempting to demonstrate that their pet medieval grammarian or philosopher thought up some technical term before somebody else's pet medieval grammarian or philosopher. Some well-meaning friends warned me that to join their ranks would be to commit professional suicide. They were wrong, I think.

On the other hand, there is also a certain snob appeal to being a front-line theoretician. Departing from their ranks to take a (more-or-less) detached view of their work appeared to many to be opting out of the only important task for a linguist: pushing back the frontiers of theory. While writing *LTA*, I was made to feel by some theoreticians like an art historian or critic who flunked out of art school and ended up living out his or her creative fantasies by passing judgment on the output of the real artist.

Nevertheless, the generally positive reception of *LTA* within the community of generative grammarians was heartening, and convinced me that there is a place for the theoretician-cum-historiographer. I've consequently devoted a fair share of my professional time since 1980 to historical questions; the articles in this volume represent, for the most part, a more in-depth look at some of the issues with which I dealt only peripherally in that book. I would also like to think that this positive reception may have played a role in encouraging other theoreticians to undertake work in the history of linguistics (see, for example, Anderson 1985 and Battistella 1990).

Individuals are not necessarily their own best biographers, so my own interpretation of *why* I turned to historiographic work has no privileged place *vis-à-vis* anybody else's. I was a student at Illinois in the late 1960s and, like most students of generative syntax at that time outside of MIT, I was drawn naturally into the framework of generative semantics. (I believe that my Ph.D. dissertation, 'English aspectual verbs', was the second one written – after Jerry Sadock's – to defend that approach.) I continued to publish in 'straight' generative semantics until around 1973, when the direction that it had started to take made me increasingly uncomfortable. I then spent several years attempting to reconcile the claims of early generative semantics, to which I was still committed, with work in the interpretivist framework. This attempt impressed absolutely nobody on either side. By late 1977, when I started work on *LTA*, I was in the 'interpretivist' camp, although it took me another few years before I had definitively lined up with Chomsky's wing, as opposed to the 'lexicalist' wing that had developed into such frameworks as generalized phrase structure grammar and lexical-functional grammar.

I spent most of the mid-1970s, then, trying to figure out where I stood. Increasingly I felt the need to review the foundations, arguments, and methodology of generative syntax. One advantage that I had was the fact that I had spent my dissertation year at MIT, thanks to the (in retrospect) happy circumstance that most of my Illinois Ph.D. committee was on leave that year. Perhaps that had left me with enough of a feel for the views of 'the other side' that I was not mentally strait-jacketed by my generative semantic training. In the autumn of 1977 I devoted a seminar to putting the debates into historical context and from there the idea of writing a book about the history of the field seemed to flow naturally. Certainly, my love of reading history had long made me fantasize about being a history writer. But whatever underlay it, the decision to write *LTA* was the most sensible of my academic life and the year I spent researching it the most pleasant.

I've divided this book, to a certain extent arbitrarily, into three parts. Part I, 'General trends', deals with issues in the history of generative grammar that span its entire history. Part II, 'The linguistic wars', focuses on the internecine debates between generative and interpretive semantics. Part III, 'Grammatical theory and second language learning', presents in historical perspective the attempt to apply the results of generative theory to understanding the process of acquiring and teaching a second language.

I will devote the rest of this introductory chapter to a short commentary on the papers to follow. I presented Chapter 2, 'Bloomfield, Jakobson, Chomsky, and the roots of generative grammar' at the First Annual Meeting of the North American Association for the History of the Language Sciences in 1988. I intended it as a corrective to the view that Chomsky was a relative latecomer to the idea of characterizing linguistic regularity by means of a formal generative grammar. *Syntactic Structures*, so the argument goes, was not published until 1957 whereas Harris and Hockett had put forward the idea of generative grammar in the early 1950s and Bloomfield and Jakobson had presented generative descriptions even a decade earlier. I argue, in rebuttal, that the first modern attempt to present a generative grammar of a language encompassing all levels of description was Chomsky's 1949 bachelor's thesis and that it is extremely unlikely that this work was influenced by either Bloomfield or Jakobson.

As Secretary-Treasurer of the Linguistic Society of America I was invited to present Chapter 3, 'The structure of the field of linguistics and its consequences for women' at a conference entitled 'Women in the Linguistics Profession'. I accepted the invitation with some trepidation, since I have no background in either women's history or feminist theory. In researching my paper, I was shocked to discover that conditions for women in academia actually worsened progressively during the first six decades of this century. It occurred to me that theoretical linguistics is unique in an interesting way. Unlike physics and chemistry, for example, it is perceived as a field which welcomes women; indeed, it is classified as part of the humanities at most universities. At the same time, however, it is a technical field that requires considerable mastery of formalism. I concluded that we might consider publicizing women's success in the field as a way of propagandizing against the idea that women face some intrinsic handicap when it comes to highly technical modes of thinking – an idea that is still more prevalent than one might wish. Chapter 3 was first published in Davison and Eckert (1990).

Probably nothing I have ever written has created a greater stir than Chapter 4, 'Has there been a "Chomskyan revolution" in linguistics?' which first appeared in *Language* (1986). I had to take on three major arguments against such an idea: first, that Chomsky's ideas were not original; second, that most of the world's linguists are not Chomskyans, so there couldn't have been a 'revolution'; and third; that if his ideas *had* been truly revolutionary, the powers-that-were in the field would have tried to suppress them. The first argument at least lends itself to rational debate; the second and third are based simply on a mistaken idea of what a scientific revolution is. Not even the most uncontroversial revolutions in science (Newton's, Darwin's) won over a majority of their field's practitioners until many decades after the central ideas had been propounded. And it has virtually *never* been the case that scientific revolutionaries have found the normal outlets for the dissemination of their ideas closed to them.

Chapter 5, 'Rules and principles in the historical development of generative syntax', was written to counteract the 'official' (Chomskyan) version of the history of generative grammar, which sees steady linear progress through a process of accretion. One can make the case, certainly, that Chomsky's thinking can be characterized in such a fashion. But the field's progress should not be confused with Chomsky's intellectual development. Twice in the past forty years Chomsky has found himself among the minority of generative syntacticians. He stood virtually alone in the late 1960s, when generative semantics ruled the roost, and the 1970s saw a flight to the lexicalist alternatives to trace theory. When we look at developments in the field as a whole, we observe a much more cyclical pattern, in which a theoretical focus on language-particular rules alternates with one emphasizing universal principles. Chapter 5 was first published in Kasher (1991).

I am happy to have had the pleasure of co-authoring Chapter 6, 'Chomsky's 1962 programme for linguistics: A retrospective', with Steve Anderson, Sandy Chung, and Jim McCloskey. We were asked to commemorate, at the Fifteenth International Congress of Linguists, the thirtieth anniversary of the paper that Chomsky had presented at the ninth congress. This paper, 'The logical basis of linguistic theory', was the first exposure of the new theory to an international audience. Our task was to document how Chomsky's ideas had evolved in the intervening thirty years. We found an amazing core of overall consistency. The principal change has been in what he has called the 'second conceptual shift' in generative grammar; a shift from a conception of a grammar as a set of rules to one in which grammatical complexity is derived from the interaction of a set of parameterized principles. Chapter 6 is currently in press.

Chapter 7, 'Linguistic diversity and universal grammar: Forty years of dynamic tension within generative grammar', deals with an analogous theme. It focuses on the question at the heart of the generativist research programme: How do we restrict the class of possible grammars, while at the same time providing sufficient empirical coverage of the incredible diversity that one finds among the 5,000-odd languages of the world? I trace the evolving answer to this question from the earliest days of transformational grammar to the present. More controversially, I take on the criticisms of generative grammarians that profess astonishment at the claim that anything can be learned about the nature of universal grammar from the study of just one language and the criticisms of the theoreticians for relying too much on an analysis of just English and a few other well-studied languages. Chapter 7 is currently in press.

Chapters 8 and 9, 'The steps to generative semantics' and 'The end of generative semantics' respectively, are excerpted from the second edition of *LTA*. Since my accounts of where generative semantics came from and why it collapsed have proved to be the most controversial aspects of that book, it seemed appropriate to reprint them in this collection. Chapter 8 stresses that generative semantics was in every sense a logical – indeed, inevitable – development in generative syntax. If one adopts uncritically the assumptions of Katz and Postal's *An Integrated Theory of Linguistic Descriptions* (1964) and Chomsky's *Aspects of the Theory of Syntax* (1965), and follows them to their logical conclusion, one is going to end up with generative semantics. Hence, there is no way that one can correctly characterize generative semantics as a 'revolution within the revolution', as was the fashion for a time. In other words, conservatism, more than any other factor, was responsible for its instant success. Chomsky's alternative programme, embodying a rich set of lexical and interpretive rules, demanded the abandoning of a fair share of the previous decade's work and theoretical machinery, and for that reason alone faced an uphill struggle for acceptance.

In Chapter 9, I document my claim that generative semantics collapsed because its central claims were refuted empirically and because its methodology increasingly prevented it from being taken seriously as a scientific approach to language. Oddly enough, when I originally wrote those sections over fifteen years ago, I had no idea that I was saying anything controversial. I took it for granted that, except in rare instances, scientists abandon ideas that they have held dear because a better (i.e., more explanatory) set comes along. That is why I came to reject generative semantics and I assumed that is why others did as well. Certainly, there are always sociopolitical factors that form a backdrop to a clash between rival theories. Such factors were present in the mid 1970s and I called attention to them. All in all, however, they just didn't seem that important.

Chapter 10 reviews Geoffrey Huck and John Goldsmith's *Ideology and Linguistic Theory: Noam Chomsky and the Deep Structure Debates*, a book which does attempt to attribute the fall of generative semantics primarily to sociopolitical factors. In Huck and Goldsmith's view, generative semantics and its interpretivist rival were at the root so similar that an argument refuting one was *ipso facto* an argument refuting the other. Hence, they conclude, we have to appeal to external factors to explain its demise. I argue that the authors are mistaken. Their conclusion is based on a mischaracterization of the essential features of generative semantics and an ahistorical view of that approach, which fails to recognize the profound changes that it underwent during the decade of its existence. When these mistakes are corrected, my conclusion that generative semantics was abandoned because its leading ideas were refuted regains all of its plausibility. Chapter 10 was written for this volume.

Chapter 11 is also a review of a book centred around generative semantics, though quite a different one from *Ideology and Linguistic Theory*. The book in question, *The Best of CLS*, assembles important papers from the Chicago Linguistic Society meetings from 1968 to 1975, the majority of which assume or defend the generative semantic framework. I focus my comments on those assumptions implicit in the papers in the collection that have failed to stand the test of time. This provides a useful yardstick, I think, for measuring the amount of progress we have made in theoretical linguistics over the past twenty years. Chapter 11 first appeared in *Language* (1989).

Steven Weinberger and I co-authored Chapter 12, 'The ontogenesis of the field of second language learning research'. We trace the crooked path of research on the processes involved in acquiring a second language, from contrastive analysis to error analysis and through to the current

programme of investigating whether universal grammar drives acquisition. As long as Eric Lenneberg's famous conclusion that the language
acquisition device 'shuts off' at puberty was maintained, there could be
no theoretical interest in second language acquisition at all. Now that this
conclusion (at least in its strongest form) appears to be discredited,
productive work is possible in exploring the degree to which innate
principles of universal grammar direct acquisition and, conversely, on
what can be concluded about universal grammar on the basis of second
language acquisition data. Chapter 12 was first published in Flynn and
O'Neil (1988).

I presented Chapter 13, 'The current convergence in linguistic theory:
Some implications for second language acquisition research', at a British
Association for Applied Linguistics meeting. I was asked to deliver some
remarks on how a second language researcher was to decide which of the
competing frameworks for syntactic analysis he or she should adopt.
Since they seemed on the face of it to be so dramatically different, their
decision would appear to have profound consequences for their work.
That set me to studying in greater depth than I had before the current
work in generalized phrase structure grammar and lexical-functional
grammar. I found to my surprise that there were profound convergences
between those approaches and that of the government-binding theory.
The former were increasingly developing an approach with a high degree
of grammar-internal modularity. In the latter, locality conditions of various sorts were playing more and more of a leading role. I concluded that
while important differences remained among the frameworks, the interesting and heartening convergences lessened to a considerable degree the
hard choices that had to be made by a researcher in an allied domain.
Chapter 13 first appeared in *Second Language Research* (1987).

The last chapter, Chapter 14, is entitled 'Competence vs. performance;
theoretical vs. applied: The development and interplay of two dicho-
tomies in modern linguistics'. In this chapter, I take as a starting point my
conclusion of Chapter 5 – that generative grammar can be divided into
specific historical stages. I then characterize three strategies for drawing
on the results of theoretical linguistics in applied work, which I call the
'mechanical', the 'terminological', and the 'implicational'. I attempt to
show that each stage in the development of the theory has spawned all of
the three strategies for researchers in applied linguistics. The inevitable
conclusion is that second language learning is still an immature discipline
– one whose reliance on the results of generative theory far overshadows
any successful attempt to develop its own programme of theory and
application. Chapter 14 first appeared in *Historiographia Linguistica* (1990).

Part I
General trends

Chapter 2

Bloomfield, Jakobson, Chomsky, and the roots of generative grammar

Three linguistic works written in this century before 1950 are generally regarded as presenting 'generative' analyses of the data that they treat.[1] They are, in chronological order of appearance, Leonard Bloomfield's 'Menomini morphophonemics' (Bloomfield 1939); Roman Jakobson's 'Russian conjugation' (Jakobson 1948); and Noam Chomsky's undergraduate honours essay, 'Morphophonemics of modern Hebrew' (Chomsky 1949). Since Chomsky's essay contained many of the principal ingredients of the theory that would exert a major influence in the field in the coming years, it is natural to enquire to what extent its ideas drew directly from the Bloomfield and Jakobson papers that preceded it.

I will argue that there is no evidence whatsoever that either 'Menomini morphophonemics' or 'Russian conjugation' played a part in the shaping of Chomsky's ideas. After attempting to establish this hypothesis, I will point to other, more plausible, influences on Chomsky's essay.

Let me begin by outlining briefly the three works in question. Bloomfield devoted a major part of his career to the analysis and historical reconstruction of the Algonquian languages. The foremost among them was Menomini, which, in fact, he had come to speak quite fluently. The 'Menomini morphophonemics' paper is a brilliant outline of the morphophonemic component of Menomini, in which a series of ordered rules is presented that map morphophonemic representations on to phonemic representations. Bloomfield, to be sure, had posited ordered rules before 1939 – they appear in his book *Language* (Bloomfield 1933) – and he was to utilize them again after 1939, although never to such an extent as in 'Menomini morphophonemics'. Also, unlike in *Language*, where morphemes are composed of phonemes alone, 'Menomini morphophonemics' makes use of special morphophonemic effect symbols which function to block particular rule applications.[2] Finally, it is worth mentioning that Bloomfield's paper notes that the 'theoretical basic forms' of Menomini (that is, the morphophonemic representations), which were set up by appealing to simplicity considerations alone, approximate the system that had been posited for proto-Algonquian, and that the rules mapping that level on to the phonemic one needed to be ordered in such a way as to mirror the presumed historical development from proto-Algonquian to modern Menomini.

Jakobson's 'Russian conjugation' paper, like Bloomfield's, presents a set of rules mapping a morphophonemic representation on to a phonemic one, although, unlike in Bloomfield's, no special morphophonemic elements are posited. Jakobson derives most of the superficial complexity of the Russian conjugation system by positing a single underlying stem for each verb along with a set of rules that allow each surface stem and desinence to be derived.

Jakobson's endeavour was a more modest one than Bloomfield's in two crucial respects. While Bloomfield posited rules *for the Menomini language*, Jakobson's rules were focused on a circumscribed subpart of Russian with the result that he did not state them with full generality. For example, several rules that he discusses, such as the vowel/zero alternation, substantive softening, and bare softening, occur elsewhere in Russian, yet they are stated in their verbal environments only. Furthermore, 'Russian conjugation' lacks the attention to rule ordering of 'Menomini morphophonemics'. There are instances, for example, of one rule being presented after another, even though the correct derivation demands its prior application.

The most noteworthy feature of 'Russian conjugation', from the point of view of linguistic historiography, is its 'un-Jakobsonianness'. For one thing, Jakobson seems to have had in general little interest in morphophonemics, and when he did consider such phenomena it was as a subpart of morphology. Only in his work on Gilyak do we find anything resembling the rule-centred analysis presented in 'Russian conjugation' (see Jakobson 1957). Jakobson had little interest in rule systems *in general* – to him, categories and their contrasts were paramount in language. The indirect evidence points to Jakobson not considering the paper to be very important. While it triggered a dozen imitations from his students – one for each Slavic language – Jakobson himself gave the paper only a couple of brief published references in the remaining thirty-four years of his career.

Jakobson's own student, Michael Shapiro, felt the need to criticize the paper for ignoring the principles that he had learned from his teacher. Shapiro condemned 'Russian conjugation' for valuing 'descriptive economy [as] a legitimate surrogate for explanation' (Shapiro 1974: 31) and called instead for a semantically based approach to Russian conjugation, grounded in a semiotic theory of markedness.[3]

Why, then, did Jakobson write 'Russian conjugation'? Halle (1988) suggests that the paper arose from discussions that Jakobson carried on with Bloomfield between 1944 and 1946. On his arrival in the United States in 1941, Jakobson had not yet read Bloomfield's *Language*. But after a few years, the two linguists had a productive working relationship. Jakobson was impressed with Bloomfield's *Spoken Russian* text, produced for the war effort (Lesnin *et al.* 1945), and suggested that the two collaborate on a Russian grammar. While the grammar never materialized, the 'Russian conjugation' paper shows the unmistakable imprint of Bloomfield's influence. Bloomfield is the only linguist Jakobson refers to in the paper (other than himself) and the analysis presented is Bloomfieldian through and through.

The hypothesis that Jakobson's goals in writing this paper were more applied than theoretical seems to be supported by his remarks in the conclusion to it. Rather than summarizing its theoretical import, he focuses entirely on the paper's relevance for pedagogy. The paper concludes: 'The rules formulated above allow the student . . . to deduce [the] whole conjugation pattern . . . . And these rules could be presented in a popular form for teaching purposes' (Jakobson 1948: 162–3).

Now let's turn to Chomsky's undergraduate honours essay, 'Morphophonemics of modern Hebrew'. Unlike Bloomfield and Jakobson, Chomsky's goal is a full generative grammar of the language, in which every sentence is provided with a structural description at the syntactic, morphological, morphophonemic, and phonemic level. In actuality, however, only rules for Hebrew syntax and morphophonemics are presented. The former is manifested by a phrase structure grammar, with indices used to handle long components. The latter map morphophonemic representations, in which extensive use is made of special 'effect' symbols, on to phonemic representations. These rules are strictly ordered; in fact, a large part of the essay is devoted to demonstrating that generality would be lost given alternative orderings of the same rules. Finally, unlike 'Menomini morphophonemics' and 'Russian conjugation', the rules are stated formally at every level.

In what ways, then, is Chomsky's essay indebted to 'Menomini morphophonemics' and 'Russian conjugation' – seemingly the only two truly generative works of the century to precede it? Chomsky maintains that the answer is 'None at all' – that he had neither seen nor heard of either paper when he was writing his essay (see Chomsky 1975a: 47; Chomsky 1979a: 112 for remarks on the Bloomfield paper; his personal communication to the author (17 November 1988 provided the information on the Jakobson paper)).

One might or might not be tempted to take Chomsky's words at face value. All of the evidence available to me, however, suggests that he is correct in his assertion. Let us take 'Menomini morphophonemics' first. It is an understatement to say that this paper was not much appreciated in American linguistics in the 1940s. In all the papers reprinted in Joos (1957) that were written in that decade, there is only one reference to 'Menomini morphophonemics' (from Harris 1942), and this is to a point of terminology rather than substance. Incredibly, Hockett (1948), when reviewing Bloomfield's Algonquian work, not only made no reference to 'Menomini morphophonemics' in the text of the article, but omitted it from a list of Bloomfield's publications on the Algonquian languages.

Chomsky comments:

> It is rather astonishing that no one at Penn suggested to me that I look at the Bloomfield article. It is not surprising that Harris didn't, given his theoretical outlook. But more surprising is that Henry Hoenigswald never mentioned it. He must have known about Bloomfield's article as well as the Paninian tradition on which it was based. The fact that none of this was ever brought to my attention in a department consisting of Bloomfield's students and close friends is quite remarkable, and tells a great deal about the mood of the times.
>
> (personal communication, 17 November 1988)

Interestingly, Zellig Harris includes an appendix to a section in which the 'Menomini morphophonemics' paper is briefly described, in his book *Methods in Structural Linguistics* (1951). In the manuscript version of the book, however, which Chomsky had worked through in 1947, that appendix does not exist.

As far as the 'Russian conjugation' paper is concerned, again Chomsky says that in 1949 he was unaware of its existence. He comments:

> It is unfortunate, but true, that in an American linguistics programme such as that at Penn, no one ever read a word of Jakobson's, on any topic. I knew he existed, but barely more. What more I 'knew' (i.e., thought I knew) came mostly from reading Harris's critique of feature theory in his long components work. I never heard of Jakobson's paper until I met Morris Halle, sometime in the early 1950s.
>
> (personal communication, 17 November 1988)

In any event, the December 1948 issue of *Word*, in which 'Russian conjugation' appeared, wasn't in the hands of its subscribers until late March 1949. Since Chomsky's essay was submitted in early June, it is prima facie implausible that the former could have had any serious influence on the latter.

So what *were* the major influences on the young Chomsky? The principal impetus – and this should hardly come as a surprise – came primarily from the work of and conversations with his adviser Zellig Harris. The last chapter of Harris's *Methods*, which, again, Chomsky had read in manuscript form as an undergraduate, contains some scattered references to what Harris calls a 'synthetic' approach to grammar, which he counterposes to the procedural approach developed in the body of the book. Loosely interpreted, it amounts to a sort of generative grammar, though Harris neither used this term, nor went into the slightest detail as to its specifics.

It was essentially this idea that Chomsky was to develop in his essay. In an interesting sense Harris's *Methods* and Chomsky's essay are inverses of each other. For Harris, the procedures are paramount, and the 'synthetic' approach is presented, on one page as a conceivable alternative to them, and on another as something that might be applied as a restatement of the grammar that results from the procedures – a novel form of 'structural restatement', if you will. Chomsky had not rejected a procedural approach in 1949 *in toto* – that would not happen until the 1950s. But his practice amounted to a rejection, since he took as his point of departure a state of affairs in which the grammarian has already completed the procedures that have led to the identification of the grammatical elements of Hebrew.

Chomsky's essay bears the unmistakable stamp of Harris in another respect – in the confidence with which it assumes that syntax can be treated within the same overall system of principles as lower levels of grammar. Bloomfield himself had put forward a 'structuralist' view of syntax: we owe the idea of immediate constituent analysis to him. But Bloomfield felt that syntax was too 'complicated and hard to describe' (Bloomfield 1933: 201) to treat as one might phonology or morphology. Other American descriptivists had presented syntactic sketches before 1949 (see, for example, Nida 1948; Pike 1943; Wells 1947). But it is only with the work of Harris – and his student Chomsky – that we get the feeling of the possibility of a uniform package, in which the rules of phrase structure and those of allophonic detail each have their assigned place.

A second major influence on the undergraduate Chomsky was work in the foundations of logic and the philosophy of science, particularly in the logical positivist variety that still held sway in the 1940s. I believe that Chomsky's essay is the first to point out that the procedures of American descriptivist linguists can be likened to the programme of Carnap's *Der Logische Aufbau der Welt* (1928), which attempts to construct, by a series of definitions, the concepts of quality, sensation, and so on, directly from slices of experience. Another influence is clearly Nelson Goodman, whose writings about elegance as a property of scientific statements Chomsky explicitly drew upon, even to the point of appealing to them as a justification for ordered rules in grammar (see Goodman 1951). And the phrase-structure rule formalism in the essay (and accompanying terminology) is unmistakably drawn from Carnap's book *The Logical Syntax of Language* (Carnap 1937).

Finally, Chomsky adopted the process morphophonemics that had formed one strand of American structuralism since Sapir, though he increased its intricacy one hundred-fold over prior analyses. Unlike other work in this genre, such as Bloomfield's (but not Sapir's), there is no trace of the dualist approach, which considered phonemes to be a real part of the language, but morphophonemes nothing more than a 'convenient way of telling about the language' (as Bloomfield put it).[4]

So, to conclude, Chomsky's 1949 undergraduate honours essay was the first modern attempt to present a generative grammar of a language encompassing all levels of description. Its most direct influence is the work of Harris, rather than the 'Menomini morphophonemics' and 'Russian conjugation' papers with which it shares important features.

While Chomsky's 'package' was a new one, in one crucial sense it did not represent a fundamental break with American descriptivist practice. That break was to come in 1955 with his 'Logical structure of linguistic theory' ('LSLT'), a break triggered more than anything by its hypothesizing fully abstract theoretical elements in the recursive component of the grammar – the syntax. This move in 'LSLT', carried to its logical conclusion, was to force one to confront the implications that purely formal grammatical structure might pose for a theory of mind.

Chapter 3

The structure of the field of linguistics and its consequences for women

In December 1924, twenty-nine prominent linguists met in New York City at the American Museum of Natural History to sign a 'call' for a society devoted exclusively to the scientific study of language.[1] The time had come, they felt, to break away from the Modern Language Association, the Philosophical Society, and other organizations that were no longer adequate for the needs of a discipline that was rapidly developing its own professional identity.

All twenty-nine of the participants were male. One's first thought might be that this fact was a simple consequence of there being no prominent women linguists at the time, but such was not the case. At least two women, Louise Pound and E. Adelaide Hahn, were in accomplishment and stature uncontroversially the equal of the majority of the twenty-nine men. There were other women scholars who arguably deserved a place among the first dozen or two linguists in America.

Why then were there no women present at the founding meeting of the Linguistic Society of America (LSA)? Martin Joos, in his history of the Society, gives a candid explanation: 'Family reasons' (Joos 1986: 9) prevented women from attending. It was apparently unthinkable sixty-five years ago that a woman with a family could leave her husband and children for a couple of days, even for such a momentous occasion as the founding of what would soon become the largest professional body of linguists in the world.

The pressures that women felt in the early years of the LSA came as much from within the organization as from society as a whole. In 1942, Louise Pound, the prominent American dialectologist, turned her back on the LSA to found the journal *American Speech*. Joos attributes her action 'to outrage at the routine ignoring of all female scholars' (1986: 9) by the LSA and its organ *Language*.

It is impossible to pin down precisely the extent to which this 'routine ignoring' took place, since one cannot estimate with any precision the number of practising women linguists in the interwar years. Most LSA members then, as now, would not have identified themselves primarily as 'linguists' and there were practically no independent linguistics departments to provide data for tabulation. Still, we can assume that women linguists met with the same fate as women in other branches of the humanities in this period. It is not a widely known fact, but conditions for women in academia worsened in the first half of the century. There were fewer women faculty members (in all areas) in 1962 than in 1890, the percentage declining from 27 per cent to 22 per cent (Pollard 1977). Likewise, while 15 per cent of all Ph.D.s were awarded to women in 1930, only 8 per cent were awarded in 1950. The percentage did not rise above the 1930 level until the mid-1970s (Wasserman *et al.* 1975: 3)

The bulk of the loss for women was in the departments of the humanities, where by the turn of the century they had established a beachhead in academia. Every imaginable excuse was used to drive women from the universities. Perhaps the most insidious was that of 'professionalization', an excuse that we have seen recently in schools of social work. The underlying idea is that the professional stature of a field is inversely proportional to the number of women in it.

Nepotism laws, which had become increasingly common by the 1920s, also worked to the disadvantage of women, since they invariably led to the forced resignation of female professors whose husbands taught at the same university. Thereby arose the phenomenon of the husband–wife 'team', in which the husband received the job, the glory, and the salary, and the wife (if she was lucky) a joint authorship of some publications.

Third, the Depression led to cutbacks in hiring and an atmosphere in which it was considered 'unfair' to hire a woman when so many qualified men were jobless. Finally, in the aftermath of World War II, academia was no different from any other area of employment. The returning GIs, the great majority of whom were male, were felt to have 'earned' any available jobs, many of which had been filled by women during the hostilities.

As a consequence, by the 1950s, a young woman professor – even in a humanities department – had become an anomaly. It is therefore hardly surprising that women linguists, in a period in which linguistics was regarded as a central discipline in the humanities, should have met the same fate as their sisters in departments of literature, history, and the arts.

Linguistics, however, began to undergo a significant change in the late 1940s, a change that accelerated greatly in the 1950s and 1960s. More and more emphasis was placed on methodology and synchronic analysis, as first Bloch and Harris and later Chomsky and his associates set high standards of rigour and formalism for linguistic descriptions. By the late 1960s, symbol manipulation, the search for abstract patterns in data, and broad theorizing had come to characterize the most prestigious area of linguistics. Linguistics had thus begun to take on a cast that was antithetical to the humanities as they had been traditionally conceived, but had more in common with the practice in mathematics and the natural sciences, fields that were (and still are) virtually all male.

It is interesting, but perhaps not surprising, that quite a few of the earliest female contributors to generative grammar had strong backgrounds in psychology. In the 1940s and 1950s, only two academic areas increased their percentage of women scholars: psychology and education. Linguistics was enriched by women entering it from these fields. Thus the interdisciplinary fields of psycholinguistics and applied linguistics, which came into their own in the early 1960s, had high percentages of women scholars from the very beginning. Until recently, very few of these women had actually been trained in linguistics departments.

When we look at the representation of women in different branches of the field, we find some expected correlations and some surprises. It does not strike one as odd, for example, that a higher percentage of women work in child language acquisition than in mathematical linguistics, given the well-understood ways that girls and women are channelled in our society. It does seem rather surprising, though, that so many women have contributed to experimental phonetics, from Eli Fischer-Jørgensen and Ilse Lehiste, who were trained decades ago, to a huge number working in this area today. One's first thought, given the usual stereotypes, is that it would be one of the last areas of linguistics to attract women, since it involves a considerable knowledge of physics and the mastery of formidable machinery. I have no explanation to offer for why women have played the role in experimental phonetics that they have.

The fact that the field of linguistics is so small, and its subfields even smaller, makes it difficult in many cases to derive women's representation in it from socially significant facts. For example, the fact that a higher percentage of women syntacticians do lexical-functional grammar (LFG) than government-binding (GB) or generalized phrase structure grammar (GPSG) is clearly due more to personal influences and role models than to the intrinsic content of these frameworks or to the social channelling of women linguists.

It is not the place of this chapter to compare the percentage of women in linguistics with that in other fields or to provide current statistics documenting the status of women within the discipline. But it seems uncontroversially true that for a technical field, women have achieved a relatively high degree of prominence. The percentage of women in mathematics, physics, and even (or especially) analytic philosophy is far lower than in even the most technical subfields of linguistics. As an anecdotal confirmation of this claim, in the five-person short list for a recent position in formal semantics at the University of Washington, the top three candidates were women.

I am certain that the relative success of women in formal linguistics is not a consequence of male linguists being inherently less sexist than men in other fields. Rather, it results from more women entering linguistics than other technical fields. This, in turn, is a consequence of there being much more mystery about what work in linguistics involves than work in, say, mathematics or the physical sciences. Since in the popular mind linguistics is not a 'man's discipline' involving supposedly 'male skills', women are not dissuaded by social pressure from seeking careers in linguistic theory. And once embarked in a programme of study in this field, women, not surprisingly, find that the subject matter and mode of argumentation present them with no intrinsic obstacles to success.

The field, of course, has never been monolithic in orientation. The 1960s saw the development of a pole of attraction away from the abstract theorizing of generative grammar. Most importantly, sociolinguistics came into prominence at this time. Sociolinguistics was very much a by-product of contemporary social movements: struggles for national liberation in the Third World; the Black and minority movements in the United States; the anti-war movement, which led many to examine social divisions in that country, and (from the early 1970s) the women's movement.

At first, parallelling the situation in other social sciences, virtually all sociolinguists were male. But a view of language came out of sociolinguistics that was congenial to many women, who saw in this subfield the possibility of integrating social and linguistic concerns in a way that generative grammar could never allow them to do. For while generative grammar explores the question of why languages are as similar to each other as they are, sociolinguistics focuses on diversity and differences, and thereby invites a search for the linguistic basis of sexual and other inequality.

The great bulk of scholarly writing on language and gender has involved empirical studies, investigating such questions as gender differences in verbal interaction, the role of women in language change, the nature and use of the female register, gender roles in bilingual communities, and so on. The vast majority of this work has been carried out by women scholars.

Others, however, have not been content simply to document the situation; rather they have attempted to reconstitute a feminist linguistics. Seeing language as the primary mechanism by which misogyny is constructed and transmitted, some feminists – more influenced by phenomenology and continental structuralism than by any mainstream current in the field of linguistics – have analysed language itself as an instrument of patriarchy and oppression.

While such an approach has generated a considerable literature and has been highly influential within the feminist scholarly community, it has had little effect on the field of linguistics itself, even on sociolinguistics. In fact, the feminist intellectual critique of linguistics has exerted less influence on this field than comparable critiques have exerted on, say, literary criticism, political science, sociology, or anthropology.

The reason for this is surely that the critique only rarely impinges on issues under debate in the field, and where it does, it is shared by many linguists, whether feminist or not. For example, while some feminists might attack the notion of an abstract 'linguistic competence' for devaluing and isolating language, so too do other (not necessarily feminist) linguists from a variety of orientations.

Only rarely do we find a feminist critique of specific positions taken within linguistic theory proper that would not also appear in the general critical literature. So, for example, Cameron (1985) attacks componential analysis and markedness for imposing a dichotomous view of the world that, she feels, can only work to the disadvantage of women.

We do find, however, established linguists appealing to feminist criteria in support of positions that they had already arrived at for other reasons. Perhaps the best known example is Robin Lakoff (1975a) attacking interpretive semantics (i.e., the 'extended standard theory' version of transformational grammar) for not being able to account for the oddness of the sentence *John is Mary's widower*. In her view, the generative semantic theory that she advocated at the time, by incorporating social facts into the grammar itself, was able to treat this sentence adequately.

Perhaps the most curious example of a *post facto* feminist motivation for an established position is found in Hintikka and Hintikka (1983). They argue that most versions of model theoretical semantics are 'sexist' because they posit a domain of discrete individuals. Only males, as they see it, tend to think in terms of independent discrete units; females are more sensitive to relational characteristics. At it turns out, their conclusion is quite congenial to the approach developed earlier in J. Hintikka (1974), in which an individual-based ontology is abandoned for a more interactive one.

Robin Lakoff, by the way, has made proposals which, if implemented, would drastically affect the organization and structure of the field in so far as women are concerned. In R. Lakoff (1974), she speculated that women might be 'inherently' indisposed to formalism; if so it could only be 'criminal' to attract them to generative grammar. And later (R. Lakoff 1989) she takes an explicitly biologist view of women's supposed inability to master formal linguistics. In a review of the 1970s debate between generative semantics and interpretive semantics, she describes the former as inherently 'interactive' and 'feminine', the latter as 'hierarchical' and 'masculine'. Indeed, she appeals to the 'feminine' nature of generative semantics as the primary factor that contributed to its downfall.

In any event, it seems fair to say that a very small percentage of women in linguistics, even those in subareas maintaining close contacts with the humanities and social sciences, are involved in addressing what one might call 'women's issues concerning language'. This presents quite a contrast with Black linguists, who, at least in the United States, generally practise a 'race-related' linguistics, focusing on such issues as Black English, pidgins and creoles, and African languages.

Feminist linguists have tended to take a 'women-in-science' approach. That is, in their scholarly work they do not challenge the foundations of the field any more than a female mathematician or physicist would. Rather, they attempt to better the status of women within the field in hiring and promotion decisions, and to improve the presentation of women within the field by calling for the elimination of sexist language from example sentences.

I will close this chapter on a more speculative note. In a little-known paper, Greenberg (1973) pointed out that linguistics has always acted as a pilot science for the social sciences and the humanities. The historical and comparative linguistics of the nineteenth century led to attempts to apply the same methods to construct 'proto' legal systems, mythologies, and cultures. Structural linguistics spawned structural analysis in anthropology, psychology, and literary criticism while generative grammar has led social scientists to seek out 'deep structures' and 'universals' in their own fields of study.

Perhaps linguistics can act as a 'pilot science' in a rather different way, not for the social sciences but for the natural sciences. The level of formalism and abstract mathematical reasoning can be as high in linguistics as in the physical sciences. The fact that women not only do well but have made outstanding contributions in every area of formal linguistics is a fact that linguists can go out of their way to advertise and thereby help to demolish the lingering myth that women are inherently unsuited to be scientists.

Chapter 4

Has there been a 'Chomskyan revolution' in linguistics?

INTRODUCTION

It was once uncontroversial to refer to a 'Chomskyan revolution' in linguistics.[1] Commentators took it for granted that the publication in 1957 of *Syntactic Structures* by Noam Chomsky ushered in an intellectual and sociological revolution in the field – a revolution that deepened with the following decade's work by Chomsky and his associates. The term 'Chomskyan revolution' has appeared in the titles of articles (Searle 1972) and book chapters (Newmeyer 1980), and an historian of linguistics has written that the work of Chomsky 'fully meets [the philosopher Thomas] Kuhn's twin criteria for a paradigm [in science]' (Koerner 1976: 709). Even Chomsky's professional opponents have acknowledged the revolutionary nature of his effect on linguistics. Geoffrey Sampson, who feels that 'the ascendancy of the Chomskyan school has been a very unfortunate development for the discipline of linguistics' (Sampson 1980), nevertheless writes that 'Chomsky is commonly said to have brought about a "revolution" in linguistics, and the political metaphor is apt' (*ibid.*: 130). And Robert Longacre, an individual who has a quite different orientation to grammar from Chomsky's, writes that 'the field was profoundly shaken by him' (Longacre 1979), and has identified the essence of the Chomskyan revolution (a term which he uses without surrounding quotes) as its commitment to the construction of an explanatory linguistic theory.

The idea that linguistics ever underwent a 'Chomskyan revolution' has, however, been challenged in recent years, and the challenges appear to be on the increase. Koerner has now reconsidered his earlier position and believes that 'upon closer inspection, the term "revolution" does not properly apply to TGG' (Koerner 1983: 152). The sociologist Stephen Murray, whose professional speciality is the informal groupings and networks within the field of linguistics (see Murray 1983), wrote that 'Chomsky did not make a revolution with [*Syntactic Structures*]' (Murray 1980: 81); rather he and his associates engineered a 'palace coup' (*ibid.*: 82) in the early 1960s. In this view, Murray echoes the opinions of Raimo Anttila, who,

with 'an increasing number of linguists, ha[s] realized that this allegedly
linguistic revolution was a social *coup d'état*' (Anttila 1975: 171) and of
Bennison Gray, who recognizes no Chomskyan revolution, but only a
situation in which, 'as all admit, transformationalists have succeeded in
capturing the organs of power' (Gray 1976: 49). Those who see the generativist ascendancy as little more than a successful 'power grab' tend to
regard generative grammar as essentially post-Bloomfieldian business as
usual. As Koerner puts it, 'TGG is basically post-Saussurean structuralism, characterized by excessive concern with "langue" . . . to the detriment
of "parole"' (Koerner 1983: 152). Others believe that Chomskyan theory
does represent a fundamental break with its antecedents, but one which
did not occur with the publication of *Syntactic Structures*. Rather, it is felt
that Chomsky only departed from earlier traditions in the early 1960s,
when he and his associates began to campaign against the autonomous
phoneme (for such a view, see Hill 1980: 75), or in the middle years of that
decade, when he began explicitly to embrace a 'rationalist' philosophical
basis for the theory (see Uhlenbeck 1975: 106–8).

   In this chapter, I will defend the position that Chomskyan theory
represents a revolutionary approach to the study of language, and one
whose revolutionary content was present in explicit form in *Syntactic
Structures*. Moreover, I will argue that sociologically as well as intellectually the field has undergone a Chomskyan revolution. Paradoxically,
however, the sociological transformation of the field has not been
accompanied by a corresponding success on the part of generative grammarians in achieving institutional power.[2] I will demonstrate that, far
from being comfortably seated on the throne after their successful 'palace
coup', generativists, as they compete for adherents with linguists of other
persuasions, find themselves well outside the walls of the palace.

THE REVOLUTIONARY NATURE OF *SYNTACTIC STRUCTURES*

What makes *Syntactic Structures* revolutionary is its conception of a grammar as a theory of a language, subject to the same constraints on construction
and evaluation as any theory in the natural sciences.[3] Prior to 1957, it was
widely considered, not just in linguistics, but throughout the humanities
and social sciences, that a formal, yet nonempiricist, theory of a human
attribute was impossible. Chomsky showed that such a theory was
possible. Indeed, the central chapter of *Syntactic Structures*, 'On the goals
of linguistic theory', is devoted to demonstrating the parallels between
linguistic theory as he conceived it and what uncontroversially would be
taken to be scientific theories. Still, *Syntactic Structures* would not have
made a revolution simply by presenting a novel theory of the nature of
grammar; the book had revolutionary consequences because it was not
merely an exercise in speculative philosophy of science. Rather, it

demonstrated the practical possibility of a nonempiricist theory of linguistic structure: half of the volume is devoted to the presentation of and defence of a formal fragment of English grammar.

Chomsky's conception of a grammar as a theory of a language allowed him to derive the major insight of earlier theorizing about language: the *langue/parole* (later competence/performance) distinction. For Saussure, who conceived of linguistics as a branch of social psychology, the distinction was merely stipulated: surely, for him there was no necessary reason why *langue* should be 'a well-defined object in the heterogeneous mass of speech facts' (Saussure 1966: 14). One can easily imagine a social system of verbal exchange in which such a 'well-defined object' is absent. For Chomsky, however, the distinction followed as a logical consequence of the assimilation of linguistics by the natural sciences. Just as physics seeks to specify precisely the class of physical processes and biology the class of biological processes, it followed that a task of linguistics would necessarily be to provide 'a precise specification of the class of formalized grammars' (Chomsky 1962a: 534). Interestingly, Chomsky's empiricist antecedents in American structural linguistics, who were in principle incapable of postulating a sharp dichotomy on the basis of observationally graded data, were forced to negate the *langue/parole* distinction by regarding the former as no more than a set of 'habits' deducible directly from speech behaviour (Hockett 1952). Not surprisingly then, Hockett's major attempt to rebut Chomsky (Hockett 1968) recognized that the question of whether or not the grammar of a language is a well-defined system was the central issue separating his view of language from Chomsky's.

The publication of *Syntactic Structures* represented a revolutionary event in the history of linguistics for a second reason: it placed syntactic relations at the centre of *langue*. By focusing on syntax, Chomsky was able to lay the groundwork for an explanation of the most distinctive aspect of human language: its creativity. The revolutionary importance of the centrality of syntax cannot be overstated. Phonological and morphological systems are essentially closed and finite; whatever their complexity or intrinsic interest, their study does not lead either to an understanding of a speaker's capacity for linguistic novelty or to an explanation of the infinitude of language. Yet earlier accounts had typically excluded syntax from *langue* altogether. For Saussure, most syntagmatic relations were consigned to *parole*, as they were for the linguists of the Prague School, who treated them from the point of view of 'functional sentence perspective'. Zellig Harris, it is true, had begun in the late 1940s to undertake a formal analysis of intersentential syntactic relations (see Harris 1957), but his empiricist commitment to developing mechanical procedures for grammatical analysis led him to overlook what the study of these relations implied for an understanding of linguistic creativity.

The fact that *Syntactic Structures* was syntax centred lay at the foundation of the interdisciplinary revolution that it initiated. Consider its effect on psychology. Psychologists had certainly taken an interest in pre-Chomskyan structural linguistics; indeed, John B. Carroll had written: 'From linguistic theory we get the notion of a hierarchy of units . . . . It may be suggested that stretches of any kind of behavior may be organized in somewhat the same fashion' (Carroll 1953: 106). Yet the approach to language to which Carroll referred, by granting the primary position to either phonology or morphology, offered little to an understanding of language processing or more general aspects of verbal behaviour. As a consequence, the results of structural linguistics were completely ignored in Skinner's *Verbal Behavior* and given only limited attention in Osgood and Sebeok's major pre-Chomskyan survey of psycholinguistics (1954). But shortly after Miller *et al.* (1960) had revealed to the community of psychologists the implications for the structure of human behaviour latent in Chomsky's theory of syntax, the 'psycholinguistic revolution' (Greene 1972: 11) was well under way.

The effect of *Syntactic Structures* on philosophy was equally profound. Although the two major schools of mid-twentieth-century philosophy – logical empiricism and ordinary language philosophy – were preoccupied with problems of language, they paid scant attention to structural linguistics. But Chomsky's syntax-centred approach, with its implications for limitless yet rule-governed creativity, had initiated a dialogue among philosophers even before he had called attention to the 'Cartesian' properties of the theory (cf. Bar-Hillel 1962; Chomsky 1962a; Putnam 1961; Scheffler 1963).

While Chomsky's conception of the nature of grammatical theory was a revolutionary one, there were, needless to say, numerous respects in which *Syntactic Structures* retained crucial conceptions of its historical antecedents. Foremost among them is Saussure's great insight that at the heart of language lies a structured interrelationship of elements characterizable as an autonomous system. Such an insight is the essence of 'structuralism' and, since it is assumed throughout *Syntactic Structures* and Chomsky's subsequent work, one can, with good reason, refer to Chomsky as a 'structuralist'.[4] Some commentators have pointed to this fact in order to dismiss the idea that there could have been a Chomskyan revolution. Since structuralism was well established years before the publication of *Syntactic Structures*, by what criteria, they ask, could it be correct to refer to a Chomskyan revolution? Thus George Lakoff concluded from Chomsky's commitment to structural analysis that early transformational grammar, rather than representing a revolutionary development, 'was a natural outgrowth of American structural linguistics' (G. Lakoff 1971a: 267–8). The same point has been made more recently by Stephen Murray, who finds 'the base of Chomsky's early work . . . in

American structural linguistics, especially as developed by Zellig Harris' (1980: 76); by Dell Hymes and John Fought, who regard *Syntactic Structures* as showing 'no evidence of basic revolutionary change' (Hymes 1964: 241; Hymes and Fought 1981: 241); and, as we have already seen, by Konrad Koerner.

Chomsky's 'structuralism', however, no more disqualifies his theory from being revolutionary than Einstein's Newtonian search for physical laws undermines the revolutionary nature of relativity theory. Saussure's victory was that of structuralism, just as Newton's victory was that of a lawful universe. We would no more expect the next revolution in linguistics to be an anti-structuralist one than we would expect the next revolution in physics to return to divine intervention as an explanatory device. Chomsky's revolution was a revolution *within* structural linguistics – one which profoundly altered our conceptions of the nature of linguistic structure and opened the way to an understanding of how its nature bears on the workings of the human mind. When Hockett wrote that 'Chomsky's outlook . . . is so radically different from Bloomfield's and from my own that there is, at present, no available frame of reference external to both within which they can be compared' (Hockett 1966: 156), one presumes that he was (correctly) ignoring the fact that the approaches of all three linguists share the property of 'structuralism'.

Chomsky's debt to his predecessors encompassed, of course, more ideas than that of a systematically structured langue. Again, his critics have pointed to these ideas to bolster the charge that the field has not undergone a Chomskyan revolution. For example, Hymes and Fought (1981: 167) stress that generative grammars were not introduced to the field in *Syntactic Structures* and note that 'if by generative theory, one means explicit formal theory, it is a whopping error to identify the concept with Chomsky and his followers'. And Koerner (1983: 159) emphasizes that Chomsky borrowed the idea of the transformational rule from his teacher, Harris.

While Hymes and Fought and Koerner are correct, their observations are irrelevant to the question of whether *Syntactic Structures* was revolutionary. No partisan of Chomskyan theory has ever suggested that the proposal of a generative grammar embodying transformational rules constituted, in 1957, a revolutionary break with past practice. Indeed, the idea that a grammar could be viewed as a set of instructions for generating the sentences of a language had been in the air for several years (Harris 1954; Hockett 1954).[5] And as far as formalism is concerned, Saussure had said in the 1890s that a linguistic description 'sera algébrique ou elle ne sera pas' (Godel 1957: 49), though he never put his pronouncement into practice in a synchronic analysis. Models have even been proposed that are faithful to the overall Chomskyan research programme but which explore alternatives to generative grammars (cf.

McCawley 1970). Chomsky's contribution to linguistics was not the proposal that generative grammars were suitable devices for representing human language; rather it was the reinterpretation of generativity within a revolutionary conception of what a linguistic theory is a theory *of*.

Correspondingly, transformational rules are not central to Chomskyan theory, nor have they ever been regarded as an innovation of the theory. Far from it: Chomsky has always credited Zellig Harris for having originated them (for example, Chomsky 1957: 6). Such rules are simply one of any number of possible devices available to syntactic theory for the expression of formal generalizations. In any event, an improved system of formalism had little, if anything, to do with what made *Syntactic Structures* revolutionary. Not surprisingly, then, frameworks for syntactic analysis have appeared since 1957 which are wholly Chomskyan in their basic worldview, but which reject outright the necessity for transformational rules (cf. Gazdar 1981; Koster 1978).

In their long discussion of the research continuities in American linguistics, Hymes and Fought do in fact identify the central distinguishing feature of Chomsky's theory, though they fail to identify it as a revolutionary innovation. They write:

> Chomsky's true argument with the Bloomfieldians was with regard to the kind of evaluation procedure, the kind of formal justification of a linguistic analysis, or linguistic theory, that should be followed. To the criterion of theoretically possible induction, he opposed the criterion of theoretically definable simplicity (generality).
>
> (Hymes and Fought 1981: 180)

But Chomsky's 'true argument' dealt with nothing less than the very nature of linguistic theory. No issue is as important as the relevant criteria for theory evaluation, since a radically revised evaluation procedure entails a theory with a radically revised ontological basis. To abandon a procedure based on induction, and to adopt one based on generality, is to break from past practice at its most fundamental point; it demands that one ceases to think about a grammar as an operationally derived synthesis of a corpus, and that one begins to regard it as a theory of a language.

THE SOCIOLOGY OF SCIENTIFIC REVOLUTIONS

We may conclude then that, intellectually, *Syntactic Structures* had a revolutionary effect on the field of linguistics. Its effect was equally revolutionary in a sociological sense, although this question is complicated by the fact that historians of science have presented conflicting criteria for identifying successful revolutions. For example, Thomas Kuhn, in his influential book *The Structure of Scientific Revolutions* (Kuhn 1970), claims that a central criterion is the resultant uniformity of belief, within the scientific community, in the new 'paradigm'. If Kuhn is correct, then *no* (scientific) revolutions have occurred in linguistics.[6] As Percival (1976) has shown, no approach to linguistic analysis, past or present, has garnered universal acceptance, and, most relevantly, 'Generative grammar does not command universal assent among linguists all over the world; it is not a conceptual framework shared by all the members of the profession' (Percival 1976: 289). The conclusion seems inescapable: the 'Chomskyan revolution', if there was one, was not a 'Kuhnian revolution'.[7]

Kuhn's theory of scientific revolutions has been subject to considerable scrutiny; and it seems fair to say that only a small number of philosophers of science accept it, even in broad outline. But of all the components of his theory, none is as vulnerable as the 'uniformity of belief' hypothesis. It is apparently the case that no scientific theory, even the most uncontroversially revolutionary one, has ever generated universal assent. As the philosopher Larry Laudan has pointed out:

> We speak of the Darwinian revolution in nineteenth-century biology, even though it is almost certainly the case that only a small fraction of working biologists in the last half of the nineteenth century were Darwinians. We speak of a Newtonian revolution in early eighteenth-century physics, even though most natural philosophers in the period were not Newtonians.

> (Laudan 1977: 137)

What sociological criterion, then, uniquely characterizes a scientific revolution? Laudan provides a compelling answer:

> . . . a scientific revolution occurs, not necessarily when all, or even a majority, of the scientific community accepts a new research tradition, but rather when a new research tradition comes along which generates enough interest (perhaps through a high initial rate of progress) that scientists in the relevant field feel, whatever their own research tradition commitments, that they have to come to terms with the budding research tradition. Newton created the stir he did because, once the *Principia* and the *Opticks* were published, almost every working physicist felt that he had to deal with the Newtonian view of the world. For many, this meant finding cogent arguments against the Newtonian system. But what was almost universally agreed was that Newton had developed a way of approaching natural phenomena which could not be ignored. Similarly, late nineteenth-century biologists, whether fervent Darwinians or confirmed anti-evolutionists, found themselves having to debate the merits of Darwinism. To put the matter in a more general fashion, I am suggesting that *a scientific revolution occurs when a research tradition, hitherto unknown to, or ignored by, scientists in a given*

field reaches a point of development where scientists in the field feel obliged to consider it seriously as a contender for the allegiance of themselves or their colleagues.

(Laudan 1977: 137–8; emphasis in original)

If Laudan is correct, there can be no question that the field has undergone a 'Chomskyan revolution'. As Dell Hymes noted the year before the publication of *Aspects of the Theory of Syntax*, 'it remains that transformational grammar has established itself as the reference point for discussion of linguistic theory . . . it remains the case that it has been Chomsky who has effectively opened the American linguistic scene to its present free and fruitful discussion' (Hymes 1964: 25). In other words, by 1964 it was Chomsky and his theory that formed the focal point for debates about how to carry out theoretical linguistics.

We know that there was a Chomskyan revolution – but not because every linguist in the world was at one time, or is now, a generative grammarian. There was a Chomskyan revolution because anyone who hopes to win general acceptance for a new theory of language is obligated to show how the theory is better than Chomsky's. Indeed, the perceived need to outdo Chomsky has led him to be the most attacked linguist in history. Presentations of alternative conceptions of grammar routinely devote entire chapters to debunking his views (cf. Givón 1979; Moore and Carling 1982; Prideaux *et al.* 1980). One can appreciate the depth of Chomsky's impact by noting that a large percentage of his opponents are Europeans; his ideas have been subjected to book-length critiques published in Britain (Robinson 1975), Holland (Uhlenbeck 1975), France (Hagège 1976), Germany (Weydt 1976), Sweden (Collinder 1970), and the Soviet Union (Akhmanova and Berezin 1980). Since only a small percentage of European linguists have ever been generative grammarians, the motivation for these attacks can be only that he is seen as the dominant figure in *world* linguistics.

THE RECEPTION OF CHOMSKY'S IDEAS

Chomsky's ideas have continued to generate resistance; but when they were first presented in the late 1950s and early 1960s, the leaders of American structural linguistics did not attempt to prevent them from being heard.[8] Quite the contrary in fact: while Chomsky's first two generativist manuscripts were rejected by publishers, all of the subsequent ones were accepted. Chomsky was, almost from the start, touted by the leaders of the field as the brightest and most original of the younger generation of linguists. Speaking invitations were extended to him even before he received his doctorate; and as early as 1962 he was granted the honour of being one of the five plenary session speakers at an International

Congress of Linguists.[9] Furthermore, Bernard Bloch, arguably the most influential American linguist of the period, concretely abetted Chomsky and his theory in a number of ways.[10]

Chomsky's undeniable ease at gaining a hearing has been proffered as an argument that instead of a genuine 'Chomskyan revolution' taking place, the field saw only a 'power grab' by him and his supporters in the mid-1960s. Murray (1980) therefore questions whether Bloch and other prominent structuralists would have accorded Chomsky access to the public organs of the field if they had seen his ideas as an intellectual threat to post-Bloomfieldianism or had regarded him as likely to form a sociological pole of attraction. Murray's case is built implicitly on the idea that no rational individual would willingly help to undermine his or her own dominant position; hence the field's leaders (being rational) must have viewed Chomsky's ideas as quite congenial to their own.

It is difficult to ascertain whether reasoning such as Murray's has its roots in anything other than a thoroughly dismal view of human nature; however, it might be attributable to a misreading of those passages in Kuhn that take on the question of the transition of power from one paradigm to the next. In his discussion of this question, Kuhn pointed out that it is 'very often' (1970: 150) the case that older workers in a scientific field do not accept revolutionary developments; to support this idea he cites examples of the non-adoption of the theories of Newton, Priestly, Kelvin, and others by the establishment in their respective fields.[11] But Kuhn never implies that the Old Guard attempt to *suppress* revolutionary new ideas, nor do they even fail to encourage such ideas (however much they may disagree with them). It is easy to fall prey to the romantic (and pessimistic) idea that in order to win a voice, a young innovator in a field must struggle heroically against the obstructionist establishment. But such a scenario does not correspond to reality, either within linguistics or within science in general. Kuhn's further point that establishment figures do not adopt new theories themselves is borne out completely by the Chomskyan revolution. With the exception of Sol Saporta and Robert Stockwell (both of whom were quite young at the time) and only a very few others, the leading structural linguists of the late 1950s did not become generative grammarians.

In any event, the published commentary on Chomsky's early work by prominent American structuralists leaves no doubt that they saw in it a fundamental challenge to their own established views of how to carry out linguistic research. For example, C. F. Voegelin recognized that the rejection of empiricist-based discovery procedures was at the heart of Chomsky's approach to both syntax and phonology, and wrote that 'if transform grammar also persuades linguists to relegate phonemics to a preliminary stage of analysis . . . and to operate in final analysis . . . exclusively with morphophonemics, it will have accomplished a

Copernican revolution' (Voegelin 1958: 229).[12] Likewise, while Martin
Joos recognized the 'structuralist' core of generative grammar, he also
recognized that it differed fundamentally from other structuralist approaches; hence he identified Chomsky's theory as a 'heresy within the
neo-Saussurean tradition rather than as a competitor to it' (Joos 1961: 17).
Why was it heretical? Because:

> [it] ignores . . . something which has been either taken for granted or
> circumvented for many years . . . this is the neo-Saussurean axiom
> which we may try to state in these words: 'Text signals its own
> structure'. From this tacit assumption there follows automatically the
> most troublesome rule of neo-Bloomfieldian methodology: the rule
> demanding 'separation of levels' . . . . But [the generativist] leaders are
> able to point out that *no other science has a parallel rule*.
>
> (*ibid.*: 17–18; emphasis added)

In short, Joos recognized that the rejection of empiricist constraints on
theory formation was at the heart of the Chomskyan movement, and that
Chomsky's thrust was to bring linguistics into accord with the natural
sciences.

I have pointed out elsewhere (Newmeyer 1980: 46–7) that Charles
Hockett, far from viewing generative grammar as a mere logical extension
of his own and others' work in the post-Bloomfieldian tradition, went so
far as to characterize the publication of *Syntactic Structures* as one of 'only
four major breakthroughs' in the history of modern linguistics (Hockett
1965: 185). He wrote:

> Between Sir William [Jones's] address and the present Thirty-Ninth
> Annual Meeting of the Linguistic Society of America there is a span of
> 178 years. Half of 178 is 89, a prime number. If we add that to 1786 [the
> date of Jones's address] we reach the year 1875, in which appeared Karl
> Verner's 'Eine Ausnahme der ersten Lautverschiebung'. Thereafter,
> two successive steps of 41 years each . . . bring us to the posthumous
> publication of Ferdinand de Saussure's *Cours de Linguistique Générale*
> and then to Noam Chomsky's *Syntactic Structures*.
>
>   I have allowed myself this bit of numerology because I know none of
> you will take it seriously. But behind this persiflage there is a sober
> intent. Our fraternity has accomplished a great deal in the short span
> of 178 years; yet, in my opinion, there have been only four major
> breakthroughs. All else that we have done relates to these four in one
> way or another.
>
> (Hockett 1965: 185)

Hockett recognized that the major breakthrough of *Syntactic Structures*
was its abandonment of empiricist constraints on theory formation and
evaluation – which, as he noted, involved distinguishing discovery from

evaluation procedures, and practical description and formal theory, and which required setting the formal requirements that a theory must meet. Hockett referred to the various components of nonempiricist theory collectively as the 'accountability hypothesis' and wrote 'that it is a breakthrough I am certain' (*ibid.*: 196).[13]

Even before the publication of Chomsky's *Aspects* in 1965, commentators began to refer to Chomsky's revolutionary effect on the field. This fact refutes the view (cf. p. 24, above) that it was only with the publication of this book that Chomsky was seen by contemporaries as departing from the mainstream post-Bloomfieldian tradition. Papers published in 1965 (and therefore presumably written before the appearance of *Aspects*) noted that 'it is a truism by now that the publication of *Syntactic Structures* marks an epoch in the development of American linguistic thought' (Levin 1965: 92); that 'a revolution of the kind Kuhn describes has recently taken place in linguistics – dating from the publication of Chomsky's [*Syntactic Structures*] in 1957' (Thorne 1965: 74); and the 'slim volume [i.e., *Syntactic Structures*] was to have a startling impact on linguistics' (Bach 1965: 111–12).

Along the same lines, overviews published after 1965 have typically pinpointed the Chomskyan revolution as an historical event marked by the appearance of *Syntactic Structures*, not of *Aspects*. While we might expect an early dating from generative grammarians, nongenerativists as well consider 1957 to mark the turning point in the field. So Thomas Sebeok describes 'the emergence, in the late 1950s, of the Chomskyan paradigm' (Sebeok 1969: vii); R. H. Robins writes that 'in 1957 the description and analysis of languages was thrown into exciting turmoil by the publication of Noam Chomsky's *Syntactic Structures*' (Robins 1971: 33); and Herman Parret notes that 'almost everybody considered the publication of *Syntactic Structures* in 1957 as a revolution in contemporary linguistics' (Parret 1974: 27).

The personal testimony of the psycholinguist Howard Maclay might be coloured in part by his sympathetic attitude towards generative grammar, but it captures a widely held sentiment. According to Maclay, 'The extraordinary and traumatic impact of the publication of *Syntactic Structures* by Noam Chomsky can hardly be appreciated by one who did not live through this upheaval' (Maclay 1971: 163).

Even R. A. Hall Jr could write that 'since 1957, especially, an extensive upheaval has resulted from the doctrines propounded by Noam Chomsky, which are in many respects diametrically opposed to those of earlier approaches' (Hall 1969: 192). According to Hall:

in the United States, counter-attacks were slower in coming [than in Europe], primarily because many established scholars did not realize, *at the outset*, the full implications of Chomskyan total 'rejectionism' and anti-scientific positions, and expected his arguments to fall of their own weight, underestimating their appeal to newcomers untrained in linguistics and imbued with our culture's superstitions concerning language.

(*ibid.*: 226; emphasis added)

THE ORGANIZATIONAL SUCCESS OF GENERATIVE GRAMMAR

Chomsky's success in setting new ground rules for linguistic debate was matched by a corresponding success in drawing a host of new recruits into the field. It is true that, in the 1960s, almost every area of American higher education expanded at a high rate; but the growth in linguistics (as measured by the number of doctoral degrees awarded) was three times the average rate of expansion for all fields. And in the early 1970s, while the number of first-year graduate students in physics declined by 41 per cent, in English by 35 per cent, and in history by 31 per cent, linguistics actually saw an increase of 49 per cent (Newmeyer 1980: 52–4). Since the promise of future financial reward could hardly have motivated students to enter a linguistics programme, it seems reasonable to attribute, to a considerable degree, the accelerated growth of the profession after 1957 to the appeal of generative grammar.

One might assume then that generative grammarians would have been equally successful in securing for themselves a dominant organizational position within American linguistics. That is, given their other successes, it seems reasonable that it should be Chomsky and his associates who make the day-to-day decisions about who gets hired, what gets published, which grants get awarded, etc. Indeed, as we have seen, Murray, Anttila, Gray, and others believe that such is their *only* true achievement – one which they ruthlessly exploit to 'silence' critics lacking tenure at their universities (Maher 1980: 6).

I find little evidence to support the idea that, organizationally, American linguistics is controlled by generative grammarians; in fact, their influence is disproportionately small.[14] To begin with, there is ample opportunity to study with nongenerativists for anyone who wishes to do so. The linguistics programmes at many major universities are dominated by nongenerativists, among which are those at California-Berkeley, Columbia, Florida, Georgetown, Harvard, Hawaii, Illinois-Chicago Circle, Michigan, Michigan State, New Mexico, Oregon, Pennsylvania, Rice, SUNY-Buffalo, and Yale. According to a recent survey sponsored by the National Research Council, the linguistics departments at California-Berkeley and Pennsylvania are among the ten best in the country. Even in the departments at Brown, Cornell, CUNY, Minnesota, Southern California, UCLA, and Wisconsin, where a majority of the faculty are generative grammarians, one is able to study with individuals who are hostile to the generativist approach.

Second, generative grammarians receive only a small minority of the grants allocated in the field. As public records show, in 1982, generativists received seven out of twenty-eight National Institute of Health Grants in Linguistics and only eleven out of forty-seven National Science Foundation Grants within their Linguistics Programme.[15] The Ford Foundation, incredibly, gives *political* motivation for its refusal to fund generativist research: it objects to the fact that generativists 'have isolated [the field] from the world of nonlinguistic events and concentrated on abstract and formal theories about the nature and structure of language' (Fox and Skolnick 1975: 6). The Ford Foundation chooses to support those linguists who 'have come to view the relevance of their discipline as most importantly defined by its ability to contribute to an understanding of society'.

So far as I have been able to determine, the two major individual grant recipients in linguistics in the past fifteen years have been William Labov and Peter Ladefoged, neither of whose work can be regarded primarily as an elaboration or a defence of Chomskyan theory.[16] The major institutional grant recipient is the Center for Applied Linguistics, where virtually no generativist-orientated research takes place, and the organizational unit within the field that has the greatest resources and personnel at its disposal appears to be the Summer Institute of Linguistics, few of whose members are generativists.

Much has been written about the military funding (direct or indirect) of generativist research in the 1960s, and there is no question that such funding played a role in the early success of the theory (for discussion see Newmeyer and Emonds 1971 and Newmeyer 1986b). But what is often forgotten is that, after the Mansfield Amendment to a late 1960s appropriations bill was passed, demanding demonstrable military relevance for all military spending, such funding came to a complete halt. Throughout the 1970s, when sociolinguists were drawing from the various agencies of the Department of Health, Education, and Welfare, and phoneticians from the National Science Foundation, the programme at MIT had to content itself with rather nonlucrative National Institute of Mental Health training grants for its graduate students.

Third, one would be hard put to identify the Linguistic Society of America as a generativist-dominated organization. Only two of the annually elected presidents in the history of the society have been generativists, and partisans of Chomskyan theory make up a minority of its Executive Committee. Indeed, there is a feeling among many generativists that the LSA is an *anti*-generativist organization – or is, at best, irrelevant to their needs. As a consequence, many do not bother to join. An inspection of the December 1984 LSA *Bulletin* (no. 106) reveals that the following prominent generative grammarians were not members: Michael Brame, Joan Bresnan, Joseph Emonds, Robert Fiengo, Osvaldo Jaeggli, Lauri Karttunen, Edward Keenan, Charles Kisseberth,

Edward Klima, Mark Liberman, Alan Prince, Paul Postal, and Edwin Williams.[17]

Likewise, *Language*, the journal published by the LSA, is not orientated towards generative grammar. While a majority of its editorial board members are generative grammarians, its editor is not. If anything, generativist strength in the field is under-represented on the pages of *Language*; only about a third of its articles reveal such an orientation. Recent years have seen an article entitled 'On the failure of generative grammar' (Gross 1979) and a single issue (58: 1, March 1982) contains an article by Ronald Langacker presenting an alternative conception of grammar from Chomsky's, a review article by Harold Schiffman that derides generative grammar for hypothesizing the 'ideal speaker/hearer' and categorial rules, and a laudatory review by Jeri Jaeger and Robert Van Valin of a book (Prideaux *et al.* 1980) that concludes that Chomsky's approach is disconfirmed by psycholinguistic experimentation.[18]

Wherever we look, we fail to find confirmation of the claim that generativists rule the field. Some journals have a generativist bias, some a non- or anti-generativist bias. Some conferences are based on generativist themes, some are not. The 1983 Linguistic Institute was orientated towards generative grammar;[19] the 1985 Linguistic Institute was not. And so on. One simply cannot avoid the conclusion that an open market for linguistic ideas exists in the United States; no single theory, framework, or orientation comes close to being in an administrative position to prevent the others from being heard.

It is interesting to speculate on the reasons why the generativists' intellectual achievements and public visibility are not matched by an accompanying organizational dominance. Several come to mind. This state of affairs is partly a simple result of the inevitable time lag between a scientific theory's being recognized as revolutionary and its institutionalization in academia. For example, Einstein had won the Nobel Prize and his name was a household word years before relativity theory was part of the core curriculum in all major physics departments and its advocates held the leading positions in the various professional societies of the field. Time lag is also the obvious explanation for the fact that only Morris Halle and Victoria Fromkin, of all generativists, have served as LSA president – few others have practised linguistics long enough to achieve the degree of distinction to merit this honorary office.

Another reason has to do with Chomsky's own perception of the field. To quote him from an interview:

> As I look back over my own relation to the field, at every point it has been completely isolated, or almost completely isolated. I do not see that the situation is very different now . . . . But I cannot think of any

time when the kind of work that I was doing was of any interest to any more than a very tiny fraction of people in the field.

(Chomsky 1982a: 42–3)

Whether Chomsky is right or wrong (and he most certainly is wrong),[20] the effect of his perception of the field has been to discourage many of those under his influence from involving themselves in its bureaucratic infrastructure. This fact no doubt explains why so few generativists have served on LSA committees, and it may even be at the root of the under-representation of generative grammar in *Language*. Generativist submissions are not rejected at a disproportionately high rate; there are simply not that many of them. Chomsky's alienation from the field has kept him from submitting a paper to that journal for almost twenty years, and, it seems, many of his colleagues have followed his example.

The lack of generativist hegemony also stems in part from the nature and scope of the field of linguistics. There are aspects of the field that the Chomskyan revolution has not touched and is unlikely ever to do so. Consider, for example, such sociolinguistic topics as the language situation in Belgium, the characterization of turn-taking behaviour in conversation, and the extent to which the prescriptively sanctioned use of masculine third-person pronouns reinforces the social position of women. One's approach to these issues seems wholly unrelated to the correct form of the theory of grammar. The same point can be made for many of the topics taken up in experimental phonetics, pragmatics, lexical semantics, and other traditional areas of linguistic study. Since many subareas of linguistics complement grammatical theory rather than challenge it, it is not surprising that the success of the Chomskyan revolution has left intact the organizational power of their practitioners.

Finally, the diversity that exists in the field today is in part a result of the extraordinary complexity of its subject matter. While some linguistic phenomena lie uncontroversially outside the realm of grammatical analysis, a host of others might be amenable to grammatical treatment – or might not be. As a consequence, a multitude of approaches to language has developed, each mustering its share of supporters and each with its own particular account of the same phenomena. Chomsky himself has put forward a 'modular' conception of language, in which complex linguistic phenomena are attributed to the interaction of many different systems, of which formal grammar is only one (see Chomsky 1965: 3–4, 1981: 1–6). But other popular points of view have ranged from the idea that grammatical systems are merely artefacts of principles of communication and cognition with no independent existence at all (cf. Givón 1979) to the opposite extreme, namely the idea that even such information as the speaker's culture, social standing, and attitudes should be incorporated into the grammar (G. Lakoff 1974a). As suggested above, advocates of such positions have invariably defined (and defended) their positions with respect to Chomsky's; but they have had no difficulty in creating institutional poles of attraction in opposition to his. Indeed, the relatively decentralized and open nature of American academia, in which there is no 'Ministry of Education' to dispense all funds and appointments, has actually encouraged the development of a multitude of competing schools of thought in the field.

To conclude: despite the fact that generative grammar is not predominant institutionally, abundant evidence exists that there has been a successful 'Chomskyan revolution'. This revolution began with the publication of *Syntactic Structures* in 1957 and has had profound effects both intellectually, for the study of language, and sociologically, for the field of linguistics.

Chapter 5

Rules and principles in the historical development of generative syntax

INTRODUCTION

A recent characterization of the history of generative syntax is one of steady progress through a process of accretion.[1] This view points to a succession of discoveries, each building on prior ones, that have steered the field on a straight course that has led inexorably to the government-binding (GB) theory of the present day. To be specific, this account characterizes the principal task of the syntactician of thirty years ago as being to construct grammars of individual languages, each consisting of a list of language-particular rules. Between that time and the present, our ever deepening understanding of the principles of universal grammar (UG) has led to a steady reduction of the complexity and language-particularity of these rules. Today, our understanding of these principles is profound; in fact, we are close to the point where we can attribute virtually all observable differences among languages to the parameterization of these principles within highly circumscribed limits.

This interpretation is largely due to Chomsky and it receives its clearest exposition in his book *Knowledge of Language* (1986b). In a discussion spanning over 100 pages, Chomsky reviews how progress in developing the principles that govern the general form of grammars has allowed first, simplification in the statement of individual rules, and then their literal elimination, to the point where now we have arrived at 'a conception of UG as a virtually rule-free system' (*ibid.*: 93).

It is clear that Chomsky views progress towards this goal as having been achieved in a fairly gradual fashion. The results that he cites as having led to the current highly developed conception of UG seem fairly evenly distributed over the past twenty-five years. From the 1960s, Chomsky cites the principle of recoverability of deletion and the A-over-A principle (Chomsky 1964b), followed by the 'island constraints' of Ross (1967). The 1970s saw the principle of subjacency (Chomsky 1973), the structure preserving constraint (Emonds 1970, 1976), and the first attempts to derive principles of rule application (Freidin 1978). From the 1980s, Chomsky makes reference to the current formulation of principles of government and binding and the projection principle. Each such development has contributed one step further towards the goal of 'reduc[ing] the recourse to rule systems' (Chomsky 1986b: 84).

This essentially linear progress-through-accumulation view of the history of generative syntax has become quite accepted, at least by those who feel that GB is on the right track. Indeed, I have endorsed it myself (Newmeyer 1986a: 198). Even introductory texts contrast favourably today's elegant model of interacting principles with the clumsy rule-dominated work of the early days. As Riemsdijk and Williams (1986) put it in their overview of GB: 'From today's perspective most research carried out before the late 1960s appears data-bound, construction-bound, and lacking in appreciation for the existence of highly general principles of linguistic organization' (*ibid.*: 175).

The purpose of this chapter is to challenge the accretionist interpretation of the history of generative syntax. While as a statement of the evolution of *Chomsky's thinking* it may well have merit, this interpretation does not characterize adequately the course of development of the field itself. One must be careful not to identify Chomsky's views at any point in time with those of the mainstream in generative syntax. At certain times the two have coincided, and at other times they have not. His current conceptions of the organization of grammar in fact do command the allegiance of the majority of generative syntacticians (as I will argue below), just as in the years following the publication of his seminal work *Syntactic Structures* in 1957 his ideas were predominant. But for at least half of the time between 1957 and the present, Chomsky has been in a minority among generative syntacticians on many major questions. And once we disregard Chomsky's minority positions and focus instead on the mainstream line of research at any given period, we will see that the accretionist interpretation has little to recommend it.

I will offer instead a more cyclical interpretation of the history of generative syntax. In place of a gradual progression from a rule-orientated conception of grammar to a principle-orientated one, I will suggest that there have been four successive stages in the development of the field, alternatingly rule-orientated and principle-orientated. Before defending this claim, however, it is essential to clarify what exactly is being implied by identifying a period as 'rule-orientated' or 'principle-orientated'. Specifically, I will characterize a period as 'rule-orientated' if the generally accepted central task is seen to be to propose, motivate, or argue against the existence of language-particular rules. The period will be identified as 'principle-orientated' if mainstream research focuses on motivating principles of UG.

Whether a period is rule-orientated or principle-orientated is tangential to which particular *research topics* happen at the time to be engaging the interest of a significant number of syntacticians. For example, in the past thirty years, topics such as the nature of the interface between syntax and semantics; that between syntax and phonology; whether syntactic processes are fundamentally distinct from morphological ones; the number of syntactic levels; the form of syntactic rules; and so on have, at various times, been at the top of the collective research agenda. Yet each can be (and has been) approached from either a rule-orientated or principle-orientated direction. The nature of a period therefore cannot be surmised simply by examining the *questions* raised at a particular point in time; rather, it is more a function of the *form of the solutions* to the problems that are put forward.

It must be stressed that there is no sensible criterion, scientific or otherwise, that would single out either a focus on motivating principles or one on motivating rules as an inherently more desirable enterprise. Indeed, both are indispensible tasks in linguistics, as are their analogues in other sciences. And, as we shall see, each successive transition in the development of generative syntax, whether from a rule-orientated period to a principle-orientated period, or in the opposite direction, has represented a major step forward in our understanding of the nature of syntactic processes.

Also, as a final qualification, motivating rules and motivating principles are not wholly incompatible tasks. One can hardly imagine a paper that put forward some new principle of UG that did not at least call attention to, and perhaps reformulate, a language-particular rule, if only to show how its application is constrained by the principle. Likewise, virtually all work that has motivated a rule or rules has done so in the context of providing support (implicit or explicit) for a particular model of grammar, that is, for a theoretical principle. The best work in generative syntax, in fact, has taken rule-motivation and principle-motivation to be entirely complementary tasks. Consider, for example, the work of Emonds (1970, 1976), which involves careful formulation of rules of English (and, to a lesser extent, of French) in the context of showing how these rules and their precise formulation bear on an important principle of UG, the structure preserving constraint. Much other work, as well, has taken rule-motivation and principle-motivation in conjunction, in some cases to the point where it is impossible to characterize it as a rule-orientated or a principle-orientated piece of research.

Nevertheless, at different times in the history of generative syntax, there have been different *priorities*, shifting conceptions of where the greatest progress can be made and thus where one should devote one's energies. At certain times attention to particular rules has been seen as the most rewarding enterprise, at other times attention to general principles. Thus it is possible to divide the history of the field into four periods, which are summarized in Figure 5.1.

Period	Nature	Years predominant	Principal inspiration
Early transformational grammar	Rule-orientated	1957–67	Chomsky, *Syntactic Structures* (1957)
Generative semantics	Principle-orientated	1967–72	Katz and Postal, *An Integrated Theory of Linguistic Descriptions* (1964)
Lexicalism	Rule-orientated	1972–80	Chomsky, 'Remarks on nominalization' (1970)
Government-binding	Principle-orientated	1980–	Chomsky, 'Conditions on transformations' (1973)

Figure 5.1 Four periods in the development of generative grammar

To summarize the evolution of the field, the publication of Chomsky's *Syntactic Structures* in 1957 ushered in the rule-orientated period of early transformational grammar that lasted until around 1967. It was replaced by a period in which the predominant framework was the principle-orientated generative semantics and which derived its main inspiration from Katz and Postal's (1964) book *An Integrated Theory of Linguistic Descriptions*. Generative semantics gave way around 1972 to the rule-orientated lexicalist period, whose course was charted by Chomsky's (1970) paper 'Remarks on nominalization', and which flourished until around 1980. Since then, we have been in the second principle-orientated period, dominated by the government-binding framework, and owing its inspiration to Chomsky's (1973) paper 'Conditions on transformations'.

It should be noted that there can be a substantial time lag between the appearance in print of the work that would form the 'principal inspiration' of a given period and that period's predominance – one of seven years, in fact, in the case of the current period.

In some cases, it is a trivial task to identify a 'principal inspiration'. The ritualistic invocation of *Syntactic Structures* in virtually all generative syntactic work published between 1957 and 1965 leaves no room for doubt as to its inspiratory effects. However, in other cases, it may not be so clear that one work can be singled out as having played this role; and, to be sure, there is no logical reason why in all cases one even *should* exist. For example, can one point to a single principal inspiration for generative semantics? Even if the answer to this question is affirmative, it is by no means obvious that it should be identified as Katz and Postal's (1964) *An Integrated Theory of Linguistic Descriptions*. Thus I will devote considerable space to arguing that it should be accorded this role, though I will conclude that generative semantics followed the path charted by that book more in an 'atavistic' than in a conscious sense.

I shall further defend a claim that I assume to be more controversial – as well as more interesting – than that there have simply been four alternating periods in the development of the field. I will argue that the *internal structure* of each period has been roughly the same. The beginning of each period is marked by a major leap in our understanding of syntactic processes and brings with it impressive publications whose fundamental insights are not diminished by subsequent research. At the same time, the field sees a burst of enthusiasm accompanied by a level of activity unknown since the beginning of the previous period. After a time, however, a levelling off begins to take place, followed by a period of stagnation. This is marked by a decline in the level of argumentation and, more seriously, by the beginnings of an entry into a phase in which mere descriptions of phenomena, divorced from serious discussion of how such descriptions might bear on the choice between competing theories, become the order of the day. When this takes place in a rule-orientated period, a rule becomes little more than a shorthand way of referring to the superficial properties of a construction in a particular language. In a principle-orientated period, a parallel shift takes place: while the rhetorical focus might remain on principles of UG, the actual practice becomes to focus on language-particular constructions without serious consideration of their relevance to these principles.

In this context, the next turn is taken: to a principle-orientated stage from a rule-orientated one, or to a rule-orientated stage from a principle-orientated one. A new upsurge takes place in the field, and the process begins anew.

THE FIRST RULE-ORIENTATED PERIOD: EARLY TRANSFORMATIONAL GRAMMAR

It is hardly necessary to go into detail here on what the publication of *Syntactic Structures* meant for the field of linguistics. By breaking from structural linguistics, both in its rigidly empiricist American version and its less rigid, though equally taxonomic, European version, the book put forward a new research programme for linguistic analysis. *Syntactic Structures* itself can hardly be characterized either as rule-orientated or principle-orientated. Indeed, it is a masterpiece of the integration of general principles of grammar with compelling detailed analyses of particular phenomena in English. As Chomsky reminds the reader:

neither the general theory nor the particular grammars are fixed for all
time, in this view. Progress and revision may come from the discovery
of new facts about particular languages, or from purely theoretical
insights about organization of linguistic data – that is, new models for
linguistic structure. But there is also no circularity in this conception.
At any given time we can attempt to formulate as precisely as possible
both the general theory and the set of associated grammars that must
meet the empirical, external conditions of adequacy.

(Chomsky 1957: 50)

In *Syntactic Structures*, there is never any question of how the rules
proposed bear on the conception of language introduced and defended in
that book: there is a constant appeal to their abstractness and complex
interaction, which Chomsky clearly regards to be of greater theoretical
significance than the precise details of their formulation. Furthermore, it
is clear that Chomsky does not regard the existence of a particular *construction* in English to be prima facie evidence that there is necessarily a
single *rule* to characterize that construction. While it is in general the case
that rules are construction-specific, there are several instances in which a
single rule is involved in the generation of more than one construction
and in which the derivation of a single construction involves the interaction
of several rules. Both are illustrated by Chomsky's ingenious analysis of
the English auxiliary. The failure of the auxiliary transformation (later
called 'affix-hopping') to apply predicts the environment for the
occurrence of supportive *do* in both negatives and questions, while the
generation of simple yes–no questions involves the application of two
rules, the auxiliary transformation and a fronting rule ('T_q'), both of
which are at work in the generation of other constructions.

Other early work in transformational syntax maintained a comparable
degree of subtle interplay between general theory and particular rule-
statement: Lees' *Grammar of English Nominalizations* (1960) and Bach's
(1962) paper 'The order of elements in a transformational grammar of
German' come to mind as particularly good illustrations of work that
comes close to matching *Syntactic Structures* in this respect.

However, as the number of people working in transformational generative grammar increased in the first decade of its existence, the emphasis
of the typical paper or thesis began gradually to shift. More and more
over this period, we find the standard appeal to *Syntactic Structures* taking
on little more than ritualistic value. Reading a random selection of this
work gives one a very different feeling for the nature of the period than
does a reading of Chomsky, Lees, Bach, and the other leading generativists of the early years. It is not just that the work is not as insightful or
as intricate in its argumentation – one would hardly expect the average
work at any point in time to exude brilliance. Rather, this work is different

conceptually. In it, one finds very little in the way of interplay between rules and principles. On the contrary, this work is almost exclusively rule-orientated. The author identified a construction, then wrote a transformational rule which came close to mimicking its surface characteristics. In other words, for many linguists, transformations had become little more than a new descriptive device to supplement those that had been provided in the past decades by structural linguistics.

In this typical work of the first decade, it is not simply a matter of questions of UG being de-emphasized; in many cases one feels that the author is not aware that such questions were even on the agenda. Only the occasional rule-ordering argument prevents this work from being in the same mould as that of Zellig Harris, in whose work transformational rules were explicitly regarded as a device for capturing surface co-occurrence relations. In other words, in mainstream generative grammar by the mid-1960s, transformations had become a vehicle for doing descriptive syntax.

One might object that since there were so few people engaged in generativist research in the first decade of its existence, generalizations such as the above are meaningless, but this is not the case. In fact, there were dozens of people working in transformational generative grammar by the early 1960s. A bibliography compiled by William Orr Dingwall in 1965 lists well over 100 contributions in this area, including theses, dissertations, and working papers, as well as published books and articles (many of which, to be sure, appeared in fairly obscure journals).[2]

Another objection that one might raise is that the work that I am referring to here was not central to the development of generativist theory; that at the time it was not considered mainstream research or even considered worthwhile by leading figures in the field. But even if that were true, it would be beside the point. My goal is to characterize the *typical* work of each period, what the 'ordinary working grammarian' (to use Fillmore's phrase) was involved in doing. In the first decade of transformational grammar, this work was overwhelmingly rule-orientated and became, as time went on, increasingly descriptivist.

Actually, the point can be made that even work by the most prominent generative grammarians in this period tended, for the most part, to emphasize rules over principles. One is struck by the relative frequency with which principles of UG were proposed in one work, then ignored in ensuing work. For example, in *Syntactic Structures*, Chomsky proposed the following general condition on derived constituent structure, one effect of which would be to guarantee that the *by*-phrase created by the passive transformation would receive the label 'PP':

> If X is a Z in the phrase structure grammar, and a string Y formed by a transformation is of the same structural form as X, then Y is also a Z.
>
> (Chomsky 1957: 73)

This principle is not even mentioned in Lees (1960), though he could have made use of it. Likewise, so far as I have been able to determine, no reference is made to Chomsky's A-over-A principle, proposed at a 1962 conference and published in 1964, until Ross's 1967 dissertation, 'Constraints on variables in syntax'.

The publication in 1965 of Chomsky's *Aspects of the Theory of Syntax* did little to change the increasingly rule-orientated and descriptivist direction that transformational generative grammar was taking in the mid-1960s. The most important and memorable part of that book is Chapter 1, 'Methodological preliminaries', in which the 'rationalist' nature of linguistic theory is defended at length and the case is made that the problems of the validation of a theory of grammar and that of the construction of a theory of language acquisition are one and the same. This chapter sparked a debate among psychologists, philosophers, and anthropologists – not to mention linguists – that has continued unabated to the present time. However, this chapter did little to affect the actual *practice* of generative syntacticians.

There were, of course, important principles of UG proposed in *Aspects*, the three most far-reaching of which were base recursion, the principle of cyclic application of transformational rules, and the separation of category-introducing rules from those of subcategorization.[3] Interestingly, however, none of these had the contagious effect of leading syntacticians in a more principle-orientated direction. In fact, they had the opposite effect. Each had the effect of 'cleaning up' the phrase-structure and transformational components of the grammar. By doing so, they made rule writing an easier and more immediately gratifying experience.

It is interesting to recall that the topic in *Aspects* that receives the longest single treatment is quite in keeping with the rule-orientated spirit of the early years of the theory: the extended and often tortuous discussion in Chapter 2, where Chomsky puts forward and evaluates a variety of formats for lexical insertion, an issue that appeared even then to many linguists to have few interesting implications for UG, and which had little impact on subsequent work in the field.

The most important analytic work wholly within the *Aspects* framework is generally regarded to be Peter Rosenbaum's 1965 MIT dissertation which was published in 1967 as *The Grammar of English Predicate Complement Constructions*, in which he provided an analysis of English subordination and associated phenomena. It was Rosenbaum's formulation of rules such as equi-NP-deletion (which he called the 'identity erasure transformation'), extraposition, and raising (essentially his 'pronoun replacement'), which, after modification in G. Lakoff (1968a), would come to represent the 'standard' analyses of these phenomena for over a decade, partly as a result of their being enshrined in Akmajian and Heny's *An Introduction to the Principles of Transformational Syntax* (1975), an important syntax textbook.

It is interesting then, considering the longevity of Rosenbaum's proposals, to recollect what his stated goals were. Rather than to motivate or to provide support for some principle of UG or to constrain the power of linguistic theory, they were far more modest. To be specific, he wrote that '[t]he aim of the present study is to develop an adequate framework for *describing* certain types of sentential complementation in English' (Rosenbaum 1967: 1; emphasis added).

While Rosenbaum's work may have been the first empirical study of significance to incorporate base recursion and the transformational cycle, it presents no *arguments* for either of these principles. Indeed, the rules would have required only the most minor revisions to work without either of them.

In short, the first decade of generative syntax was a highly rule-orientated one. More and more in this period, descriptive goals came to outweigh explanatory ones. In much of the work in this period – perhaps largely outside of the MIT mainstream, but nevertheless numerically significant – transformational grammar had become little more than descriptive linguistics with a transformational veneer.

It was in this context that an approach to grammar whose rhetorical emphasis valued explanatory principles over detailed formulation of language-particular rules was bound to fall on welcome ears, and to present a pole of attraction for those whose interest in current work was flagging. That model was generative semantics.

THE FIRST PRINCIPLE-ORIENTATED PERIOD: GENERATIVE SEMANTICS

The shift from a rule-orientated to a principle-orientated approach to grammar had begun to be felt around 1966 and 1967, when works appeared that were devoted in their entirety to the motivation of a single principle of UG or a set of related principles. The two most important of these, while not full-blown generative semantics themselves, were to set the stage for this framework through their successful demonstration that there were impressive pay-offs to be had in emphasizing principles over rules. They are Ross's 1967 doctoral dissertation, 'Constraints on variables in syntax', and Postal's *Cross-Over Phenomena*, circulated in mimeographed form in 1968 and published as a book in 1971.[4] Ross's work was to underlie all subsequent studies of movement constraints, while Postal's, in addition to providing a wealth of interesting generalizations that would occupy syntacticians' attention for years, would turn out to provide some of the best evidence for movement rules leaving traces at the site of extraction (see Chomsky 1975c; Wasow 1972).

These works by Ross and Postal are perfect illustrations of the above claim that the major contributions at the *beginning* of each period balance the postulation of principles of UG with solid motivations of language-particular rules. Both Ross's and Postal's essays are principle-orientated, but they nevertheless contain dozens of formulations of transformational rules, many of which undergo modification as the principles argued for undergo refinement.

The impressive quality of these works helped to ensure that Ross and Postal, along with George Lakoff and James McCawley (among others), would have little difficulty weaning most syntacticians away from the kind of work that had characterized early transformational syntax and towards the new framework of generative semantics that they were in the process of developing.

There are many ways in which generative semantics can be compared with the earlier work that preceded it and with the lexicalist model that by the mid-1970s had supplanted it, but I feel that the most important way is typically overlooked or downplayed. Generative semantics was, first and foremost, a *principle-orientated* approach to grammar. Virtually every paper written in that framework put forth some novel principle governing UG or sought to provide evidence for some principle which had already been proposed. At the same time, language-particular rules were downplayed to the point where, in most generative semantic work, not a single one was formalized.

The typical research strategy in the generative semantic period was to motivate some broad principle by showing that a number of already accepted lesser principles led to analyses that suggested its correctness. Consider a position that generative semanticists had come to in the late 1960s, namely that the inventory of syntactic categories is isomorphic to the categories of predicate logic (see especially McCawley 1967; 1968b). This principle is certainly an interesting one, although subsequent research has shown it to be untenable. How was it motivated? For the most part, by pointing to earlier analyses which *themselves* were motivated on the basis of an appeal to principles.

Let me offer a concrete example. The idea that syntactic categories are mirrored by logical categories presumably entails that there is no category 'Auxiliary' (Aux). Hence, McCawley (1967) appealed to the conclusion of Ross (1969b) that the auxiliary is a subclass of the category 'Verb' (V), which itself can reasonably be regarded as isomorphic to the predicate of logic. Ross justified this conclusion by arguing that to deny it would fly in the face of other, independently motivated, principles. One such principle would be widely accepted today, namely that rules can refer only to constituents. This led Ross to reject the *Syntactic Structures* treatment of the auxiliary, in which the subcomponents of the category Aux represented in (1) are referred to in the rules forming yes–no questions and simple negatives, even though they do not form a constituent:

(1)

$$Tense \left(\left\{ \begin{array}{l} M \\ have \\ be \end{array} \right\} \right)$$

Ross advocated instead replacing the elements in (1) with the category V, which would have the features [+V, +Aux].

Another principle that led Ross to his conclusion was never put in explicit form, though it guided a great deal of generative semantic research. It can be stated roughly as in (2):

(2) If two lexical items occurring in similar environments appear to undergo the same rule, then they must belong to the same syntactic category.

In fact, before features ranging over the major lexical categories became part of the theory (an idea that was hinted at, but not developed, in Chomsky 1970c), there was little alternative to principle (2) if one wished to avoid disjunctive elements in the structural descriptions of transformational rules. On the basis of this principle, Ross concluded that copula *be* belongs to the category V since it seems to share with true verbs the property of undergoing the rule of gapping (cf. 3a–b); to complete the argument, since auxiliaries share with the copula (now established to be a V), the property of allowing quantifiers to 'hop' over them (cf. 4a–b), they too must belong to the category V:

(3) a. *I ate fish, and Bill ___ steak*
    b. *I am American, and Bill ___ Canadian*

(4) a. *They all/both/each are handsome → They are all/both/each handsome*
    b. *They all/both/each have gone/must go → They have all/both/each gone/They must all/both/each go*

Some of the principles put forward by generative semanticists were genuinely interesting and challenging, and provided an air of excitement to the enterprise of doing syntactic research that had been missing a few years earlier. One might be tempted to downplay the contributions of that framework or even to dismiss it out of hand, given that many of the principles that it put forward proved to be empirically deficient and also that by the mid-1970s the body of practitioners of that framework had dissolved almost completely. But that would be a serious mistake. The fact that many of its ideas resurfaced in modified form in later work suggests that they contained more than a small kernel of correctness.

Let us consider three examples of generative semantic principles of UG that were adapted subsequently by later frameworks. The first is the conception that there exists a word-internal syntax that parallels in crucial respects phrase-internal syntax (McCawley 1968a; Postal 1970; Weinreich 1966), an idea which, in generative semantics, was manifested through the device of lexical decomposition. This conception promised to provide the first generative characterization of the notion 'possible lexical item'. While generative semanticists were unsuccessful in getting this idea to work, subsequent approaches to grammar have not fared any better in finding a syntactic or semantic basis for distinguishing possible from impossible words in a language. Furthermore, current research in a variety of frameworks has resurrected the idea of word/phrase syntactic parallels in various ways (see Baker 1988; Dowty 1979; McCawley 1968a; Postal 1970; Selkirk 1982), and even lexical decomposition itself has reappeared in semantic theories such as that presented in Jackendoff (1983).

A second generative semantic principle worth mentioning is the idea that syntactic rules (or at least a large subset of them) are stated in terms of semantic rather than syntactic categories (see especially Green 1974; Newmeyer 1974). Again, this principle, could it be maintained, would have placed a strong constraint on syntactic operations. While, of course, it could not be maintained, the germ of the idea survives in theories of the lexicon that posit that the rules applying in that component are sensitive to – or are actually stated in terms of – the thematic roles of the elements involved (see Anderson 1977; Williams 1981).

Finally, the generative semantic principle that at one syntactic level sentences are disambiguated in terms of the scope of their logical elements (G. Lakoff 1971a; McCawley 1968b) has become a mainstay of the government-binding framework (see May 1977 and much subsequent work).

It is perhaps inviting, given the spectacular rise of generative semantics in the late 1960s and its equally spectacular collapse less than a decade later, to dismiss it as little more than a phenomenon to be attributed to sociological or personal factors. While such factors were clearly involved (for discussion, see Newmeyer 1986a: 101–3, 126–7, 137–8), there was an intellectually far more respectable reason for its success, however short-lived. Generative semantics promised to ground syntax in a theory of universal principles in a way that its precursor of the first decade of generative syntax did not and that its emergent rival, the lexicalist model, was perceived not to.

Rules played an ever-decreasing role in generative semantics in the period that it flourished and were almost never formulated precisely. Transformations such as passive, predicate raising, nominalization, equi and others were often referred to, but rarely received any motivation beyond the observation that they seemed a necessary intermediary between two structural configurations whose correctness had already been decided for independent reasons. That is, whenever generative semanticists needed a transformation to collapse two clauses, they postulated predicate raising at work; to raise a noun phrase to a higher clause, raising; to make an object a subject, passive. Little independent motivation for the application of these rules was ever given, aside from the need to relate predetermined structures (for further discussion, see Newmeyer 1986a: 129).

In an early generative semantics paper, George Lakoff made explicit the marginality of rules and their motivations in this framework. After positing essentially identical deep structures for the sentences *Seymour sliced the salami with a knife* and *Seymour used a knife to slice the salami* on the basis of their shared semantic properties, Lakoff wrote:

> Due to the nature of the definition of deep structure, one can provide arguments for the identity of deep structures without proposing what these deep structures are *and without proposing any transformational derivations*. This type of argument differs considerably from the type of argument that has been used in transformational research so far. To date, research in transformational grammar has been oriented toward proposing rules. Arguments concerning generalizations of deep structure selectional restrictions and cooccurrences have been brought up only in support of some given set of rules. What we have done here is to show that arguments of this sort can be used by themselves *without discussion of rules at all*.
>
> (G. Lakoff 1968b: 24; emphasis added)

By 1972, many generative semanticists had abandoned even *in principle* the possibility of motivating and formalizing grammatical rules. In that year, Ann Borkin edited a manuscript that was devoted to criticizing the rule-formulations in Burt (1971), but offered no alternatives to them. George Lakoff wrote in the foreword that 'the old goal of actually writing a complete grammar for a language has become at best a hope for future centuries and at worst a joke' (G. Lakoff 1972b: i).[5] In an interview that year, Lakoff offered the opinion that 'the time has come to return to the tradition of informal descriptions of exotic languages' (G. Lakoff 1974a: 169).

Generative semantics owes its primary inspiration not so much to the works by Ross and Postal referred to above, but to a book that had been published several years earlier: Katz and Postal's *An Integrated Theory of Linguistic Descriptions* (1964). This book must be considered the intellectual antecedent of generative semantics for three reasons.[6] First, it was fundamentally different in its general orientation from work in the first decade of generative syntax, yet it presaged the spirit of research that would come to characterize the generative semantic period. Katz and Postal's primary goal was not to motivate a language-particular rule or set of rules. Rather, the book was devoted in its entirety to motivating a principle of UG, namely that transformational rules do not affect meaning, or, otherwise stated, that underlying syntactic representations contain all information necessary for semantic interpretation. (This principle has come to be known informally as the 'Katz–Postal hypothesis'.) Some language-particular rules are discussed, and a few of them are formalized, but, significantly, this is undertaken only if they appear to be troublesome for the principle!

The second reason why Katz and Postal must be regarded as proto-generative semantics is that the *particular* principle proposed there, the Katz–Postal hypothesis, would underlie all generative semantic theorizing. Indeed, it is argued in Newmeyer (1986a) that if this principle is followed consistently, there is no way to avoid arriving at generative semantics.

Third, that book proposes a novel heuristic for 'investigating syntactic structure' that would guarantee that work which followed it would downplay the importance of rules. Katz and Postal phrase their heuristic as follows:

> Given a sentence for which a syntactic derivation is needed, look for simple paraphrases by virtue of synonymous expressions; on finding them, construct grammatical rules that relate the original sentence and its paraphrases in such a way that each of these sentences has the same sequence of underlying P-markers. Of course, having constructed such rules, it is still necessary to find independent syntactic justification for them.

> (Katz and Postal 1964: 157)

This heuristic seemed to suggest that doing syntax involves four steps: first, formulating some seemingly reasonable principle of UG (in this case the principle of meaning-preservation); second, positing structures that support the principle; third, filling in the rules as needed; and, fourth, looking to see whatever other evidence might support these rules. In practice, however, the heuristic led to a diminution of the importance of rules by making them a sort of afterthought in the process of grammar construction. After all, given two levels of structure in advance, it is a trivial enterprise to construct rules linking them. As a consequence, in the fully developed generative semantics of the late 1960s and early 1970s, the third step was rarely taken, much less the fourth.[7]

Interestingly, the Katz–Postal book differs from the works that formed the principal inspirations of the other three periods in that few, if any, contemporary researchers explicitly recognized it as having played that role. In his major foundational statement of generative semantics, G. Lakoff (1971a) mentions the Katz–Postal book only to dismiss it with the opinion that as a result of it, 'a precedent had been set for the use of arbitrary markers, though that precedent was never justified' (*ibid*.: 288).

By 1972, there were a number of signs that the hegemony of generative semantics was drawing to a close; by 1975 or 1976, the community of practitioners of that framework had collapsed utterly. Increasingly, the principles propounded by this framework proved to have serious empirical deficiencies (for extensive discussion, see Newmeyer 1986a: 126–38), leading many linguists to question its theoretical foundations and to look elsewhere for a model in which to work.

For our purposes here, the interest lies in how the leading generative semanticists chose to deal with the empirical problems. For the most part, their general reaction was not to deny that they existed. Instead, it was to conclude that they would admit to a solution only if the types of data relevant for syntactic theory were expanded. So, for example, difficulties with the Katz–Postal hypothesis led generative semanticists to propose global derivational constraints (G. Lakoff 1970a), which allowed transformations to have access to derivationally remote grammatical structures, in particular to semantic structures. Since there was no obstacle to encoding presuppositional information in the semantic representation of the sentence (G. Lakoff 1971b), it was an easy step to take to allow individual rules access to such information. Thus, the presuppositions of a sentence had now become data of relevance to syntax.

To give another example, by 1970 it was clear that the principle that every anaphoric expression should have a structural antecedent in the sentence was untenable, if one were to accept the rather 'shallow' conception of structure that had predominated to that time. The solution proposed by generative semanticists like Ross (1970) and Sadock (1974) was not to reject the principle, but to conclude that it could be saved if the nature of the speech act represented by the sentence is encoded in the syntactic structure. As a consequence, information about speech acts had become syntactic data as well.

This broadening of the data base for syntactic theory had disastrous consequences. By 1972, the conclusion had been reached that virtually everything affecting a speaker's judgement about a sentence is a matter for syntactic analysis (for an explicit statement to this effect, see G. Lakoff 1974a: 159–61). There was now so much data to be accounted for, and of such diverse types, that there was no way that it could be assimilated, much less integrated into a formal theory. As a consequence, papers in late generative semantics were often no more than lists of unanalysed sentences that a theory might have to deal with, or were fascinating observations about language in use that were felt to have some bearing on the operation of a grammatical principle. Even important papers by leading practitioners of that framework had become little more than lists of sentences differing slightly from each other in their acceptability (G. Lakoff 1973) or a series of anecdotes about discourse conventions governing such matters as politeness (R. Lakoff 1973).

In short, by 1972 or 1973, generative semantics, which was born in the rejection of the turn towards descriptivism that was more and more characterizing work in early transformational grammar, had itself come to abandon theory-construction for a purely descriptively orientated approach to linguistic phenomena.

Where would generative syntacticians now turn? At the time, essentially two options were offered. One was relational grammar. It is hardly an exaggeration to claim that this framework was born out of the wreckage of generative semantics. Its two leading figures, Paul Postal and David Perlmutter, were generative semanticists who had never abandoned the commitment to search for abstract principles of UG – the kind of commitment that had driven early work in that framework.[8] A number of other former generative semanticists flirted for a time with relational grammar in the mid- and late 1970s.[9]

This is not the place to discuss the difficulties that relational grammar had in winning a substantial body of adherents, whether they had been generative semanticists or not (the matter is taken up in Newmeyer 1986a: 218). Suffice it to say, however, that it was the other option that formed the basis for the next turn in generative syntax. For the remainder of the 1970s, the model for syntactic research was the paper 'Remarks on nominalization' (henceforth 'Remarks'), written by Chomsky in 1967 and published in 1970. This paper, and to a lesser extent Chomsky's 1971 paper 'Deep structure, surface structure, and semantic interpretation' (henceforth 'DSSSSI'), were to usher in the second rule-orientated period in generative syntax.

THE SECOND RULE-ORIENTATED PERIOD: LEXICALISM

By the mid-1970s, mainstream work in generative syntax had again become rule-orientated. That is, the majority of papers were devoted to motivating or demotivating the existence of some particular rule in some language, or to arguing at what level a particular rule should apply. Most linguists carrying out such a programme explicitly saw themselves as carrying out the 'lexicalist' programme initiated in the 'Remarks' paper and/or the 'interpretivist' programme of 'DSSSSI'.[10]

Reading these two papers, it is not immediately obvious why the orientation resulting from them should have turned out to be directed towards rules rather than principles. 'Remarks' and 'DSSSSI', like all period-initiating work, were skilful blends of arguments for general principles of UG in the context of careful attention to specific grammatical processes. The former paper contributed the idea of a richly structured lexicon along with the first proposal of X-bar theory within generative grammar. The latter argued that superficial levels of syntactic structure are relevant for semantic interpretation. In fact, a moral of both papers was that there is more of theoretical interest 'close' to surface structure than had previously been considered to be the case.

The question, then, is why they should have initiated a rule-orientated period rather than a principle-orientated one. The answer owes as much to the tactical needs of the minority within the field that agreed with these papers as to purely intellectual factors. Chomsky undoubtedly felt that the most effective way to fight the then predominant generative se-mantics framework was to bring syntax down to earth, so to speak, by subjecting one particular process to detailed examination. Despite the major theoretical innovations of 'Remarks', the bulk of this long intricate paper is devoted to arguing that *one* grammatical phenomenon, namely nominalization, is to be handled in the lexicon rather than via a transfor-mational rule. The idea was that success in demolishing a nominalization transformation would challenge generative semantics as a whole, just as a card house can be toppled by removing one supporting card. The fact that Chomsky did not achieve instant success with this paper, i.e., that few generative semanticists were convinced to abandon their ideas as a result of it, led Chomsky's supporters to pick *other* rules and attempt the same sort of demolition. Hence, 'Remarks' had a profound influence in shifting attention back towards language-particular rules. Once this process was set in motion, it continued even after generative semantics had fallen by the wayside.

'DSSSSI' had the same effect for a somewhat different reason. The possibility that semantic rules might apply to more than one level of syntactic structure raised the question for each particular semantic rule of where it would apply. Hence it engendered a detailed look at individual rules of this sort to determine their point of application. Thus 'DSSSSI' presents an interesting contrast with Katz and Postal's book: both are concerned with the question of the level at which semantic interpretation takes place, but the conclusions of the latter drew linguists' attention *away* from language-particular rules; if one accepts that semantic rules all apply at a single level and that syntactic rules have no effect on meaning, then that provides one less reason to be concerned with individual rules, whether semantic or syntactic. But if neither the semantic consequences of a syntactic rule nor the syntactic level at which a semantic rule applies are an automatic consequence of the theory, it becomes an essential task to study each one individually.

Two other factors steered this period in a rule-orientated direction. The first is the concern aroused by the results of Peters and Ritchie (1969, 1971, 1973), who proved that transformational grammars, as they were then conceived, had the weak generative capacity of an unrestricted rewriting system (Turing machine). What this was interpreted to mean was that the then-current conception of transformational rules was so unconstrained that transformational grammar made no claim at all about any human languages except that its sentences could be generated by some set of rules. Peters and Ritchie further showed that the situation was not alleviated either by the recoverability condition or by the principle of cyclic application. Many linguists therefore felt that there was little point in constraining transformational rules, i.e., in developing principles of UG to limit their power. They concluded instead that the best hope was to *eliminate* them entirely by replacing them with presumably less powerful lexical rules. Hence transformational rule after transformational rule was subject to microscopic examination, essentially in the hope that evidence might be thereby forthcoming for its nonexistence.[11]

Second, the mid-1970s saw a dramatic increase in interest in formal semantics among linguists, particularly in semantics of the modeltheoretic variety that had been pioneered by Richard Montague. Montague himself had no interest in searching for syntactic principles of UG; in fact, he wrote: 'I fail to see any great interest in syntax except as a preliminary to semantics' (Montague 1970: 373). Many linguists in this period were attracted to this idea, albeit perhaps not in such strong terms. But the attitude of many seemed to be to get syntax over with as rapidly as possible, to postulate some formal rules generating the syntactic constructions of the language and get on to the interesting work – the semantics. Thus their work in syntax, such as it was, was entirely rule-orientatated.

Whatever the virtues of the two Chomsky papers, they did little at first to dislodge generative semantics from its position of hegemony. Aside from winning over the students at MIT to his position – never a difficult task for Chomsky! – they had little immediate effect in engendering significant movement among syntacticians as a whole to adopt the new approach to syntax.

To many syntacticians this work seemed like a vain attempt to prolong the life of descriptively orientated early transformational grammar at a time when generative semantics was putting forward challenging principles of UG. Since in the common view of the time, the more distant a structure was from the surface, the closer it was to (universal) semantic representation, the generative semanticists were able to take full rhetorical advantage of the fact that their framework grounded syntax in meaning, contrasting it favourably with the rival Chomskyan school, whose attention to close-to-the-surface syntax seemed guaranteed to emphasize language-particularity at the expense of universality.

For a time, the majority of syntacticians agreed with George Lakoff's charge that Chomskyan work was not worth considering, given that 'the elements used in [its] grammatical descriptions [were] arbitrary' (G. Lakoff 1972a: 76), as opposed to the elements of generative semantics which had a 'natural [i.e., semantic] basis' (*ibid.*). And indeed a superficial examination of the 'Remarks' paper, for example, which was certainly all that many generative semanticists bothered to grant to it, does convey a feeling of plodding detail, rather than the excitement of discovery that we find in many papers in the generative semantic framework.

As the principles of generative semantics came increasingly to be regarded as untenable, however, the lexicalist work of the preceding years began to attract the attention that had been denied to it when it had first appeared. It did not take long for this work to fill the vacuum left by the collapse of generative semantics, and, for the reasons discussed above, the new period that this work ushered in would be a rule-orientated one.

It was as true for the third period of generative syntactic research as it was for the first two that much of the most outstanding work produced was in the early days of the period. Actually, what are probably the two most impressive pieces of scholarship in the lexicalist framework were written while generative semantics was still in its heyday: MIT dissertations by Ray Jackendoff in 1969 and Joseph Emonds in 1970. While they were published later (in 1972 and 1976 respectively) under different titles, their original titles reveal their fundamentally rule-orientated nature: 'Some rules of semantic interpretation for English' and 'Root and structure preserving transformations'. Both are painstaking works devoted to detailed examination of particular rules in the context of defending the lexicalist alternative to the then predominant generative semantics. The former discusses the general nature of rules of semantic interpretation along with their precise formulation and point of application; the latter argues that the structural effects of transformational rules are to a large extent predictable on the basis of their structural descriptions.

As the lexicalist period progressed, however, publications whose central theme was devoted to some general principle became increasingly rare, while those that focused on a language-particular rule or rules became increasingly common. In keeping with a principal theme of the 'Remarks' paper, it became standard practice for several years to write papers demonstrating that a particular process should not be handled by means of a transformational rule or, usually equivalently, to argue that the deep and surface structures of some constructions are coincidental.

A look at some of the MIT Ph.D. dissertations written from 1972 onwards confirms both the rule-orientated nature of the period and the zeal with which the existence of once uncontroversial transformations was called into question. A five-year period saw a series of dissertations devoted to arguing that particular transformations should be greatly restricted in their scope or eliminated entirely, including pronominalization (Wasow 1972); complementizer placement (Bresnan 1972); negative placement (Lasnik 1972); *there*-insertion (Jenkins 1972); a variety of transformations (Bowers 1973); pseudo-cleft (Higgins 1973), and dative movement (Oehrle 1976). In general, the prior transformational account was replaced either by one involving base generation accompanied by a lexical rule relating the constructions or by a surface structure rule of semantic interpretation.

The contemporary spirit of demolishing long-accepted transformational rules rapidly extended beyond MIT. At the 1977 annual meeting of the Linguistic Society of America, over half of the generative syntax papers presented were devoted to showing that some grammatical process in some language should not be captured by means of a transformational rule.

The most common strategy used in this period to demonstrate that a process was to be handled lexically rather than transformationally appealed to the principle outlined in *Aspects*: that the lexicon is the repository of irregularity in language. This meant that many papers provided sets of examples showing that the process in question is not fully regular. So, for example, Oehrle (1976) appealed to the many apparent exceptions to the one-time well-accepted transformational rule of dative movement, some of which are illustrated in the examples below, to argue that the process should be handled lexically:

(5) a. *I'll get a ticket for you / I'll get you a ticket*
     b. *I'll obtain a ticket for you / *I'll obtain you a ticket*

(6) a. *You should give back the package to the owner / You should give the owner back the package*
     b. *You should return the package to the owner / *You should return the owner the package*

Now it needs to be stressed that there is nothing more intrinsically 'principled' or 'explanatory' about a transformational analysis of a phenomenon than a lexical one. Nevertheless, the advocacy of a lexical solution to syntactic problems in this period tended to lead syntactic research into a new phase of emphasizing description over explanation, a phase that was accompanied by the same marked decline in standards of argumentation that was witnessed by the first two periods. This came about for two closely related reasons: first, because it led linguists to be more concerned with surface irregularity in language than with abstract generalizations; and, second, because it tended to downplay the search for independent but interacting principles to handle complex data.

The concern with irregularity – the demonstration of which was considered to be the linchpin of the argumentation for a lexical treatment – became an obsession of the period. Many linguists of the time seemed to glory in it as, exaggerating a bit, linguistics for them had now become the search for irregularity in language. For example, Hust produced a paper arguing against a transformational account of the 'unpassive' construction, which is essentially a 35-page list of the irregularities and idiosyncracies of the construction (Hust 1977).

At the same time, once a process was attributed to the lexicon, the wide-spread conception of that component as being little more than an elaborate list provided little incentive for many linguists to probe further to see if some deeper generalizations might be at work to account for at least some of the irregularities that had led to its being placed there. Thus having argued that a construction was not to be handled transformationally, many linguists were content simply to characterize it by means of item-specific subcategorization frames in the lexicon.

To make matters worse, as time went on, the *criteria* for transformationhood were set so stringently that no process could hope to meet them. For example, Brame (1978) was even able to argue against a transformational rule of *wh*-movement on the basis of 'irregularities' such as the following:

(7) a. *What the hell did you see?*
     b. **You saw something the hell*
     c. **You saw what the hell?*

In other words, by the end of this period, 'discovering' that a process was not transformational in nature had become no more than a logical consequence of the assumptions that guided the investigation.

The obsession with irregularity, and the descriptivist consequences that accompanied it, even affected work in this period which was not addressed to the question of the transformationality of a process. For example, a crucial argument in Pullum and Wilson (1977) for categorial reanalysis of the English auxiliaries depends on the irregular behaviour of the marginal modals *dare, need,* and *ought.*

In other words, from the assumption that the lexicon is the repository of irregularity in language, many lexicalists seemed to derive the conclusion that language is one great warehouse of irregularity.

The bias towards lexical solutions was so great that there was rarely any attempt to show that the apparent irregularity threatening a transformational account was in reality a consequence of some independent principle. For example, to Freidin (1975), the absence of passives of the verbs *cost, resemble,* and *weigh,* illustrated in (8), was prima facie evidence against a transformational rule of passive:

(8) a. **Ten dollars was cost by the book*
     b. **Mary is resembled by her sister*
     c. **A whole lot was weighed by the bag of groceries*

In his lexical analysis, these verbs were simply to be listed in the lexicon as unsubcategorized for passive. Yet an independent explanation for the ungrammaticality of sentences like (8a–c) had been put forward several years earlier. Jackendoff (1972), whom Freidin did not cite, attributed the ungrammaticality of these passives to their violating the 'thematic hierarchy condition', which also accounted for unexpectedly bad reflexive and raising constructions, and at the same time explained many of the cross-over facts treated in Postal (1971).[12]

To give another example of how lexical solutions went hand in hand with a lack of interest in the search for general principles, consider the extended argument in Brame (1976) against verbs like *want* with surface VP complements (as in (9a)) embedding full sentences, whether with lexical subjects (9b) or pronominal ones (9c):

(9) a. *John wanted* [$_{VP}$*to leave*]
     b. *John wanted* [$_S$*John to leave*]
     c. *John wanted* [$_S$ *PRO to leave*]

Brame argued that (9a) is simply base generated, i.e., the verb *want* is subcategorized in the lexicon to take a VP complement. We need not dwell on Brame's arguments against (9b), since by 1976 it had become well accepted that there is no rule of equi-NP-deletion deleting an embedded lexical subject under identity to a higher NP (for arguments to this effect, see Jackendoff 1972, Chapter 5). It is interesting, however, to consider why he rejected (9c). His most telling argument was that if *want* were to allow its complement to take a PRO (or dummy) embedded subject in deep structure, then nothing would prevent (10a) from being transformed by the rule of *there*-insertion into ungrammatical (10b):

(10) a. *John wanted* [$_S$ *PRO to be in class on time*]
      b. **John wanted* [$_S$*there to be PRO in class on time*]

Brame posed the issue clearly: the ungrammaticality of (10b) could be attributed either to *want* being subcategorized for VP or to a principle that prevents PRO from occurring in nonsubject positions. It is clear that Brame took the former possibility to be the null hypothesis, since he made no attempt to formulate such a principle. Now he can hardly be faulted for not anticipating government theory (Chomsky 1980a, 1981), which would explain not only (10b), but also a host of other, seemingly disparate, phenomena. It is instructive, however, that, in keeping with the times, he chose the former alternative and opted for the most 'visible' descriptive generalization, instead of searching for a broader principle at work.

Brame's solution to the problem of the complement structure of *want* illustrates the importance attributed to subcategorization features in the lexicalist period, at one and the same time the most descriptive and least explanatory way of handling any phenomenon. The message of the later lexicalist period seemed to be that since *some* grammatical phenomena have to be listed, rather than being attributed to some general principle, it is desirable that *all* should be listed.

It had become clear by the late 1970s that the nihilistic direction in which lexicalist work had been heading could not last forever. If this rule-orientated period were to survive, positive proposals for rule-based systems that still maintained the lexicalists' principal results would have to be forthcoming. The year 1978 saw the publication of two such proposals: Bresnan's paper 'A realistic transformational grammar' and Brame's book *Base Generated Syntax*.

Both publications created a flurry of interest – particularly the former – but they probably had the effect of hastening the end of the second rule-orientated period. Bresnan's lexical entries paired subcategorization frames and functional structures in a manner that seemed to mimic directly the structural descriptions and structural changes of transformational rules. In fact, the mechanics of producing an interpretation in her theory seemed little different in content from that which would be produced by the application of intrinsically ordered transformational rules. Many linguists seemed to share Greg Carlson's 'lukewarm' reaction and his feeling that the paper 'did not contribute substantially to our understanding of language but instead showed that things done one way could be done another' (Carlson 1983: 261).

Brame's book focused on interpretive alternatives to long-distance transformational rules such as *wh*-movement and topicalization, which he replaced by a process of 'operator-binding'. But, as Kac (1980) pointed out, the notion of 'operator' was too obscure for it to be ascertained whether Brame had presented a coherent alternative to a transformational account.

By the end of the 1970s, the rule-orientated lexicalist period had run its course.[13] At the same time, a second principle-orientated approach had arisen to replace it. This approach had its roots in Chomsky's 1973 paper 'Conditions on transformations' (henceforth 'Conditions').

THE SECOND PRINCIPLE-ORIENTATED PERIOD: GOVERNMENT-BINDING

Chomsky's 'Conditions' paper presented a marked contrast from the 'Remarks' and 'DSSSSI' papers that had preceded it by only a few years. The latter focused linguists' attention on lexical processes and close-to-the-surface generalizations in language. The focus of 'Conditions', however, was almost wholly on abstract principles governing the general form of grammars. The paper opens with Chomsky assuming the correctness of one principle, that of blind application of transformational rules. From that point, the reader is led inexorably to further principles, from the tensed-S and specified subject conditions to subjacency, to the principle that movement rules leave traces at their extraction sites, and to a half dozen more of lesser importance.

Chomsky had even less immediate success in winning over substantial sections of the population of syntacticians to the 'Conditions' framework than he had had with the 'Remarks' framework. Generative semanticists, most of whom by 1973 had ceased paying attention to anything that Chomsky produced, by and large ignored it. They were open to the idea of searching for general principles, it is true, but to them such principles had to be 'natural' ones, i.e., ones grounded in semantics or perhaps in the processing of speech. Thus those who cared enough about Chomsky's ideas to read the 'Conditions' paper at all dismissed it out of hand for its 'unnatural', i.e., strictly syntactic, principles of UG.

Lexicalists, on the other hand, were appalled at a framework that seemed to grant centrality to transformational rules, even if its general thrust was to propose ways in which such rules might be constrained. What is more, the abstractness of the principles in the 'Conditions' framework clashed head on with the increasingly concrete surface-orientated direction that lexicalists were taking.

Some lexicalists even saw in the 'Conditions' framework a return to generative semantics (see Bach 1977; Brame 1979; Gazdar 1982). Some of the analogies that were drawn between the two frameworks seem disingenuous as, for example, identifying traces as similar in principle to the global rules of generative semantics. There is a vast difference between a theory that says that every movement rule must leave behind a trace and one that allows global rules to be constructed at will between any two random stages of a derivation. The former does not lead to a more powerful theory, only to a different theory; the latter, on the other hand, leads to a vastly more powerful theory (for more extensive discussion of the question of traces *vis-à-vis* global rules, see Chomsky 1975c: 117–18).

There is a real sense, however, in which the 'Conditions' framework, and the government-binding theory that it gave rise to, *are* like generative semantics. They share a commitment to prioritizing the postulation of a set of general explanatory principles governing UG. This has led both of them to look at the big picture first, to concentrate on the general form of grammars at the expense of constructing actual grammar fragments containing formalized rules. Both generative semanticists twenty years ago and GB practitioners today would willingly plead guilty to downplaying the language-particular, and would argue that doing so permits one to grasp more effectively the general principles of language organization.

In any event, throughout the 1970s, the 'Conditions' framework was very much overshadowed by lexicalism. There were, to be sure, a handful of people developing it outside MIT, and almost from the beginning Chomsky was able to attract a following in Europe to his new approach to syntax. Numerically, however, the body of linguists following and developing 'Conditions' was considerably smaller than that which the 'Remarks' paper had attracted.

What then caused the turn to this framework around 1980? Two factors were responsible. First, as pointed out in the previous section (pp. 59–61), the lexicalist movement had sunk into a deep decline and had, for the most part, ceased to act as a major pole of attraction for students entering linguistics. But even more importantly, a qualitative change had occurred in the rival Chomskyan framework.

The publication of the paper 'On binding' in 1980 and, much more importantly, the launching of GB in the following year by the publication of the book *Lectures on Government and Binding* (*LGB*), represented a quantum leap forward in the development of the 'Conditions' framework. These works seemed to unify a great number of seemingly disparate grammatical phenomena in a conceptually simple and elegant overall framework of principles. In particular, the principles of *LGB* succeeded in subsuming many of the most troublesome and *ad hoc* features of the 1970s papers that had followed 'Conditions', in particular the bulk of the idiosyncratic filters that had been proposed.

The effect of *LGB* was explosive. It seemed as if overnight ten times as many people were working in GB as had been involved in its antecedent 'Conditions' framework in the year before its publication; indeed, it seemed almost as if ten times as many people were doing generative syntax as had been before. And *LGB* had another interesting result: for the first time in over fifteen years, the majority of people doing syntax were working within the framework currently being developed by Chomsky.

The fourth period of generative syntax followed the first three in the degree to which substantial progress was made in its initial years of predominance. Many early studies which were coincident with the advent of GB or which appeared soon afterwards have become classics: one thinks of Borer (1980) showing that the set of permissible 'landing sites' for movement rules follows from the θ-criterion; the demonstration in Rizzi (1982) that the principle of subjacency can be maintained for Italian if it admits a slight degree of parameterization; and the Huang (1984) zero topic analysis of empty subjects in Chinese, Japanese, and other languages. In one 26-month period (July 1980 to September 1982) MIT dissertations appeared by Joseph Aoun, Hagit Borer, Denis Bouchard, Luigi Burzio, Osvaldo Jaeggli, Alec Marantz, David Pesetsky, Kenneth Safir, Timothy Stowell, and Maria-Luisa Zubizarreta. Each of them has left its mark on the shape of GB theory.

My characterization of the 1980s as a principle-orientated period might seem to be contradicted by the appearance of the frameworks of lexical-functional grammar (LFG) (see Bresnan 1982a) and generalized phrase structure grammar (GPSG) (see Gazdar *et al.* 1985) almost simultaneously with that of GB. Both give the appearance of being lexicalist and rule-orientated; indeed, LFG appears to be a rule-orientated theory *par excellence*. The typical paper in this latter framework (Andrews 1982 could serve as an example) devotes most of its space to detailed examination of the linking, much of it language-particular, between grammatical relations, constituent structure, morphological markings, thematic roles, and functional structure.

Two points are in order. The first is that even if the characterization of both LFG and GPSG as rule-orientated is correct, given that so few people actually work in these frameworks, the fact is of little consequence. The body of linguists that works in LFG has barely transcended the circle around Joan Bresnan. A great many more linguists work in GPSG than in LFG, but even their number is relatively small. I compiled a list of what was published in 7 journals and presented at 4 conferences in 1986 and found 72 GB papers, but only 10 in GPSG and 2 in LFG (there were also 2 papers that attempted to unify GPSG and LFG).[14] There were actually more papers published and presented in relational grammar (8 in all) than in LFG, despite the popular wisdom that relational grammar was still-born in the 1970s.

The second point is that while LFG is clearly a rule-orientated theory, this characterization is less clearly true of GPSG. In its early stages, it is true that it essentially recapitulated the rule/construction homomorphism of early generative grammar: for the most part, each phrase structure rule or metarule served to characterize a particular construction in the language. But this is not true today; now a wide variety of interacting principles must be appealed to in the derivation of any single construction (see, for example, the discussion of the English 'fronted auxiliary' construction in Gazdar *et al.* 1985: 60–5, in which four separate principles interact to yield the surface forms, only two of which are particular to the construction). Likewise, there are a number of cases in GPSG in which a single principle is involved in the generation of several constructions. For example, its foot feature principle is at work in the derivation of questions, relative clauses, reflexives, and reciprocals.

I have claimed that the first three periods, despite the solid advances that accompanied their coming into being, ultimately degenerated into little more than a form of descriptive linguistics with a generative veneer. Has this happened to the fourth period as well? I would answer this question in the negative, though it is clear that the potential is there for such a development. Ideally, GB should develop in the following manner: with each passing year the principles should broaden in scope, gradually subsuming what in previous work had to be stated in terms of a language-particular rule. At the same time, the degree to which each principle admits parameterization should come to be circumscribed within well-defined limits. In other words, in the ideal case, the deductive structure of the theory should become ever more profound.

It is easy to see what the alternative to this ideal case would be. In this worst-case scenario, the amount of parametric variation postulated among languages and the number of possible settings for each parameter would grow so large that the term 'parameter' would end up being nothing but jargon for language-particular rule. In this scenario, as many different parameters and parameter-settings would be needed as there are construction-types in language. Thus doing GB would become nothing more than listing a set of 'parameters', each one a description of a recalcitrant fact in some language.

In fact, in a 1984 GLOW Newsletter, Bennis and Koster warned of this very possibility:

> Parametric syntax and phonology have quickly become very popular. Of necessity, this has led to some excesses: too often ill-understood differences among languages are simply attributed to some new *ad hoc* parameter.
>
> (Bennis and Koster 1984: 6)

One does feel uneasy at the language-specificity of some parameters that have been proposed within GB. Consider the papers from the Fifteenth Annual Meeting of the North Eastern Linguistic Society in 1985, in which six papers propose parameters of variation. Some of these in fact do seem fairly general, including one distinguishing nominative/accusative languages from ergative/absolutive languages; a parameter that states that, in some languages, prepositions govern only elements in their subcategorization frames; and one that states that nominative case is assigned inherently in languages with no category AGR (Agreement). But others have the appearance of being uncomfortably language-particular, including one that states that Finnish is immune to the Case filter; one which has *wh*-movement pass through INFL in Yoruba; and a parameter that states that a preposition must be properly governed in Dutch in order to be a proper governor itself.

It seems clear that the future success of GB – in particular, its success in avoiding the fate that befell the predominant frameworks in the three antecedent periods of generative syntax – will be determined in large part by its ability to constrain the language-particular parameterization of principles.

CONCLUSION

In this chapter, I have suggested that we rethink the nature of the historical development of generative syntax. It is tempting to think that the history of this field can be interpreted as a straight-line development from *Syntactic Structures* to present-day theorizing, through which in gradual fashion principles of UG have allowed language-particular rules to be simplified and, ultimately, eliminated. But this tempting account is not a factual one. Instead, the field has seen alternating rule-orientated and principle orientated periods, each of which has followed a remarkably similar course of development.

Chapter 6

Chomsky's 1962 programme for linguistics

A retrospective

Co-authored with Stephen R. Anderson, Sandra Chung and James McCloskey

'THE LOGICAL BASIS OF LINGUISTIC THEORY'

The historical setting

Thirty years ago Noam Chomsky presented a paper at the Ninth International Congress of Linguists entitled 'The logical basis of linguistic theory' (henceforth 'LBLT'). In this paper, he outlined his programme for linguistic theory, an approach to language then known to all and still known to some as 'transformational generative grammar'. This paper was particularly memorable for a number of reasons. First, it marked the first international exposure for the theory and the first international recognition for the 33-year-old Chomsky, whose fledgling theory had been encapsulated five years earlier in the monograph *Syntactic Structures* (Chomsky 1957). Chomsky was one of only five plenary speakers at the Congress, the others being the European luminaries Jerzy Kurylowicz, Emile Benveniste, André Martinet, and N. D. Andreyev. Second, 'LBLT' introduced several important theoretical innovations that were to affect profoundly the shape of the theory and technical terms that were to become everyday generative parlance. And finally, the paper is famous – 'notorious' is perhaps a better word – for the internecine polemics that it engendered, though surely not over those aspects that Chomsky would have considered most central. It was primarily as a result of 'LBLT' that generative grammarians acquired the reputation of relishing – indeed, seeking – intellectual combat to defend their views and challenge those of their opponents.

The goals of this chapter are to present the 'LBLT' theory and to discuss the extent to which its conceptions have been maintained in current generative work. It might be worth mentioning briefly the circumstances under which Chomsky came to give a plenary address. The Congress was held in Cambridge, Massachusetts, with the venue alternating between MIT and Harvard. The organizers' original plan was to have Zellig Harris as a plenary speaker and therefore for him to represent, so to speak,

American linguistics. But Harris wavered for weeks over whether or not to accept his invitation and by the time that he finally turned it down, the meeting was rapidly approaching. With time running out, the three MIT linguists on the local organizing committee, Morris Halle, Roman Jakobson, and William Locke, coaxed Chomsky into replacing Harris. Chomsky, never an avid conference-goer, agreed, though his entire contact with the meeting was limited to the drive into Cambridge the morning of his presentation, staying for a late afternoon reception, and driving back that evening.

So there was an element of serendipity in Chomsky's having the opportunity to come across as the *de facto* spokesperson for American linguistics, though the organizing committee had hardly chosen a relative unknown to replace Harris. Not only had *Syntactic Structures* made a big splash, but Chomsky's review of Skinner's *Verbal Behavior* (Chomsky 1959) had extended his reputation far beyond the narrow circle of professional linguists. Likewise, his presentation and defence of transformational generative grammar at the Third Texas Conference on Problems of Linguistic Analysis in English in 1958 (see Chomsky 1962b), a conference called 'an important historic event' by Koerner and Tajima (1986: 10), had left no doubt as to his possession of the rhetorical skills that one would expect of a plenary speaker at an international congress.

The 'LBLT' programme for linguistics

To outline briefly the contents of 'LBLT': the first section elucidates Chomsky's conception of the goals of linguistic theory, stressing that speakers' unbounded ability to produce and understand novel sentences and learners' limited input lead to the conclusion that linguistic competence must be highly structured, abstract, and to a significant extent, innate. The section repeatedly stresses that the transformational model is a formalization of features implicit in traditional grammars, amply illustrated by untranslated quotes from von Humboldt.[1] In Section 2, 'Levels of success for grammatical description', Chomsky introduces the trichotomy observational-descriptive–explanatory adequacy. Many concrete illustrations are given from phonology, syntax, and (to a limited degree) semantics to illustrate the character of an explanatorily adequate theory, that is, one which provides a principled reason, independent of any particular language, for choosing the descriptively adequate grammar of each language. The brief Section 3 is methodological, challenging the then still widespread idea that operational criteria for establishing the 'correctness' of linguistic data enjoy a privileged position. Section 4, entitled 'The nature of structural descriptions', is just that – an account of the levels and rule types in phonology and syntax. But it is remembered primarily for subsection 4.3, 'Taxonomic phonemics', a lengthy and blistering attack on post-Bloomfieldian and other structuralist approaches to phonology, an attack which practitioners of these approaches were equally strident in maintaining to be an utter misrepresentation on Chomsky's part (see, for example, Householder 1965; Lamb 1966; and the replies in Chomsky 1966; Chomsky and Halle 1965; and Postal 1968). Section 5 concludes the paper with a brief discussion of the relationship between linguistic theory and models of perception and acquisition.

Any historical account of 'LBLT' and its importance has to deal with the fact that no fewer than four versions of the paper were in circulation, three of them published. The preprint was passed around, mimeographed, and discussed for two years before the somewhat amplified version which Chomsky presented was published in 1964 as part of the Congress proceedings, along with a transcript of the discussion session that followed (Chomsky 1964c). But 1964 also saw the publication of the paper in two revised forms, both called 'Current issues in linguistic theory', one a chapter in Fodor and Katz (1964) (Chomsky 1964b), the other a monograph published by Mouton (Chomsky 1964a). By comparing the latter two with the former, we can see the rapid pace of development of linguistic theory in that period and catch a glimpse of Chomsky's own evolving interests. The 'Current issues' papers expand on his increased attention to the rationalist philosophical antecedents of generative grammar, give even more space to Humboldt, and point to the importance of the views of Descartes and the Port-Royal grammarians. More importantly, however, they incorporated the work of Jerrold Katz, Jerry Fodor, and Paul Postal which was devoted to the treatment of semantics within generative grammar and the determination of the level at which syntactic structures are interpreted semantically (Katz and Fodor 1963; Katz and Postal 1964). The 'Current issues' anthology paper added a discussion of the semantic component, while the book referred for the first time to the notions 'deep structure' and 'surface structure'.

Three decades of overall consistency

It is remarkable how constant Chomsky's explananda have remained during the past thirty years. In 1962, the 'central fact' to be explained was that:

> a mature speaker can produce a new sentence of his language on the appropriate occasion, and other speakers can understand it immediately, though it is equally new to them . . . . On the basis of a limited experience with the data of speech, each normal human has developed for himself a thorough competence in his native language.
>
> (Chomsky 1962: 914–15)

This fact has now been recast as 'Plato's problem', the fact that 'we can know so much [about language] given that we have such limited evidence' (Chomsky 1986b: xxv). The 'three basic questions' that arise in this regard – 'What constitutes knowledge of language? How is knowledge of language acquired? How is knowledge of language put to use?' (Chomsky 1986b: 3) – are posed as explicitly in 'LBLT' as they were to be in *Knowledge of Language*.

Likewise, the essential structure of the programme to answer such questions remains unchanged. The 'explanatorily adequate' theory to strive for of 1963 evolved into the maximally restrictive theory of universal grammar of later years, one 'learnable' on the basis of the limited and degenerate evidence presented to the child. Again, contrast passages from 'LBLT' and *Knowledge of Language*:

> The learning model B is a device which constructs a theory G (i.e., a generative grammar G of a certain *langue*) as its output, on the basis of the primary linguistic data . . . as input. To perform this task, it utilizes its . . . innate specification of certain heuristic procedures and certain built-in constraints on the character of the task to be performed. We can think of a general linguistic theory as an attempt to specify the character of the device B . . . . [An explanatorily adequate linguistic theory] can be interpreted as asserting that data of the observed kind will enable a speaker whose intrinsic capacities are as represented in this general theory to construct for himself a grammar that characterizes [his] linguistic intuition.
>
> (Chomsky 1964c: 923–4)

> UG [i.e. universal grammar] may be regarded as a characterization of the genetically determined language faculty. One may think of this faculty as a 'language acquisition device', an innate component of the human mind that yields a particular language through interaction with presented experience, a device that converts experience into a system of knowledge attained: knowledge of one or another language.
>
> (Chomsky 1986b: 3)

Nothing has changed but terminology.

At a more rhetorical level as well, we see consistency in the tenor of Chomsky's writing. 'LBLT' foreshadows the books he would write later with a broader audience in mind than those already committed to his version of generative grammar, that is, books such as *Reflections on Language* (1975c), *Rules and Representations* (1980c), and *Knowledge of Language* (1986b). In all of these works we find the broadest theoretical overview presenting the goals and methodology of linguistic theory in something close to educated laypersons' language sandwiched around technical detail probably intelligible to few but his own advanced graduate students. We suspect that the reaction of the Congress participants of 1962 to Chomsky's formulation and discussion of the A-over-A principle was little different from that of later readers engrossed in the discussion of Plato's problem in *Knowledge of Language* who find themselves having to confront the spectacle of clitics moving in LF!

Chomsky has also been consistent in the selective manner in which he picks particular opponents to debate. One could argue that neither his post-Bloomfieldian targets in 'LBLT' nor the philosophers whom he takes on today have ever represented the views of the majority who misunderstand or reject generative grammar. It seems evident that Chomsky has always challenged publically not those alien ideas with the greatest number of adherents, but those he respects sufficiently to merit his attention.

THE 'LBLT' PROGRAMME FOR SYNTAX

The syntactic goals of 'LBLT'

Syntax plays a relatively minor role in 'LBLT'. None the less, it puts forward certain metatheoretical positions that continue to shape theoretical inquiry today, and it maps out certain empirical domains that were to prove central to syntactic research in the years following 1962.

At the metatheoretical level, the discussion of syntax – like the much longer and more controversial discussion of phonology – is grounded in an essentially polemical stance: the insistence that a simple parse of the surface string, and the organization of its elements into steadily more inclusive hierarchical groupings, will never suffice to achieve insightful analysis. If that is so, the argument goes, then a satisfactory syntactic theory will necessarily be more complex and abstract than the taxonomic model would lead one to expect. Indeed, the basic goal of syntactic enquiry is precisely the search for abstract organizing principles of grammar. As Chomsky puts it: 'The general theory . . . would have to make possible the formulation of the underlying generalizations that account for this arrangement of empirical data, and to distinguish these real and significant generalizations from vacuous pseudosimplifications that have no linguistic consequences' (1964c: 928); it must find a principled basis for the factually correct description. One consequence of this goal – also alluded to in' LBLT' – is that a certain tension arises between the empirical coverage of the theory and the attempt to formulate principles that are sufficiently general and abstract. This tension has been, and will continue to be, a fact of life for generative syntacticians, for whom it is at times a source of great frustration. None the less, it is one of the facets of the theory that make the generative enterprise intellectually challenging – and one of the things that make the enterprise difficult.

This view of the fundamental goal of syntactic theory has, we believe, remained constant within generative grammar since 1962.[2] Another element of constancy has been the general programme for syntactic research put forward in 'LBLT': the overall way of viewing what the task of syntactic analysis consists of. Many assumptions of the programme we have in mind are quite specific, and can in no way be said to follow from the metatheoretical imperative just described. Despite this, the programme itself has remained essentially unchanged over the last thirty years.

The programme takes as its point of departure the idea that sentences exhibit complex arrays of overlapping grammatical relationships. A particular element of a sentence, a noun phrase (NP) for instance, may enter into many such relations simultaneously. To take a somewhat oversimplified example, in the sentence *Who might eat everything?*, the NP *who* is the subject of the sentence and an argument of the verb *eat*. It is also an operator that can be assumed to bind a variable in subject position, and a quantifier that takes the NP *everything* in its scope.

The central assumption of the programme is that there is a canonical way of representing these relations: all of them can (and should) be represented phrase structurally, via phrase structure trees annotated with indexings. It follows that if an element of a sentence participates in such a relation, this can only be because the sentence has some representation – not necessarily one that directly reflects the audible surface string – in which the relation is encoded in its canonical form. What do these representations consist of? Crucially, each is constructed from the same vocabulary as all the others, and by way of the same combinatorial processes. What counts as the full syntactic analysis of a sentence is then an ordered set of such representations. More generally, the study of syntax becomes, in large part, the attempt to uncover what those representations are, and what rules or other mechanisms of grammar relate to them.

This overall conception of the objects of syntactic analysis was not much different in 1992 from what it was in 1962. This is not to say that nothing at all has happened within the intervening thirty years. To mention only those aspects of the programme that have endured would be to pass over some of the most interesting developments that have occurred within the theory. It is to these that we turn next.

Syntactic developments since 'LBLT'

To many syntacticians who entered the profession in the 1960s and 1970s (as did the authors of this paper), the task of syntactic enquiry now seems far more difficult and demanding than it once did. The observation immediately suggests two questions. Why should syntax be harder to do now than it was in the early days of transformational grammar? And, accepting that this is so, what might it reveal about the progress of generative grammar over the last thirty years? Exploring these questions is one way to assess what has happened to the programme for syntax since 1962.

Although the representations that serve to encode syntactic relations within generative grammar have remained relatively constant since 1962, the way in which sentences are derived (that is, how the various representations associated with a sentence are licensed) has undergone a radical reorientation. During the 1960s and even the 1970s, enquiry was focused on achieving the goal of descriptive adequacy with respect to a broad range of syntactic constructions, primarily in English. The approach taken to this goal stressed the centrality of transformations and other language-particular rules in relating the different representations contained within a derivation; it also tended to analyse each individual construction more or less independently of all the rest. As a result, a veritable zoo of descriptive devices came to be invoked in syntactic analyses: several types of transformations, their associated conditions (some of these not formalized in any sense), global and – even – trans-derivational constraints, to name only a few. This was a zoo that it was clearly in the interests of the theory to tame.

Considerations of this sort led to several conceptual shifts within the generative programme, the most radical of which occurred in the early 1980s; it can be localized specifically to Chomsky's *Lectures on Government and Binding* which was published in 1981. Today, well into the aftermath, the generative approach to syntax has a noticeably different feel. The older emphasis on rules has been replaced by a more exclusive focus on representations – representations constrained by principles and sub-theories that are hypothesized to be universal. These universal principles interact with language-specific settings of their parameters to produce the constructions that were formerly derived by more parochial transformations. The task of the syntactician has likewise shifted, away from the discovery of language-particular rules and towards the investigation of principles that are, by hypothesis, universal – yet another reason why syntax seems hard to do.[3]

The conceptual shift of the early 1980s grew out of aims articulated by Chomsky in the late 1950s and early 1960s, among them the goal of achieving explanatory adequacy, thereby accounting for how language acquisition can occur at all. But, as has been recognized from the start, the more abstract sorts of explanation now aspired to by syntacticians come with a price attached. As we had occasion to remark above, there seems to be an unavoidable tension between theoretical generality on the one hand and empirical coverage on the other. So it should come as no surprise that current generative syntax has experienced some losses at the descriptive end. Various constructions that once figured prominently in theoretical debate, including *wh*-clefts, comparatives, gapping, and other ellipsis processes, are today largely ignored (and unaccounted for), because the descriptive mechanisms they appear to require fall outside the reach of the principles recognized by the current theory. Admittedly some losses have been recouped: a notable example is the post-1980s analysis of English auxiliaries and negation initiated by Pollock (1989). Still, that there has been some overall empirical slippage is undeniable. A related development has been that, as the theory has tightened to exclude certain possibilities in principle, several constructions whose analysis was once thought to be settled – including the famous *John is easy to please* – now appear to be more recalcitrant.

On the more positive side, the increase in theoretical sophistication within the empirical domains that *can* be described has made it possible to account for facts of increasing subtlety. For instance, a major pre-occupation today is a concern with varying degrees of grammaticality, which were often noted, but rarely analysed, in the early transformational literature.[4] Further, the focus on universal principles has explicitly extended the range of enquiry to languages other than English. The extended enquiry has led to great advances in the understanding of so-called 'major world languages' (e.g., Chinese, French, German, Italian, Japanese), but has achieved far less where other languages of the world are concerned. The discrepancy can be attributed at least in part to the theory's reliance on the linguistic intuitions of the native speaker, a reliance that seems to require there to be a substantial pool of native-speaker linguists in order for serious syntactic investigation to proceed. Whatever the cause, however, the paucity of in-depth results on the 'nonmajor' languages of the world can only be viewed as regrettable.

What we have described so far goes a fair way towards explicating what we mean when we say that it seems hard to do syntax these days. The focus on general and universal principles, the subtlety of the level of description expected, the problems faced by those (like ourselves) who work on languages that they do not speak natively – all contribute, in one way or another, to the difficulties faced by the working syntactician. At the same time, these are precisely the elements of current generative syntax that can make the enterprise challenging and exciting.

We should also observe that – while by no means fully formed in the generative syntax of 1962 – these particular elements of the programme could probably have been anticipated then. As we have tried to suggest, their conceptual origins can be found in 'LBLT', and their subsequent development can, in some sense, be viewed as a natural consequence of the earliest metatheoretical commitments of transformational grammar.

Finally, it is worth mentioning that in certain ways, Chomsky's most recent work (Chomsky 1993) represents a *return* to ideas that he held in 'LBLT' and before, ideas that he then abandoned for twenty years or more. Nowhere is this as true as in his latest views on grammatical organization, which explicitly re-embrace many of the features he first proposed in his unpublished 'The logical structure of linguistic theory' (Chomsky 1955) and maintained until the 'standard theory' of 1965. In his current model, base recursion has given way to the older conception of generalized transformations, rendering a distinct level of d(eep)-structure unformulable. His current work also abandons the level of S-structure, which in a certain sense hearkens back to his 'LBLT' view, given that S-structure, as a level more abstract than surface structure (itself proposed only in the revised versions of 'LBLT' and then replaced by phonetic form (PF)), was a construct dating from the 1970s. However, since in 1962 there was no explicit characterization of the syntax–phonology interface, it is not quite accurate to write that Chomsky has 'returned' to the theory of 'LBLT' in this regard.

THE 'LBLT' PROGRAMME FOR PHONOLOGY

From representations to rules

Chomsky's 1962 programmes for syntax and for phonology necessarily differ in their later evolution as a consequence of the fact that Chomsky himself has not really paid a great deal of attention to phonological issues since the publication of *The Sound Pattern of English* (Chomsky and Halle 1968). As a result, it is difficult to address questions of the continuity (or lack thereof) in his subsequent development of this area. Plenty of other people have been more than willing to contribute to the exploration of what was essentially his programme, however, and indeed we can well ask whether the field might not have been better served had he continued his interest in sound structure.

In 1962, syntax was a field that was just beginning to emerge from the province of traditional grammar to become part of the genuinely scientific study of natural language. Phonology, in contrast, was a vibrantly active field: the core of structuralist linguistics, and the home of its most significant claim to the status of a science, the phonemic principle. An understanding of the impact of Chomsky's paper on phonological research must therefore start from a characterization of just what phonologists were actually doing in the 1950s and early 1960s. By and large, this consisted in elaborating the notion of (what Chomsky refers to as a 'taxonomic') phonemic analysis of the sound system of a language, and preparing analyses of particular languages in these terms. Such an analysis is a transcription system for the representation of utterances in the language. It consists primarily of a set of elements (phonemes) in terms of which the transcription is composed, each defined by its relation to concrete phonetic segments which are its realization. Additional statements of the distribution of phonemes relative to each other were construed primarily as constraints on well-formed phonemic sequences. The entire theory was focused almost exclusively on questions of representation (in the terms of Anderson 1985).

Why was such a representational theory considered important? Because it was related to what was considered a fundamental scientific insight: the centrality of the contrastive function of linguistic elements. It was this notion that was being touted as the model for other behavioural and social sciences, which could achieve real scientific status if they could come up with a kind of analysis that resulted in contrastive invariants the way phonemics did. 'LBLT', of course, argued against this goal: such a representation is probably incoherent, and there is no reliable 'scientific' procedure for arriving at it on the basis of raw phonetic data.

It was this attack on phonemic representation that most outraged the structuralist establishment of the time. Indeed, Chomsky (and Halle)'s reorientation of phonological research did involve the abandonment of concerns for a level of representation that expressed all, and only, the contrastive functions of sound elements. But this was almost accidental: it came as a by-product of a more radical change, the shift of focus from questions of representation to questions of the nature of rules.

Part of the discussion of phonology in 'LBLT' is directed towards showing that the conditions that were supposed to define a phonemic representation (including complementary distribution, locally deter- mined biuniqueness, linearity, etc.) were inconsistent or incoherent in some cases and led to (or at least allowed) absurd analyses in others. But far more important than these was a series of arguments whose core was that interposing a phonemic level between the morphophonemic ('systematic phonemic') and ('systematic') phonetic levels led to a loss of generality in the formulation of the rule-governed regularities of the language. The flavour of these arguments can be suggested by quotes such as the following: 'clearly in this case the critical factors are, once again, the generality and independent motivation of the rules [vowel length before voiced obstruents, intervocalic flapping], and the relation of the forms in question to others . . .' (1964c: 959); 'Halle has pointed out that it is generally impossible to provide a level of representation meeting the biuniqueness condition without destroying the generality of rules, when the sound system has an asymmetry' (*ibid.*); etc.

Arguments of this sort were a novelty: previous discussion of phono- logical structure had more or less disregarded the form of rules. But Chomsky's focus on language as a mental reality required that we treat a characterization of what a speaker knows as the central object of a des- cription, and that meant paying serious attention to the formulation of rules. And thus a theoretical position that led to the impossibility of formulating rule-governed regularities in a satisfactory way is un- acceptable.

Analyses of the sort Chomsky (and Halle) suggested were not in themselves new: Sapir, for example, had proposed similar accounts of various phonological facts (Sapir 1969 [1933]). In fact, if one wanted to, one could perhaps even have maintained a taxonomic phonemic representation in parallel with the account advocated by Chomsky, so long as this was not required to be produced as an intermediate step between phonological and phonetic form. But what actually happened was that Chomsky's arguments convinced phonologists to shift their attention away from defining questions concerning a level of representation, to focusing on the formulation of rules. 'LBLT' initiated a period in which research attention was devoted to the question of how to formalize phonological rules and their interactions. The two central projects that occupied phonological theorists in the period between roughly the early 1960s and the late 1970s were notational conventions for phonological rules and rule ordering in phonology.

A minor irony is thus to be found in the fact that by the late 1970s, paralleling the trend in syntax, concern began to shift back to questions of representation. This was due to the introduction of notions of auto-segmental (and later, metrical) phonology, and has resulted in today's focus on questions of feature geometry and prosodic structure. Questions of the explicit formulation of rules have come largely to be ignored or assumed to be trivial. Likewise questions of ordering. Now, of course, the questions of representation thus addressed are extremely interesting and important, but it is worth while to speculate on why questions of the explicit formulation of rules seem to have disappeared from linguists' attention as a concomitant of the focus on representations. Is this because the issues of the 1960s and 1970s have been resolved? No, rather the opposite is true. They have not been resolved; in fact, at the time, they seemed increasingly impossible to address in a satisfying way, with the result that something more interesting came along and grabbed people's attention. But there was another trend that converged with this.

Explanation in phonology and the evaluation metric

The other important redirection of research that came about from the programme announced in 'LBLT' was a concern with explanation. Previous phonologists had been concerned to develop a theory that was capable of describing the phonemic systems of all of the languages of the world. The problem was to have a theory that was rich enough to describe all languages, a problem that became more and more severe as the empirical basis of linguistic discussion expanded. By focusing attention on knowledge of language as a mental reality, however, and on the problem of how that knowledge is acquired, Chomsky made it not only respectable but necessary to talk about questions of explanation. It was no longer sufficient to have a theory that could describe a set of facts: given a theory that could describe any of the languages of the world, it seemed likely that it would provide many more than just a single description consistent with a given finite set of factual observations, which meant that one had to account for why one particular description corresponded to a speaker's knowledge, while another one (also allowed by the theory) did not.

Thus, as in syntax, a tension was born between questions of the descriptive coverage of a theory and questions of explanation. As more phenomena were uncovered, it seemed necessary to admit more possibilities within the system – but the more possibilities a theory allows, the more difficult the problem of accounting for the choice of some particular description as corresponding to the internalized knowledge of speakers.

Chomsky's proposal for dealing with this tension was to supplement the formal descriptive framework with an evaluation metric over descriptions framed in it. That is, given two possible descriptions, each consistent with the same set of observed facts, one needed a procedure for comparing them. Such a procedure should yield a preference in each such case for one or the other of the candidate descriptions.[5]

The concrete implementation of such an evaluation metric was the procedure of 'feature counting'. It would take too long to explore this here, but it should be pointed out that minimizing the length of descriptions was not at all an end in itself: rather it provided the basis of a descriptive language into which one could translate the statement of particular proposals for an appropriate evaluation metric. That is, the issue for an explanatory theory was the nature of 'linguistically significant generalizations'. A linguist argued that such-and-such a situation constituted a linguistically significant generalization by proposing a formalism in which descriptions embodying that state of affairs were formally more compact than observationally equivalent descriptions not embodying it, and then showing that given a choice, speakers actually do incorporate generalizations of the form in question into their internalized grammars.

This notion was not only rather subtle, but extremely difficult to work out in practice: only a tiny number of actual arguments of this form were ever produced. The best known was Chomsky and Halle's observation about the formulation of morpheme structure rules (more or less the same as phonotactic statements) in terms of features rather than atomic segments (Chomsky and Halle 1968). They argue that the most compact description of English consonant clusters consistent with the observed facts allows for some unattested forms, but not others. The fact that English speakers readily agree that *blick* is a possible (though unattested) word, while *bnick* is not, supports this conclusion. Therefore one way to approach the resolution of the tension between concerns of description and of explanation is to supplement the descriptive framework with an evaluation metric, and phonologists paid lip service to this notion throughout the 1960s and 1970s. But arguments of this general sort are hard to construct, and few were actually offered (for some examples, see Anderson 1974). What is important to note about the structure of the theory Chomsky proposed is that matters of description and of explanation are treated as logically separable, though intimately related. A descriptive framework which allows for the formulation of a rich array of possible regularities is supplemented by an independent notion of linguistically significant generalization, with descriptions over the descriptive vocabulary taken to be plausible to the extent that they embody such generalization (as assessed by the evaluation metric). Subsequent research, however, has tended to conflate description and explanation into a single set of questions.

And thus we arrive at a second irony in the working out of Chomsky's 1962 programme for phonology. Recognizing the importance of explanatory concerns, there is another way to resolve the tension referred to above: limit the descriptive power of the theoretical framework directly. It is therefore in this form that the programme of achieving explanatory adequacy has been pursued. For instance, the descriptive power of rule ordering relations, to which a good part of the phonological sections of 'LBLT' is devoted to supporting, could be reduced if all ordering relations were predictable. So it is now widely asserted that 'extrinsic ordering' is an undesirable enrichment of descriptive capacity, and therefore illicit. But this conclusion does not in fact follow in a theoretical context that provides another device which actually excludes explicit ordering statements except when the facts require them – thus allowing us a descriptive option which seems motivated in some instances, without weakening the explanatory account of the more natural state of affairs that obtains elsewhere.

In our opinion, much of the limitation that current phonology assumes about the descriptive power of phonological formalisms is arbitrary and ultimately illusory. It results in part from (and, in its turn, reinforces) first, the general failure to provide explicit formalizations of rules and second, an arbitrary choice with respect to the concerns of explanation: instead of addressing the question of what constitutes a linguistically significant generalization directly through the development of a procedure for comparing alternative observationally equivalent descriptions, it simply assumes that the framework can be so constrained as to provide at most one description for any set of facts. Of course, if that can be achieved it would be a highly desirable result; but it is not obviously true.

One possible conclusion is the following: phonological theory might be better served by a return to the core of Chomsky's 1962 programme, including (a) a concern for the explicit formulation of rules and their interactions, as well as for the properties of representations; and (b) an approach to the tension between description and explanation that does not prejudge its resolution by assuming that only a single description will be provided for a given set of facts.

THE 'LBLT' PROGRAMME FOR SEMANTICS

One aspect of current linguistic theory that could not have been anticipated in 1962 can be found in its discussion of semantics and its role in syntactic analysis. Semantics is dealt with only cursorily in 'LBLT'. What little discussion there is seems to intimate that at least some semantic issues may ultimately fall under the purview of syntactic theory ('as syntactic description becomes deeper, what appear to be semantic questions fall increasingly within its scope' (1964c: 936)).[6] At the time, there was little to indicate that a completely independent semantic theory – the so-called extended Montague grammar – would come to occupy roughly an equivalent position within the study of semantics to that which generative grammar occupies within the study of syntax. Today, generative syntactic analyses are increasingly informed by advances in semantics made within the Montague programme. A case in point concerns the intuition that interrogative phrases such as *what* are a type of indefinite – a claim put forward, in fact, in 'LBLT'. Chomsky's 1962 discussion offers some elegant argumentation in support of this claim, but cannot do much more than stipulate the result. Current discussions of the syntax and semantics of interrogative phrases (such as Aissen 1992; Berman 1991; Li 1992; Nishigauchi 1990) have pushed the analysis considerably farther by adopting certain ideas from formal semantics, particularly the theory of indefinites developed by Heim (1988). From the perspective of 'LBLT', this intrusion of semantics into syntax (rather than vice versa) is unexpected. It strikes us as a particularly welcome development.

CONCLUSION

Chomsky's address to the Ninth International Congress of Linguists was one of the events that helped to create a new paradigm. It was surrounded by the kind of acrimony, excitement, and agitation that often accompanies the birth of new paradigms. What we have seen over the past thirty years has been the working through of that paradigm. There have been conceptual shifts in that period which are interesting in their own right and which have had a major impact on the working lives of generative grammarians. But these shifts, important as they have been, had their origins in concerns and aims that were clearly articulated in 1962. When one steps back a little from the noise of debate, the picture that emerges is one of foundational stability and continuity.

Chapter 7

Linguistic diversity and universal grammar

Forty years of dynamic tension within generative grammar

INTRODUCTION: DIVERSITY AND UNITY

The theme of this conference, 'From the diversity of languages to the unity of language', could equally serve as the theme for generative grammar throughout its forty-year development. From the start, the central generativist research project has been to extract unity from diversity, to uncover those principles of organization common to *all* of the 5,000-odd languages of the world.

As Chomsky noted in 1986, however, there is a tension between providing an adequate description of this diversity and providing a general explanation of the mechanisms that make it possible:

> there is a tension between the demands of descriptive and explanatory adequacy. To achieve the latter, it is necessary to restrict available descriptive mechanisms so that few languages are accessible . . . . To achieve descriptive adequacy, however, the available devices must be rich and diverse enough to deal with the phenomena exhibited in the possible human languages. We therefore face conflicting requirements. *We might identify the field of generative grammar, as an area of research, with the domain in which this tension remains unresolved.*
>
> (Chomsky 1986b: 55–6; emphasis added)

My remarks will be devoted to the history of the controversies surrounding this tension. In particular, I will focus on the reaction in the field as a whole to the generativist strategy for resolving it (pp. 81–85), on the consequences of the so-called 'second conceptual shift' in generative grammar for language description (pp. 85–89), on the fierce debate about whether significant properties of universal grammar (UG) can be deduced from the study of one language (pp. 89–91), and on the charge that generative grammar has been orientated to English and other familiar western languages (pp. 91–97).

DESCRIPTION AND EXPLANATION

Chomsky's 1986 quote is basically a rewording of the first paragraph of the first chapter of his 1955 manuscript, 'The logical structure of linguistic theory' (for similar remarks, see also Chomsky 1957: 50; 1964a: 54):

> Descriptive linguistics is concerned with three fundamental problems. On the one hand, the descriptive linguist is interested in constructing grammars for particular languages. At the same time, he is interested in giving a general theory of linguistic structure of which each of these grammars is an exemplification. Finally, he must be concerned with the problems of justifying and validating the results of his inquiries, and demonstrating that the grammars that he constructs are in some sense the correct ones. All three of these problems will occupy us in this investigation of linguistic structure.
>
> (Chomsky 1955: i–6; for the published version, see Chomsky 1975b: 77)

Notice that both quotes make it clear that description and explanation go hand-in-hand. Chomsky would therefore probably disagree with Robert H. Robins' conclusion that generative grammar represents a 'theory-oriented' stage in the history of linguistics, rather than a 'data-oriented' stage (Robins 1973).

Nevertheless, critiques of generative grammarians for over-attention to theory at the expense of data are legion. For example, in one of the first published attacks on generative grammar, Bolinger (1960) chastized Chomsky for going so far in this direction that the final product resembled 'engineering' rather than science.

Generativists have tended to resist not only the characterization of their work as 'theory-oriented', but the dichotomy itself. Lees (1965), in a reply to Bolinger, noted that observations are meaningless unless we know what regularity they are supposed to illustrate; furthermore, 'one single productive rule is at once more data-oriented and more model-oriented than the largest collection of examples one could write down' (*ibid.*: 23).

Admittedly, Chomsky has never felt that there is a lack of critical data; if anything we have *so much* data at our immediate disposal that we tend to be blinded by its sheer enormity. Data are too easy to come by for comfort:

> gross coverage of data is much too easily obtained, in too many different ways. There are a million ways in which you can give a kind of rough characterization of a lot of data, and therefore you don't learn anything about the principles at all.
>
> (Chomsky 1982a: 82–3)

The idea that we have enough data at our disposal to formulate profound universals of language has been anathema to most linguists outside
the generative tradition and to a goodly percentage within it. As for the
latter group, one can almost date a particular linguist's abandonment of
the generativist programme with his or her first published attack on the
'narrow' data base of the theory. The year 1972, for example, saw
erstwhile generativists Charles Fillmore and George Lakoff declaring that
'the ordinary working grammarian finds himself in the age of what we
might call the New Taxonomy, an era of a new and exuberant cataloging
of the enormous range of facts that linguists need eventually to find
theories to deal with' (Fillmore 1972: 6) and that 'I think that the time has
come to return to the tradition of informal descriptions of exotic
languages' (G. Lakoff 1974a: 153, from a 1972 interview).

To nongenerativists, particularly Europeans, the reaction to
Chomsky's view on the sufficiency of the data has at times over the years
reached the level of vehemence. The Belgian Eric Buyssens, responding to
Emmon Bach's call for linguistics to pass from the 'natural history' stage
of science to the 'deductively formulated theory' stage (Bach 1965: 135),
remarked that 'On n'a jamais connu le stade de l'histoire naturelle en
linguistique; au contraire, on a toujours été encombré de théories basées
sur une observation insuffisante' (Buyssens 1969: 857). The Frenchman
Claude Hagège writes that as a result of the preoccupation with
universals in generative grammar, our knowledge of individual language
'demeure stationnaire', and their diversity 'se gomme pour ouvrir le
champ aux quêtes hâtives de traits universels' (Hagège 1976: 227–8). And
the Dutch linguist A. H. Kuipers condemned American linguists for their
'theory-oriented, fact-despising approach', which 'constitutes a real
cultural danger' (Kuipers 1968: 84). According to Kuipers:

> Zoologists have given us guides to the birds of North America which
> contain more information on bird calls than linguists have given us on
> the Bella Coola language of British Columbia. These guides can be very
> useful in linguistic field-work, if only the linguists would come down
> from their bird-watching in Nephelococcygia [Cloud-cuckoo land].
>
> (Kuipers 1968: 85)

Given that Chomsky sees description and explanation as complementary tasks, where do opinions like those of Buyssens, Hagège, and
Kuipers come from? Why are they so widespread? The answer is, surely,
that for Chomsky, all data are not equal. He has stressed, at least since the
early 1960s, that 'data [is] of interest primarily in so far as it has bearing
on the choice among alternative theories' (Chomsky 1964a: 98–9). Or,
more recently, while he has 'consciously tried to extend the range of data,
with whatever success, . . . explanation is much more important than
gross coverage of data' (Chomsky 1982a: 82).

To drive the point home, he has been more than willing to develop Kuipers' natural history analogy. Any publication whose primary goal is to extend coverage of data without at the same time pushing back the frontiers of theory he likens to 'a wild flower guide that organizes flowers in terms of colors, number of petals, etc . . . . If I am taking a walk in the meadow, [such] is far more valuable for me than a textbook of molecular biology. If I am trying to understand the nature of life, the opposite is the case' (Chomsky 1991b: 43).

Generativists have therefore shown no compunction at putting on the back burner data that might have the potential to prove troublesome for an otherwise elegant and well-motivated theoretical proposal. In this regard, Chomsky has commented:

> If some remarkable flash of insight were suddenly to yield the absolutely true theory of universal grammar (or English, etc.), there is no doubt that it would at once be 'refuted' by innumerable observations from a wide range of languages . . . . One reason is that we have little a priori insight into the demarcation of relevant facts . . . . For another reason, the particular data may be misconstrued in the context of irrelevant grammars. In short, linguistics would perhaps profit by taking to heart a familiar lesson of the natural sciences. Apparent counterexamples and unexplained phenomena should be carefully noted, but it is often rational to put them aside when principles of a certain degree of explanatory power are at stake.[1]
>
> (Chomsky 1980a: 2)

According to Chomsky, one can 'divide linguists into two types . . . . There is one type whose immediate intuitive reaction is to look for counterexamples because they do not want to believe in [intellectually interesting] ideas; they are the overwhelming majority' (Chomsky 1982a: 45). There is another (very small) group who refuse to be daunted by data that superficially appear to refute a deep theoretical proposal.

Into the first group Chomsky has placed the generative semanticists Paul Postal, James McCawley, John Ross, and George Lakoff, as well as Charles Fillmore, who 'is doing very good work in descriptive semantics . . . . [but who] does not want to base his work on any comprehensive and explicit theory of language' (Chomsky 1979a: 148–9).[2]

Chomsky holds up the Italian linguist Luigi Rizzi as typifying the second group. Rizzi took Italian data that appeared to refute the principle of subjacency in that language, and was able to show (Rizzi 1978) that if the principle were modified in certain ways, it not only held in Italian but extended to handle a variety of phenomena for which it was not originally conceived.

Put simply, the goal of Chomsky and his co-thinkers is not, and never has been, to provide a descriptive account of all the facts pertaining to some circumscribed domain of grammar; rather it is to deepen our knowledge of the properties of universal grammar. As he has put it tersely: 'the *central and critical* problem for linguistics is to use empirical evidence from particular languages to refine the principles of universal grammar' (Chomsky 1967: 439; emphasis added). This goal might very well result in the ignoring of:

> masses of linguistic data that lie beyond the scope of an explicit generative grammar, proposed for some fragment of a language. It is no criticism of such a grammar to point to data that is not encompassed by its rules, where this data has no demonstrated bearing on the correctness of alternative formulations of the grammar of this language or on alternative theories of language.
>
> (Chomsky 1964a: 54)

Remarks such as these seem to have been most successful when there exists basic agreement about the scope of the theory and the fundamental features of a linguistic analysis. But when two theories differ as to their explananda, it is often the case that data that are not encompassed by the principles of one turn out to be fundamental facts which can be explained by the alternative. So George Lakoff, in his late generative semantics phase, argued that since 'generative semantics and the extended standard theory don't even come close to having the same subject matter' (G. Lakoff 1974a: 175), it *is* valid criticism to point to data not handled by some set of rules. Generative semantics sets out to explain, Lakoff argued, natural logic, pragmatics, and fuzzy grammar, which, in his opinion, 'Chomsky and other lexicalists don't even consider . . . to be part of the study of the structure of language' (*ibid.*).

Along the same lines, one might interpret Langacker's condemnation of generativists for ignoring categorial prototypicality judgements, conventional expressions, and other phenomena which form the explananda of cognitive grammar in just this spirit (see Langacker 1987: 35). As Langacker notes, different conceptions of the data and their relevance follow from different theoretical outlooks; the greater the differences between theories, the greater the gap between which data are deemed relevant. Thus all sides would agree that it is necessary, when comparing profoundly different theories, such as generative and cognitive grammar, to compare both the depth of principles involved and the extent to which such principles subsume the data.

While I think that it is fair to say that descriptive coverage has broadened as the theory has evolved (one thinks of the wealth of binding facts from a variety of languages, which were virtually unknown before the 1970s), the generativist strategy has resulted in descriptive losses as well as gains. Various constructions that once figured prominently in theoretical debate, including *wh*-clefts, comparatives, gapping, and other ellipsis processes, are today largely ignored (and unaccounted for), because the descriptive mechanisms they appear to require fall outside the reach of the principles recognized by the current theory.[3]

To be sure, some losses have been recouped: a notable example is the post-1980s analysis of English auxiliaries and negation initiated by Pollock (1989). Still, that there has been some overall empirical slippage is undeniable. A related development has been that, as the theory has tightened to exclude certain possibilities in principle, several constructions whose analysis was once thought to be settled – including the famous *John is easy to please* – now appear more recalcitrant.

CONSEQUENCES OF THE SECOND CONCEPTUAL SHIFT

Chomsky (1986b) refers to two major conceptual shifts in the recent history of linguistics. The first, ushered in by the advent of generative grammar, 'shifted the focus of attention from actual or potential behavior to the system of knowledge that underlies the use and understanding of language, and more deeply, to the innate endowment that makes it possible for humans to attain such knowledge' (*ibid*.: 24). The second conceptual shift is represented by the government-binding (or principles-and-parameters) model of Chomsky (1981). In this approach, the idea that language is an elaborate rule system is abandoned. Rather, the internal structure of the grammar is modular; syntactic complexity results from the interaction of grammatical subsystems, each characterizable in terms of its own set of general principles. The central goal of syntactic theory thus becomes to identify such systems and to characterize the degree to which they may vary (be 'parameterized') from language to language.

This shift has had important consequences for the description–explanation interplay that concerns us. Early work in transformational grammar presented direct descriptions of particular constructions. In general, the author identified a construction, then formulated a transformational rule coming as close as possible to mimicking its surface characteristics: passives were derived by the passive transformation, relative clauses by the relative clause formation transformation, and so on. As Riemsdijk and Williams (1986: 175) note: 'From today's perspective most work carried out before the late 1960s appears data-bound, construction bound, and lacking in the appreciation for the existence of highly general principles of linguistic organization.'

Since the mechanisms of linguistic theory provided a direct means of characterizing the constructions of the language, it was easy for transformational rules to become used as convenient descriptive tools, i.e., as new descriptive devices to supplement those that had been provided in the past decades by structural linguistics. It is undoubtedly for this reason that individuals such as Robert Hall and Charles Hockett, who were otherwise quite hostile to generative grammar, made approving remarks about transformational rules themselves (see Hall 1965; Hockett 1968).

However, in current generative work in the principles-and-parameters framework, the relationship between grammatical constructions and theoretical constructs is remote, so grammatical analysis fails to provide a direct description of the various structural types found in language. That is, constructions are simply artefacts, 'perhaps useful for descriptive taxonomy, but nothing more' (Chomsky 1991a: 24). Chomsky notes, by the way, that this conceptual shift has resulted in the theory's manifesting to a much smaller degree the flavour of traditional grammar (*ibid.*: 20–4).

Even before the second conceptual shift, some linguists opposed generative grammar for downplaying the importance of the grammatical construction. For example, in another early critique of generativism, Dwight Bolinger called for a direct inventory of the constructions for each language: 'Speakers do not "produce" constructions, but rather "reach for them", from a preestablished inventory' (Bolinger 1961: 381; see the reply in Chomsky 1964a: 54). Since the shift, however, the fact that a grammatical analysis fails to provide a detailed description of particular constructions has been the subject of a voluminous critique, and has even engendered a framework labelled 'construction grammar', one of whose principal goals is to provide direct descriptions of the constructions of the language (see Fillmore 1985; Fillmore *et al.* 1988 and, for arguments couched in terms of generative grammar that constructions are not epiphenomenal, see Pullum and Zwicky 1991 and Zwicky 1987).

Chomsky, as one might expect, is not impressed by the argument that there is any profit in cataloguing the properties of grammatical constructions. He does not question ' . . . a vast array of phenomena of language lie far beyond our current understanding. In these areas we can do nothing but construct descriptive rules, generally language-particular and construction-particular' (Chomsky 1991b: 42). However, he goes on to dismiss this fact as 'an inevitable contingency of empirical inquiry', not as setting a research goal for linguists:

> The phenomena that surround us in the real world of ordinary experience are generally not understood in any clear manner; they are too complex, they involve too many interacting factors, and our understanding is too limited for principled theories to explain a great deal of what is happening before our eyes. Most data fail to help us to attain insight into underlying principles and structure and are therefore uninteresting for the purpose of attaining rational understanding, however valuable they may be for many other aspects of human life.
>
> (Chomsky 1991b: 42)

One interesting consequence of the second conceptual shift has been to spur on the investigation of a wide variety of languages, particularly those with structures markedly different from some of the more familiar western ones. The explanation for this is straightforward. Before the shift (to oversimplify somewhat), one wrote a grammar of English, a grammar of Thai, a grammar of Cherokee, and so on, and attempted to extract universal properties of grammars from the principles one found in common among these constructed grammars. But now the essential unity of all grammars, within the limits of parametric variation, is taken as a *starting point*. One cannot even begin to address the grammar of some language without asking the question of how principles of Case, binding, bounding, and so on are parameterized in that language. But this is impossible unless one has a rough feel for the degree of parameterization possible for the principle. As Chomsky notes, to delimit the domain of core grammar, we 'rely heavily on grammar-internal considerations and *comparative evidence*, that is, on the possibilities for constructing a reasonable theory of UG *and considering its explanatory power in a variety of language types*, with an eye open to the eventual possibility of adducing evidence of other kinds' (Chomsky 1981: 9; emphasis added).

The need to base a theory of parametric variation on a wide variety of languages has resulted in what Bernard Comrie has referred to approvingly as 'one of the most interesting recent developments in linguistic typology . . . the entry of generative syntax into the field' (Comrie 1988: 458). Comparative studies of the null-subject parameter, binding domains, configurationality, and so on are now routine and provide a generative interpretation of the kind of cross-linguistic study that was initiated by the work of Joseph Greenberg in the early 1960s (see Greenberg 1963).

In this regard, it is instructive to observe Chomsky's changing attitude to Greenbergian typological work. In 1965 it was dismissed for its attention to surface structure, and attributed no more promise than the discovery of statistical tendencies (Chomsky 1965: 118). In 1982 he wrote that 'Greenbergian universals . . . are ultimately going to be very rich . . . . They have all the difficulties that people know, they are "surfacy", they are statistical, and so on and so forth, but nevertheless they are very suggestive' (Chomsky 1982a: 111). And by 1986, they are 'important, . . . yielding many generalizations that require explanation . . . ' (Chomsky 1986b: 21). A perusal of the workaday generative literature reveals that Greenberg's pioneering study from the 1960s has evolved in the past fifteen years from unknown to most generativists to among the most important of the period to cite and analyse.

So, we have seen that the second conceptual shift has represented a move away from the descriptivism that early transformational grammar tended to lapse into. It is a bit ironic, then, that this shift has its own seeds for a tilting to the descriptivist end in the description vs. explanation tug-of-war. It could happen in the following way. In the worst-case scenario, as investigation of the properties of hundreds of languages around the world deepens, the amount of parametric variation postulated among languages and the number of possible settings for each parameter could grow so large that the term 'parameter' would end up being nothing but jargon for language-particular rule. In this scenario, as many different parameters and parameter-settings would be needed as there are construction-types in language. Thus doing GB would become nothing more than listing a set of 'parameters', each one a description of a recalcitrant fact in some language. Bennis and Koster warned of this very possibility in a 1984 GLOW Newsletter:

> Parametric syntax and phonology have quickly become very popular. Of necessity, this has led to some exesses: too often ill-understood differences among languages are simply attributed to some new *ad hoc* parameter.
>
> (Bennis and Koster 1984: 6)

One does feel uneasy at the language-specificity of some parameters that have been proposed within GB. Consider the papers from NELS-15 in 1985, in which several papers propose parameters of variation. Some of these in fact do seem fairly general, including one distinguishing nominative/accusative languages from ergative/absolutive languages. But others have the appearance of being uncomfortably language-particular, including one that states that Finnish is immune to the Case filter; one which has *wh*-movement pass through INFL in Yoruba; and a parameter that states that a preposition must be properly governed in Dutch in order to be a proper governor itself.

The major steps in the direction of a corrective to this latent return to descriptivism have been taken by David Lightfoot, in his book *How to Set Parameters*. Lightfoot poses the problem by observing:

> For more than ten years generative grammarians have construed language acquisition as a matter of setting parameters – that is, of fixing option points defined in Universal Grammar. They have busily constructed 'parametric differences' between various languages, while drum rolls and trumpet fanfares have heralded a major conceptual shift . . . . [It is] surprising that so little attention has been paid to what it takes to set these parameters. Sometimes this lack of attention undermines the claims being made, as when an alleged parametric difference is based entirely on data unavailable to children, on negative data, or on data about subtleties of quantifier scope. My most general goal here is to begin to correct this omission by making some claims about the child's triggering experience and about how parameters are set.
>
> (Lightfoot 1991: ix)

Lightfoot goes on to develop a constrained view of parameter setting that would prevent the notion of 'parameter' from being little more than a construct of descriptive typology and, in doing so, probably rules out well over half of the proposed 'parameters' of the previous decade.

THE 'ONE LANGUAGE AND UG' ISSUE

If a survey of the critical literature is any indication, no remark of Chomsky's with respect to the interplay of description and explanation has outraged the linguistic community as much as the following:

> I have not hesitated to propose a general [i.e., universal: F. J. N.] principle of linguistic structure on the basis of observation of a single language.
>
> (Chomsky 1980b: 48)

Esa Itkonen's reaction has not been atypical:

> Those working outside the Chomskyan paradigm have found this type of statement rather preposterous . . . . It looks self-evident that Chomsky is merely repeating the mistakes of his predecessors [who tried to construct a theory of universal grammar based on Latin or French].
>
> (Itkonen 1992: 69)

One might conclude, then, along with Itkonen, that 'the assumption of linguistic universals is not based on data, but rather on conceptual arguments' (Itkonen 1991: 306–7).

But if we take a look at the continuation of Chomsky's passage it perhaps puts the matter in a different light:

> The inference is legitimate, on the assumption that humans are not specifically adapted to learn one rather than another human language . . . . Assuming that the genetically determined language faculty is a common human possession, we may conclude that a principle of language is universal if we are led to postulate it as a 'precondition' for the acquisition of a single language . . . . *To test such a conclusion, we will naturally want to investigate other languages in comparable detail. We may find that our inference is refuted by such investigation.*
>
> (Chomsky 1980b: 48; emphasis added)

In other words, any claim about universals based on a single language makes a testable falsifiable hypothesis. And tested and falsified they are, with great regularity! There hardly exists an issue of a generative-orientated journal that does not propose the modification or abandonment of a hypothesized principle of UG on the basis of data from a previously uninvestigated language. (For what it's worth, to put this claim to an informal test, I opened a random issue of the journal *Natural Language and Linguistic Theory* at a random page and landed in the middle of an article by Carol Georgopoulos arguing for a modification of the empty category principle based on data from Palauan (Georgopoulos 1991).)

To take a criticism in a similar vein to that of Itkonen's, Henry Hiż's negative review of *Aspects of the Theory of Syntax* in 1967 included the complaint that 'Chomsky presents no more than English and an isolated property of Mohawk to substantiate some grammatical universals' (Hiż' 1967: 71). Chomsky replied by analogizing the study of languages with the study of organisms:

> I certainly agree that one should study as many languages as possible. Still, a caveat should be entered . . . . If someone feels that the base of data is too narrow, what he should do is show that some of the material omitted refutes the principles that have been formulated. Otherwise, the criticism has no more force than a criticism of modern genetics for basing its theoretical formulations on the detailed investigations of only a few organisms.
>
> (Chomsky 1972a: 188–9)

The reaction of adherents of the Greenbergian–surface typology school to remarks such as these has been to question the analogy between language and natural objects. So, Comrie writes:

> A priori, there seems to be no reason to assume either that language universals research should require a wide range of languages . . . or that it should not . . . . For instance, if one wanted to study the chemical properties of iron, then presumably one would concentrate on analyzing a single sample of iron, rather than on analyzing vast numbers of pieces of iron, still less attempting to obtain a representative sample of the world's iron . . . . On the other hand, if one wanted to study human behavior under stress, then presumably one would not concentrate on analyzing the behavior of just a single individual, since we know from experience that different people behave differently under similar conditions of stress . . . . Since one of the things we want to find in work on language universals is the range of variation found across languages and the limits placed on this variation, it would be a serious methodological error to build into our research programme aprioristic assumptions about the range of variation.
>
> (Comrie 1981: 5)

While to the best of my knowledge, Comrie's points have not been replied to by any generativists (but see Coopmans 1983 for a general critique), it seems clear that they would reject what Comrie takes as self-evident, namely that the study of UG has more in common with the study of people under stress than with that of the chemical properties of iron. Since, in the generativist view, investigation of a number of languages *has* revealed fundamental principles of organization in common *and* this can plausibly be linked to biological necessity, the analogy to genetic or chemical investigation stands unchallenged. And perhaps it is the case that while *behaviour* under stress varies widely from individual to individual and from culture to culture, the neurophysiological changes in the stressed individual are relatively constant. If this is so, then Comrie has unwittingly suggested an even more appropriate analogy: generativists study the neurophysiology of stress, typologists its behavioural manifestations.

In any event, generativists do not 'build into [their] research programme aprioristic assumptions about the range of variation', since they make no assumptions at all about the range of variation. As far as surface variation is concerned – and this is what Comrie is calling attention to – generativists have made no assumptions because the matter is of no particular theoretical interest to them. And if parametric variation in UG is at stake, no 'assumptions' have been made, only hypotheses based on empirical investigation.

THE 'ENGLISH-ONLY QUESTION'

In *theory*, therefore, much can be learned about the nature of UG from the study of one language. What has been the actual *practice* of generative linguists in this regard? It would seem that the critical literature has reached a near consensus – that the practice fully exemplifies the principle and that the language of exemplification is English. Scores of publications have attacked the putatively English-orientated nature of work in generative grammar and have gone on to draw a variety of negative conclusions from that fact (see, for example, Collinder 1970: 3; Comrie 1988: 458–9; Givón 1979: 42; Hagège 1976: 43–51; Hall 1977: 75; Itkonen 1992: 69, Longacre 1967: 324, and so on).

The most extended attack on the supposed Anglocentric bias of generative grammar is found in Hagège (1976). Hagège asserts that generative grammar is a 'lit de Procuste' that results in 'les traitements générativistes dans lesquels les langues particulières ressemblent au modèle anglais' (*ibid.*: 45–6). Some of the examples that he adduces to support this assertion appear to be based on misunderstandings. For example, he objects to the phrase structure rule in Chomsky (1970c) that places a specifier before the specified element, on the grounds that in Japanese the specifier follows the head, and to attention paid in textbooks to English tag sentences, since such structures are rare, if even existent, in other languages. But, of course, English was being analysed, with no implications for universals.

Admittedly, Hagège also points out overt properties of English that generativists have discovered covertly in other languages, such as an (underlying) copula for Hungarian, obligatory subjects for Finnish, and verbal complements for Sonrai. We will return to this matter below.

Another objection that Hagège puts forward is the clumsy way in which English grammatical terms have been translated into French. So 'performance' is translated directly as *performance*, even though the French word lacks the sense of 'realization', and 'natural language' comes out as *langue naturelle*, which, according to Hagège, has connotations of primitiveness that the English lacks. All of this leads Hagège to give qualified agreement to the view expressed by Martinet (in a *Le Monde* interview) that, due to Chomsky, the field is under the grip of 'l'impérialisme linguistique de l'anglais' (Hagège 1976: 47).

Certainly if we confine our attention to Chomsky's principal publications, there would appear to be merit in the charge that the principles of generative syntax have been English-based. While Chomsky's first generative work was in Hebrew, not English (Chomsky 1951), his examples illustrating proposed universals of UG have in subsequent years been drawn primarily from English. Before going on to discuss the consequences of this fact, it is worth pointing out that it has been *generally* the case that presentations of new models of syntax have taken their illustrative material either from English, from the author's native language, or a combination of the two. Certainly that applies to the great bulk of the nongenerative approaches to syntax that have been put forward over the past fifty years, including those listed in Table 7.1.

One could argue that there are good practical reasons for presenting novel theories using illustrative examples that are likely to be familiar to the reader. Mastering the intricacies of a new theory is difficult enough; adding the challenge of making sense of bewildering and unfamiliar data compounds the problem enormously. Those who have attempted to learn tagmemics from Longacre's *Grammar Discovery Procedures* (Longacre 1964) or, to take a more recent example, role-and-reference grammar from Foley and Van Valin's *Functional Syntax and Universal Grammar* (Foley and Van Valin 1984), will understand what I mean. One is never sure if one's failure to understand a given point is due to a failure to follow properly the exotic language examples, but then again one is never sure that the data are reliable or representative.

Once we move away from Chomsky's work, a very different picture emerges – one that challenges the picture of generative grammar as being rooted in incidental properties of English. Even the earliest work, before there were any significant numbers of adherents of generative grammar outside the United States, was not as English-centred as many believe. For example, of the six faculty members in the MIT Linguistics Department in the late 1960s, four were known primarily for their work in languages other than English: Kenneth Hale for Amerindian and Australian; G. Hubert Matthews for Amerindian; Paul Kiparsky for general Indo-European; and Morris Halle for Russian. And, once again, Chomsky wrote a partial generative grammar of modern Hebrew before attacking

Table 7.1 The languages of illustrative examples in some expositions of syntactic theory

Author's name	Date of publication	Title of text	Languages analysed
Tesnière, Lucien	1959	*Eléments de syntaxe structurale*	(Almost all French)
Martinet, André	1960	*Eléments de linguistique générale*	(Almost all French)
Guillaume, Gustave	1964	*Langage et science du langage*	(All French)
Daneš, František	1964	*A Three-Level Approach to Syntax*	(Virtually all Czech and English)
Lamb, Sydney M.	1966	*Outline of Stratificational Grammar*	(All English)
Dijk, Teun van	1972	*Some Aspects of Text Grammars*	(Almost all English)
Shaumyan, S. K.	1977	*Applicational Grammar as a Semantic Theory of Natural Language*	(All Russian)
Dik, Simon C.	1981	*Functional Grammar*	(Mostly English and Dutch)
Halliday, M. A. K.	1985	*An Introduction to Functional Grammar*	(Almost all English)
Kuno, Susumu	1987	*Functional Syntax: Anaphora, discourse, and empathy*	(Almost all English and Japanese)
Langacker, Ronald	1987	*Foundations of Cognitive Grammar, Vol. 1: Theoretical prerequisites*	(Almost all English)

English. Of the twenty-eight doctoral dissertations written in linguistics at MIT in the 1960s, seventeen (or 61 per cent) dealt primarily with languages other than English, including those by Stephen Anderson (West Scandinavian), George Bedell (Japanese), Thomas Bever (Menomini), James Fidelholtz (Micmac), James Foley (Spanish), James Harris (Spanish), Richard Kayne (French), Paul Kiparsky (various languages), Sige-Yuki Kuroda (Japanese), Theodore Lightner (Russian), James McCawley (Japanese), Anthony Naro (Portuguese), David Perlmutter (various languages), Sanford Schane (French), Richard Stanley (Navajo), Nancy Woo (various languages), and Arnold Zwicky (Sanskrit).

If we look at current work in generative syntax, we find little support for the idea that it is primarily the province of Americans at American universities analysing English. I examined articles from 1990 to 1992 in what are arguably the three most influential publications in this area: *Linguistic Inquiry, Natural Language and Linguistic Theory*, and *Linguistic Review*. I found that out of the sixty-three papers whose theoretical framework is the principles-and-parameters theory, only thirteen (21 per cent) fit this pattern. Actually, only twenty-one, or one-third of the total, focus on English at all. Table 7.2 presents my findings.

What about the charges that incidental structural properties of English are wantonly taken to be universal and thereby imposed on all the languages of the world? Of course, one can find examples of properties of UG that were hypothesized on the basis of an examination of English and then modified as more languages were investigated in depth: principles of extraction and the characterization of binding domains are obvious examples. Are there structural features of English (and closely related languages) that generative syntacticians still (incorrectly) take to be universal? Perhaps, though their doing so is reprehensible only if sufficient evidence exists that they should not be, and such evidence would necessarily involve more than a cursory look at some surface feature of another language. Hagège might or might not be correct that it is a mistake to analyse Hungarian with an (underlying) copula; the fact that it lacks one on the surface is only one piece of evidence relevant to the question.

It seems to me that there are at least as many analyses of English that attribute to it features not overtly found in that language as there are features of English that have turned up in the analyses of other languages. For example, English has been analysed as possessing a complementizer in main clauses (Bresnan 1970), making it look like Arabic; as possessing a subject to complements of verbs like *try* (Koster and May 1982), making it look like the Balkan languages; as possessing a rich Case system for noun phrases (Rouveret and Vergnaud 1980), making it look like Russian; and as possessing a canonical structure in which the subject follows the inflectional element (Koopman and Sportiche 1991), making it look like Irish. Has English been 'forced into the mould' of Arabic, Serbo-Croatian, Russian, and Irish? That seems implausible; rather, deep analysis of English has simply led to the conclusion that it possesses certain features common to these languages, just as deep analysis of some other languages has led to the conclusion that they share surprising properties with English.

There is also another side to the charge that a focus on English, if one were to exist, would represent a form of Anglocentric (or America-centric) linguistic imperialism. Perhaps it is the case that at one time the majority of published works in generative syntax dealt with English. Surely that would be no more than a reflection of the fact that at one time the great majority of generative syntacticians were native English speakers. Katz and Postal took note of this very fact:

Table 7.2 Languages treated in three generative journals, 1990–92

Nationality of author(s)	Residence of author(s)	Language(s) treated	Number of papers
USA	USA	English	13
USA	USA	Yiddish	2
USA	USA	Portuguese	1
USA	USA	Chamorro	1
USA	USA	English, Vata, Chinese, Japanese	1
USA	USA	Jacaltec, Niuean, Chamorro	1
USA	USA	Romance	1
USA	USA	Palauan	1
USA	Canada	Mohawk	1
USA	France	Chadic	1
USA	Switzerland	English	1
USA/Canada	USA/Canada	English	1
USA/Germany	USA	English	1
USA/Canada	USA	English	1
USA/Canada	USA/Canada	Austronesian	1
USA/Israel/China	USA	Chinese	1
Canada	USA	English	1
Canada	Canada	French	1
Canada	Canada	Inuktitut	1
Israel	Canada	Moore	1
Israel	Israel	Hebrew	1
Israel	Canada	Hebrew	1
Israel	Switzerland	Hebrew, Arabic	1
France	France	French	1
France	France	Attie	1
France	USA	Haitian Creole	1
France/Paraguay	USA	French, English	1
Netherlands	Netherlands	Dutch	1
Netherlands	Netherlands	Romance, Germanic	1
Netherlands	USA	Bambara	1
Japan	Japan	English	1
Japan	USA	English	1
Japan	USA	Japanese	1
Spain	Spain	Catalan	1
Spain/Portugal	USA	Romance	1
China	USA	Chinese	1
China	USA	Bantu	1
Norway	Germany	Norwegian, English	2
Morocco	UK	various	1
Argentina	USA	Italian	1
Belgium	Switzerland	Flemish	1
Romania	France	Romanian	1
Switzerland	Switzerland	Swiss German	1
Italy	Italy	Italian	1
Iceland	Iceland	Icelandic	1
India	USA	Hindi	1
Germany/Sweden	Germany/Sweden	German	1
(N) Ireland	(N) Ireland	English	1

> Although the discussion in this study primarily concerns abstract questions about the nature of language, rather than questions about the description of specific natural languages, the examples upon which our answers to these questions are based are drawn almost exclusively from English. We have not overlooked the task of testing our theory against examples drawn from a wide variety of languages. However, we are here concerned more with the formulation and presentation of our theory than with its defense. Moreover, a full-scale empirical test of a theory such as ours is obviously not possible at the present time, because other languages have not received an extensive enough formal description for them to provide the kind of examples needed.
>
> (Katz and Postal 1964: 5)

The alternative, to work on languages that one does not know very well, has its own dangers, and they are not just the dangers of a poor linguistic analysis. As I have noted elsewhere (Newmeyer 1983: 71–2), there are negative social consequences of drawing hasty theoretical conclusions from a perfunctory examination of some poorly studied languages, the great majority of which are spoken by nonwhite inhabitants of the developing countries. By not subjecting such languages to the same degree of detailed analysis as western languages, the linguist stands to reinforce the idea that the western languages – and therefore, by implication, their speakers – are in some fundamental sense more sophisticated and advanced than those of the nonwestern world.

In fact, a tremendous amount of work in the typological tradition initiated by Greenberg bases its data on the most informal sources: brief century-old grammars written by missionaries with no linguistic training; example sentences culled from previously published work; out-of-context questions posed to native speakers found in the university or the community; and so on. All of this gives rise to what Lightfoot (1979) has called the 'Ebeling principle', after the Dutch structuralist Carl E. Ebeling. Ebeling (1960: 43–4) noted that the German linguist Hintze found German syllable structure intractible, although syllable structure presented no analytic problems for him in Kpelle, Ful, and Sahidic-Coptic. Ebeling went on to express bemusement that the American Kenneth Pike could write that 'In phonemic theory today considerable uncertainty remains . . . although . . . it is fortunate that one seldom finds [these difficulties] as strikingly . . . as in English' (Pike 1947: 63–4). Ebeling remarked:

> As to myself, I am inclined to concede to Dutch the honor of putting up the most stubborn resistance to current phonemic analysis, but I am convinced that when a Tübatulabal Indian masters the technique, he will soon notice that it works perfectly for all languages except Tübatulabal.
>
> (Ebeling 1960: 44)

In short, the historical tendency for individual generative syntacticians to focus on their native languages as opposed to seeking broad coverage of as many languages as possible is by no means obviously ill-founded, either linguistically or socially. The more in-depth work accomplished by more native speakers on more languages, the deeper will be our understanding of universal grammar.

CONCLUSION

To conclude briefly, generative grammarians have seen the tasks of description and explanation as wholly complementary. But no description is theory-neutral. The practice, therefore, has been to appeal to language-particular facts only in so far as they bear on a theoretical proposal; theoretical proposals have been judged successful in part to the extent to which they have in turn led to coverage of a wider variety of language-particular facts.

Part II
The linguistic wars

Chapter 8

The steps to generative semantics

AN UNSTABLE SITUATION

Until around 1965, generative theoreticians had been united on virtually every important issue. In one sense, this is hardly surprising – *Aspects* was written by Chomsky with constant feedback from the faculty and students at MIT, who made up at least 90 per cent of the transformational grammarians in the world at that time. Yet, even by late 1965, the first public signs of division had appeared. In the autumn of that year, Paul Postal argued at a colloquium held at MIT that adjectives were members of the category 'Verb' – a conclusion quite uncongenial to Chomsky's view of English syntax. The following spring, John Robert Ross, a graduate student and instructor at MIT, and George Lakoff, a part-time instructor at Harvard and associate in its computation laboratory, organized a series of Friday afternoon seminars in Harvard's William James Building, devoted to challenging analyses then favoured by Chomsky. In the autumn of 1966, with Chomsky on leave in Berkeley, Ross and Lakoff brought their opposition into the open in their classes. Ross's class in universal grammar at MIT drew dozens of students; Lakoff's in syntactic theory at Harvard well over one hundred.

The real fight began upon Chomsky's return to MIT early in 1967. For several years, however, the sides were very uneven. Aside from Chomsky and his current students at MIT (most of whom speedily reconverted from their infatuation with the Ross–Lakoff approach), a large majority of theoretical linguists held positions very much at odds with those of the field's founder and driving force. The rift grew throughout the late 1960s, as measured both by the intensity of feeling of the participants and by the number of theoretical issues at stake.

The primary point of contention at that time centred around the *abstractness* of underlying syntactic structure. While all grammatical structures are 'abstract', the notion 'degree of abstractness' came to be identified with 'degree of distance of deep structure from surface structure', or as contemporary eyes saw the issue, with 'degree of closeness of deep structure to semantic representation'. By this criterion the deep structures posited by many linguists were becoming very abstract indeed. To give one typical (and much discussed) example, Ross and Lakoff argued that the deep structure of (1) was not (2) – as an analysis along the lines sketched in *Aspects* would suggest – but rather the highly abstract (3):

(1) *Floyd broke the glass*

(2)

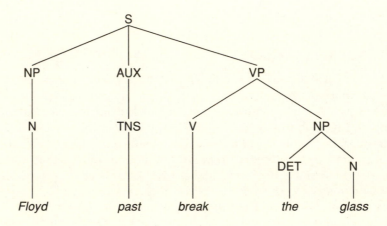

(3)   (See opposite page)

Going hand-in-hand with abstract deep structures was a drastic reduction in the inventory of grammatical categories. For example, abstract syntacticians argued that adjectives, prepositions, auxiliaries, and negative elements were all members of the category 'Verb' in deep structure. In addition, numerous arguments were adduced for 'lexical decomposition' – the structural representation of a word's component elements in the underlying phrase-marker. Example (3) illustrates lexical decomposition. The verb *break* is derived from (roughly) *cause + come about + be + broken*. Under abstract syntax, sentences with radically different surface structures were typically analysed as identical at the deepest level of syntactic representation, as was the case with (4a) and (4b):

(4)   a. *Seymour sliced the salami with a knife*
      b. *Seymour used a knife to slice the salami*

Before the end of the decade, abstract syntacticians had come to abandon the concept of an independent level of deep structure entirely – this level

(3)

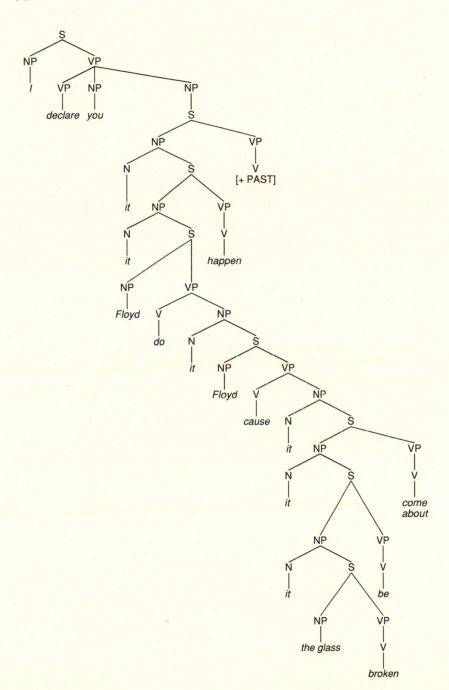

had been driven back so far that it made no theoretical sense to distinguish it from semantic representation. The new deep structureless model of grammar, dubbed 'generative semantics' by its practitioners, won virtually all abstract syntacticians to its banner.

As we will see, these radical conclusions were arrived at almost entirely by recourse to the assumptions of Katz and Postal's *Integrated Theory of Linguistic Descriptions* and Chomsky's *Aspects*. This fact alone, needless to say, accounts in large part for their widespread acceptance. The counterattack, initiated by Chomsky's lectures in the spring of 1967 (which were published as Chomsky 1970c), required an abandonment of certain of these assumptions, and for that reason, if for no other, Chomsky was faced with an uphill struggle. It was not until the mid-1970s, in fact, that the nonabstract alternative was to reassert itself as the dominant model of syntactic description (for an outline of its development, see Newmeyer 1986a: Ch. 6).

In the remainder of this chapter, I will outline in some detail the reasoning which led to the conclusion that deep structures were highly abstract. I have often chosen the expository device of presenting these arguments by paraphrasing the authors' own words, without providing immediate critical commentary on their adequacy. The reader should not, however, conclude from my doing so that I either endorse the assumptions underlying the arguments, or feel that the arguments go through even granting the assumptions. In fact, I do neither. For the sake of historical continuity, however, it seems best to withhold their evaluation at this point.

THE KATZ–POSTAL CONTRIBUTION TO GENERATIVE SEMANTICS

By far the main impetus for the adoption of highly abstract deep structures came from the Katz–Postal hypothesis. This might seem surprising: there is nothing in the notion that all interpretation takes place at deep structure which, *per se*, leads to abstractness. One can imagine a model consistent with Katz–Postal in which deep structures are quite 'shallow', and are mapped on to their respective meanings by a rich set of interpretive rules. In fact, the possibility of semantic rules actually contributing to meaning is not ruled out under the Katz–Postal hypothesis. But consider the trivial nature of the projection rules as proposed in the seminal Katz–Fodor paper (Katz and Fodor 1963). Their triviality led syntacticians simply to ignore them, and invited them to search for a syntactic solution to every semantic problem. Furthermore, whatever Chomsky's actual views may have been in 1965, many interpreted his comment that 'the syntactic component of a grammar must specify, for each sentence, a *deep structure* that determines its semantic interpretation' (Chomsky 1965: 16) as an endorsement of the position that it was reasonable to appeal to meaning in constructing syntactic rules and representations. Hence syntacticians began to posit deep structures which represented every aspect of the meaning of the sentence under investigation – a practice that led to ever more abstract deep structures.

It follows logically from the Katz–Postal hypothesis and the Katz–Fodor conception of the projection rules that every ambiguity must be represented by a deep structure difference. A few arguments for abstract deep structures, which were motivated by the assumption that such structures should be semantically unique, are paraphrased below. In all cases, previous analyses would have derived the sentence in question from only a single deep structure:

> Sentences like (5a), which contain both a reason adverbial and a negative, are ambiguous between one reading in which the adverbial has wider scope and another in which the negative has wider scope. A natural way of representing this ambiguity in deep structure is by phrase-markers (5b) and (5c), respectively.
>
> (*Paraphrasing* G. Lakoff 1970b: 169–71)

(5)   a. *I don't steal from John because I like him*
      b.

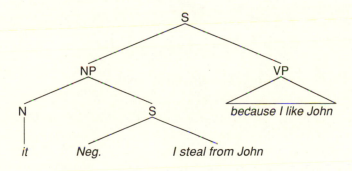

      c.

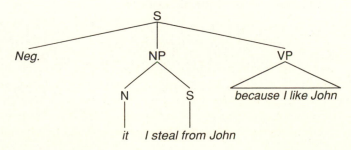

Sentences like (6) are ambiguous between one reading in which *John* and *Mary* left jointly and another in which they left separately. Therefore two deep structures must be posited for such sentences, one capturing the joint reading (7a) and one capturing the separate reading (7b).

(*Paraphrasing* G. Lakoff and Peters 1969: 113–20)

(6) *John and Mary left*

(7) a.

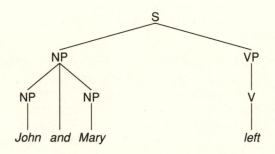

b.

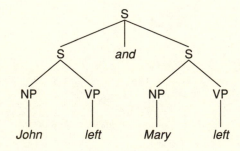

It also followed that since projection rules did not supply any aspect of the meaning, anything *understood* as part of the meaning had to occur in the deep structure. Two examples follow of arguments constructed to represent syntactically a semantically understood element:

(8) contains a nonovert but understood verbal sense of performing some activity with respect to the book. (9), in which this verbal sense is syntactically encoded, is a reasonable candidate for the deep structure of (8).

(*Paraphrasing* Newmeyer 1975: 40–4)

(8) *John began the book*

(9)

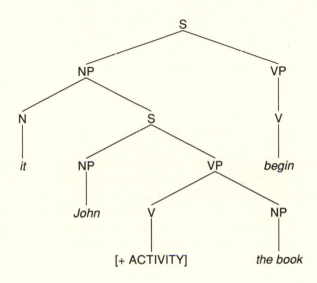

Consider (10):

(10) *John agreed that Harry was an idiot*

One cannot simply 'agree'; one must agree with *someone*. Hence, the deep structure of (10) is roughly (11).

                              (*Paraphrasing* G. Lakoff and Peters 1969: 118–19)

(11)

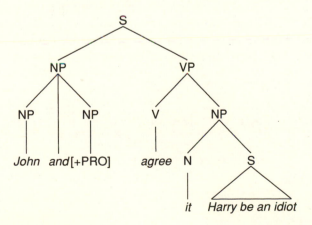

THE *ASPECTS* CONTRIBUTION TO GENERATIVE SEMANTICS

Even the assumptions of Katz–Postal and Katz–Fodor, taken together, were not sufficient to secure the generative semantic conclusion that there exists no level of deep structure distinct from semantic representation. This is because there is nothing in them that demands that if two sentences are paraphrases, then they must have identical deep structures. Take for example the following two sentences, which, for purposes of illustration, are assumed to be perfect paraphrases:

(12) a. *Mary sold the book to John*
      b. *John bought the book from Mary*

It is consistent with Katz–Postal and Katz–Fodor that these sentences could have strikingly different deep structures, yet could be mapped on to identical semantic representations by the projection rules.

Ironically, it was a proposal that Chomsky put forward himself in *Aspects* (however hesitantly) that facilitated the final step to generative semantics. In that book, it will be recalled, he suggested that selectional restrictions be handled at the level of deep structure by means of subcategorization features of lexical entries. That is, a verb like *persuade* might be entered with a feature requiring it to co-occur with a human subject and a complement sequence consisting of a human direct object followed by a clause denoting a concept. As it turns out, the great majority of syntacticians in the late 1960s accepted the idea of deep structure selection without question, and found that, carried to its logical conclusion, it led to the virtual annihilation of deep structure as an independent level. Typically, arguments constructed on the basis of selectional restrictions took the following form:

> The selectional restrictions holding between A and B in sentence S and between C and D in sentence S′ are essentially the same. We can capture this within the *Aspects* framework by positing substructures within S and S′ where A and C, and B and D, have the same representation. The restriction now need be stated only once.

Here is an example from George Lakoff:

> Consider sentences (13a) and (13b). Prior analyses would most likely have derived them from deep structures (14a) and (14b), respectively:

(13) a. *Seymour sliced the salami with a knife*
      b. *Seymour used a knife to slice the salami*

(14) a.

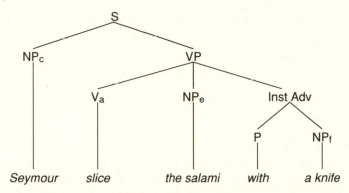

b.

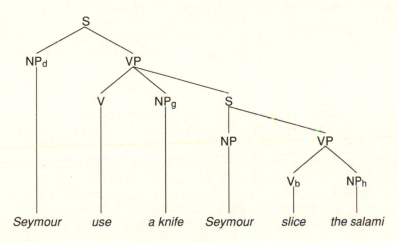

But notice the internal selectional correspondences that the two sentences share. The class V*a* that occurs before instrumental adverbs is
identical to the class V*b*, which can occur as the main verb of the
complement to *use*. Animate nouns alone can be NP*c* in (14a); likewise
only animates can be NP*d* in (14b). The same coreferentiality restrictions that block NP*e* = NP*f* and NP*c* = NP*f* in (14a) seem to block NP*g* =
NP*h* and NP*d* = NP*g* in (14b). And so on. Clearly, it would be undesirable
to have to state these restrictions once for structures like (14a) and
again for structures like (14b). Yet this is what would be necessary if
the sentences were derived from two different deep structures. Therefore both (13a) and (13b) are derived from (14b), and the selectional
restrictions need to be stated but once.

(*Paraphrasing* G. Lakoff 1968b: 4–29)

And here is another example from Paul Postal:

Observe the parallels between (15a), (15b), and (15c):

(15) a. *America attacked Cuba*
  b. *The American attack on Cuba (was outrageous)*
  c. *America's attack on Cuba (was outrageous)*

Clearly, the possible noun phrase subjects of the verb *attack* in sentences like (15a) and the possible prenominal pseudo-adjectives and possessives in sentences like (15b) and (15c) respectively are, in an intuitive sense, the same. In other words, the verb *attack* and the noun *attack* share selectional restrictions. Yet a nonabstract approach to syntax would treat the restriction in (15a) as one between a noun phrase and a verb, in (15b) as one between an adjective and a noun, and in (15c) as one between a noun phrase and a noun. How can the statement of three separate selectional restrictions be avoided? Quite simply, by deriving them all from the same deep structure. The noun *attack* should be derived from its homophonous verb and the pseudo-adjective *American* from the noun *America*. In such an analysis, the selectional restriction would need to be stated only once, as a subject–verb restriction.

(Paraphrasing Postal 1969: 219–24)

Arguments based on selectional restrictions led irrecoverably to the conclusion that every meaning identity had to be represented as a deep structure identity. To see why, let us consider sentences (12a) and (12b) once again. Clearly, if the sentences are true paraphrases, the possible subjects of *buy* are identical to the possible indirect objects of *sell*, the possible subjects of *sell* are identical to the possible indirect objects of *buy*, and so on. In other words, these sentences manifest identical selectional restrictions. The obvious way to avoid this situation would be to derive both sentences from the same deep structure, so that the selectional restrictions would require only one statement.

In other words, two conclusions had been reached: meaning differences were reflected by deep structure differences and meaning similarities were reflected by deep structure similarities. These two conclusions invited a third: there was no appreciable difference between a deep structure representation and a semantic representation, and hence little reason to continue positing an independent syntactic level of deep structure.

THE BIRTH OF GENERATIVE SEMANTICS

Up to about 1967, a battery of arguments had led consistently in one direction – to deep structures that exhibited semantic relations far more straightforwardly than the rather shallow ones of earlier work. Yet in no way had the fundamental *assumptions* of Katz and Postal (1964) and

Chomsky (1965) been challenged. Quite the contrary, in fact – as we have seen, the abstract analyses arrived at were based explicitly on the theory put forward in those works. Paradoxically, however, the more abstract deep structures became, the more difficulties were created for another well accepted proposal put forward in *Aspects*, namely the hypothesis that deep structure is the level at which lexical items enter the derivation. The seriousness of this problem became evident as a result of the conclusion (G. Lakoff 1970b) that if the theory were to account for the selectional restrictions holding *between* lexical items, it would also have to account for those *within* lexical items. For example, Lakoff argued that since selectional arguments demanded deriving *John thickened the sauce* from (roughly) *John caused – the sauce thicken*, it was necessary to derive *John killed Bill* from (roughly) *John caused – Bill die*. Otherwise, two separate (and unrelated) projection rules would be necessary to interpret causative sentences. But since Lakoff had not yet questioned the *Aspects* assumption that lexical items were inserted at deep structure, he had no choice but to posit deep structure (16) for *John killed Bill*:

(16)

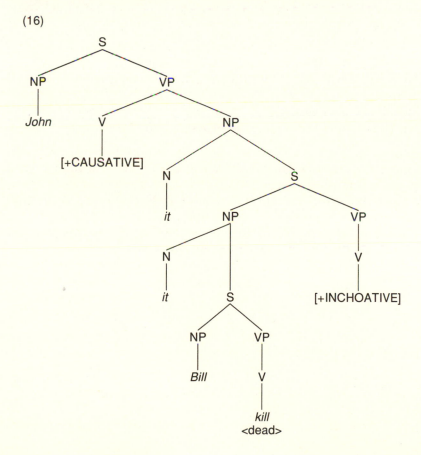

Since lexical items were assumed to be in the phrase marker before the first application of a transformation, *kill* had to be inserted in the deep structure prior to the transformations collapsing the triclausal structure into a uniclausal one. Furthermore, it was necessary to enter the word *kill* with the meaning 'dead' (where else would that meaning be represented?) and supply it with a feature to ensure that in such a circumstance it would obligatorily undergo the collapsing transformations. Such consequences made it clear that the presence of *kill* in the deep structure prior to the application of the collapsing rules was undesirable.

The obvious solution was to formulate deep structure representations strictly in terms of semantic features and to insert *kill* and other lexical items only after the collapsing rule (soon to be christened 'predicate raising') applied. The fact that, by 1967, deep structure had come virtually to represent meaning anyway made this step a completely natural one to take.

The idea of getting rid of deep structure as an independent level was first suggested in a widely circulated letter which George Lakoff and John Robert Ross wrote to Arnold Zwicky in March 1967 (now published as G. Lakoff and Ross 1976).[1] As they saw it, the level of deep structure, as defined in *Aspects*, possessed the following four properties. Deep structure was:

1 The base of the simplest syntactic component.
2 The place where subcategorization and selectional restrictions were defined.
3 The place where basic grammatical relations were defined.
4 The place where lexical items were inserted from the lexicon.

But, they argued, all the evidence pointed to 1, 2, and 3 being properties of semantic representation, not of some intermediate level of deep structure, while as far as 4 was concerned, they pointed to examples like those discussed above to illustrate that some transformations had to apply before lexical items entered the derivation.[2]

With the abandonment of an independent deep structure, the first major rift among generative grammarians was firmly established.

Chapter 9

The end of generative semantics

GENERATIVE SEMANTICS UNDER ATTACK

A period of acrimony

It is hard today to appreciate the vehemence with which the debate between generative semanticists and partisans of the extended standard theory ('interpretivists') was carried out in the late 1960s and early 1970s. At times, its heat grew so intense that even in print the rhetoric exceeded the bounds of normal partisan scholarship – witness the description of a paper of McCawley's as 'Machiavellian' (Dougherty 1974: 267) and the accusation that Chomsky 'fights dirty when he argues. He uses every trick in the book' (G. Lakoff 1972c: 70L). As can easily be imagined, the discussion sessions after conference papers provided an arena for far stronger sentiments. The high point (or low point) surely followed the presentation of George Lakoff's 'Global rules' paper at the 1969 Linguistic Society of America meeting, in which for several minutes he and Ray Jackendoff hurled amplified obscenities at each other before 200 embarassed onlookers. There is hardly a need to mention the personal animosities engendered, some of which smoulder still.

As might be expected, hiring-decision controversies provided a particularly bitter aspect of the internecine warfare. For example, the replacement of two generative semanticists at the University of Massachusetts by interpretivists served to solidify partisans of the former model in their opposition to interpretivism. On the other side of the fence, the hiring of a noninterpretivist by MIT in 1970 to fill a vacant position had an analogous effect on the students at that institution, who almost unanimously would have preferred an interpretivist.

In the following pages, I will attempt to identify the more substantive issues of the debate, and explain why generative semantics came away very much the loser.

The question of category membership

The generative semantic arguments that were by far the most vulnerable (and therefore the first to be attacked by their opponents) were those that led to the conclusion that the inventory of syntactic categories could be reduced to three. Yet such a conclusion was vital to generative semantics, given its commitment to identifying syntactic categories with those of predicate logic. It was easy to show that generative semanticists succeeded in eliminating categories by recognizing only *sufficient* conditions for conflating two categories into one, never *necessary* conditions (a point acknowledged by McCawley 1977). To take a typical example, Ross (1969a), making the then well-accepted assumption that definite pronouns refer only to full noun phrases, concluded on the basis of sentence (1) that adjective phrases are really members of the category NP:

(1) *John is happy, but he doesn't look it*

For Ross, (1) provided sufficient justification for *happy* being an NP. He felt no obligation to discuss the prima-facie counterexamples (2a–c), in which *it* does not refer to *happy*.

(2) a. **John is happy, but I can't imagine why he is it*
     b. **John isn't happy, but he hopes to become it*
     c. **John is happy and I'm it, too*

In any event, Chomsky (1971) later demonstrated that the antecedent of *it* need not even be a constituent, much less a noun phrase.

The assumption that if two categories share some syntactic feature then they are in reality members of the same category also contributed to the generative semantic reduction in the inventory of syntactic categories. For example, George Lakoff (1970b) subsumed adjectives into the class of verbs on the basis of their both being subcategorized for the features [± STATIVE] and ± [_____S] (the ability to occur before a sentential complement). But Chomsky (1970c) and Culicover (1977) pointed out in response that it is not just adjectives and verbs that share the feature stative, but nouns can be stative or nonstative as well:

(3) *Be a hero* [–STATIVE]
(4) **Be a person* [+STATIVE]

Analogous reasoning should have led logically to nouns, adjectives, and verbs all being considered to be in the same category. While such a conclusion was not necessarily repellent to generative semanticists – Bach (1968), in fact, had proposed it on independent grounds – the same type of test could have been used to conflate all categories into one, a conclusion that few, if any, would have found acceptable.

Finally, it was pointed out that even if generative semantics had been successful in reducing the *underlying* set of categories to three members, it did not succeed in reducing the *total* number to three. There is a difference between nouns, verbs, adjectives, adverbs, quantifiers, prepositions, and so on in surface structure, regardless of what is needed at the most underlying level. Hence, there seemed to be no substance to the generative semantic claim that it had succeeded in reducing the inventory of substantive universals. How would generative semantics distinguish nouns from verbs? As McCawley explained: 'The difference between nouns and verbs is that nouns but not verbs are subject to a transformation which replaces a relative clause by its predicate element' (1970:169–70). But as Bresnan (1972:198) pointed out, such an approach is really nothing more than using a class of transformations as categories in disguise. Nothing is gained by replacing *ad hoc* (if such they be) categories by *ad hoc* transformations. Bresnan discussed the problem at length, arguing that an approach positing deep structure and a variety of categories makes an important prediction that the generative semantic approach does not, namely, that syntactic properties should cluster around the distinct categories. Given the generative semantic approach, such a clustering is not predicted to occur.

The question of deep structure

Needless to say, the generative semantic abandonment of deep structure was an issue that caused its share of rancour. Since the most persuasive refutations of the existence of this level involved arguments for syntactic lexical decomposition, it was on lexical decomposition that the interpretivists most frequently trained their guns. They claimed to be able to show, and by and large were perceived as successful in doing so, that neither the syntactic nor the semantic behaviour of lexical items matches those of their supposed syntactic sources, thereby invalidating the strongest argument for lexical decomposition.

For example, Fodor (1970) argued that if transitive *melt* were derived from something like 'cause to melt', (5b) should be grammatical and a paraphrase of (5a):

(5) a. *Floyd caused the glass to melt on Sunday by heating it on Saturday*
     b. **Floyd melted the glass on Sunday by heating it on Saturday*

However, contrary to the prediction implicit in an analysis involving lexical decomposition, (5b) is unacceptable.

Analogously, Bowers (1970) pointed out that Postal's treatment of *remind* predicts that the contradictory nature of (6a) should entail (6b) being contradictory as well. But it is not, as (6c) (in which modifiers have been added for clarity) illustrates:

(6) a. *I perceive that Larry is similar to Winston Churchill, although I perceive that Larry is not similar to Winston Churchill*
     b. *Larry reminds me of Winston Churchill, although I perceive that Larry is not similar to Winston Churchill*
     c. *For some reason Larry reminds me of Winston Churchill, although I perceive that Larry is not really similar to him at all*

Many more arguments of a similar nature were constructed against lexical decomposition. The generative semanticists' only recourse was to say that the lexical items *melt, remind*, etc. do not have exactly the same semantic representations as *cause to melt, perceive to be similar*, etc., but have meanings which are either more restricted or less restricted. While nobody denied that such was the case, having to posit distinct structures for lexical items and their phrasal near-paraphrases undercut the justification for having lexical decomposition in the first place.

Generative semanticists also attempted to motivate syntactic lexical decomposition by pointing to the fact that their crucial rule of predicate raising applied uncontroversially in languages as diverse as Japanese, Eskimo, and Blackfoot (see Frantz 1974). Hence, they claimed, it followed that English should also have the rule. But such reasoning was not regarded as compelling. Indeed, it seemed to be the case that whenever generative semanticists needed a prelexical transformation to collapse two clauses, they postulated predicate raising at work; to raise a noun phrase to a higher clause, subject raising; to make an object a subject, passive. No motivation for the application of these rules was ever given, aside from the need to get from point A (semantic representation) to point B (a constituent which a lexical item could replace). But as many linguists came to realize in the mid-1970s, given enough ingenuity and enough rules for whose application no formal statement nor external motivation was required, and whose application could be assumed to be optional or obligatory at will, there would never be a problem in getting from A to B.

The internal modification arguments for lexical decomposition fared little better than the others. Chomsky (1972b) and Kac (1972) pointed out that lexical decomposition predicts many more ambiguities than actually occur. If the ambiguity of *John almost killed Bill* is an argument for the decomposition of *kill*, then the fact that the sentence is not obviously four (or more) ways ambiguous should count as an argument against it, since, for generative semanticists, the semantic representation of *kill* contained (at least) *cause-become not-alive*, each of which was in principle modifiable by *almost*.

But by far the most intractable problem for the generative semanticists was accounting for the primary function of the renounced level of deep structure – the specification of morpheme order. As most syntacticians soon realized, the order of articles, adjectives, negatives, numerals, nouns, and noun complements within a noun phrase is not predictable (or even stable) on semantic grounds. How then could generative semantics state morpheme order? Only, it seemed, by supplementing the transformational rules with a close-to-the-surface filter that functioned to mimic the phrase structure rules of a theory with the level of deep structure. Thus despite its rhetorical abandonment of deep structure, generative semantics would end up slipping that level in through the back door.[1]

The question of globality

One of the most emotional issues between generative semanticists and interpretivists involved the question of the existence of global rules. This might seem strange, since even prior to the birth of generative semantics it had been taken for granted that the history of the derivation often played a role in determining the applicability of a transformation (see Lees 1960). Also, Chomsky had discussed in some detail a 'rather abstract condition that takes into account not only the structure to which the operation applies but also the history of derivation of this structure' (1968:28). Furthermore, even during the debate over global rules, nobody denied that transformations needed to be supplemented with rules of a different formal nature. Why then did the claim that some rules were global engender such heated controversy?

Global rules were controversial because their thrust was an entirely negative one. George Lakoff (whose position came to be identifed with the 'official' generative semantic line) repeatedly implied that to claim that a phenomenon was to be handled by a global rule was to make no claim at all about it, other than the negative one that a transformational rule could not handle it. Since neither Lakoff nor any other generative semanticist made a serious attempt to constrain global rules, the expression 'global rule' became a catchall phrase for a disparate collection of mysterious phenomena which defied ready explanation. More and more, it seemed, when a generative semanticist invoked globality, he or she had simply given up trying to explain what was going on.

It is instructive to contrast the alternative interpretivist account of 'global' phenomena. As far as Greek case agreement is concerned, Baker and Brame (1972) and Quicoli (1972, 1982) proposed the following solution: an index is assigned to an NP and its modifiers which indicates their being in the same simple S; a late rule assigns case to the modifier based on that of its co-indexed NP. For *be* contraction, Selkirk (1972) proposed that transformations that move or delete constituents do not move or delete the word boundaries associated with them, and that the presence of these word boundaries blocks stress reduction and contraction.

In one sense, the above proposals were little more than formalizations of the global rules they were intended to replace. After all, they recognized that 'standard' transformational approaches were insufficient for handling the phenomena and, in their own distinct ways, allowed generalizations to be stated involving nonadjacent phrase-markers. At a more metatheoretical level, however, they were profoundly different from global solutions, and came to be seen as preferable to them. Devices such as co-indexing between heads and modifiers and special conventions regarding the deletion of word boundaries involve the most minimal extensions of already existing mechanisms. It seemed that solutions involving them could be achieved without increasing the power of the theory. Whatever grey areas an indexing/word boundary approach might contain, such an approach came to be more and more favoured, since, if nothing else, it at least enabled the phenomenon under investigation to be concretized and, in many cases, pointed the way to a principled solution.

The question of grammatical theory and pragmatics

Virtually nobody today accepts a strictly grammatical explanation of all pragmatic phenomena. The mid- and late 1970s saw an ever-increasing number of papers and books which convincingly cast into doubt the possibility of one homogeneous syntax–semantics–pragmatics and the consequent abandonment of the competence–performance distinction.

The syntactic arguments for the performative hypothesis were challenged almost immediately and in many papers (see Anderson 1971; Banfield 1973; Fraser 1974; Heal 1977; Gazdar 1979; Gildin 1978).[2] All concluded that there was no syntactic motivation for positing an abstract performative verb of declaring, requesting, commanding, or whatever at the deepest level of syntactic representation. Fraser, for example, pointed out that Ross's argument based on the distribution of reflexive pronouns (see Newmeyer 1986a: §5.2.1) is invalidated by the possibility of a reflexive occurring in the performative clause itself:

(7) a. *You are hereby authorized by John and myself to buy that ship*
     b. *You are hereby advised by Mary and myself that we are married*
     c. *The court rejects any such remarks directed at the other jurors
         and myself*

Others challenged George Lakoff's view that conversationally implied aspects of meaning could be analysed as entailments. For example, Gazdar (1979) demonstrated that there is no relationship of semantic entailment between a speech act and its felicity conditions. If Lakoff were right, he argued, (8a) should entail (8b):

(8) a. *Sue requested of Tom that he meet Harry*
     b. *Sue attempted to get Tom to meet Harry*

But if there were such an entailment relation, Gazdar argued, (9a) should make Sue sound irrational, and (9b) should be contradictory:

(9) a. *Sue requested of Tom that he meet Harry, because it was the only way she knew of preventing him from doing so*
     b. *Sue requested of Tom that he meet Harry, but she was only attempting to shock him*

Since (9a) and (9b) do not behave as predicted by Lakoff, it follows that the relationship between a speech act and its felicity conditions cannot be one of entailment. Thus a pragmatic rather than a grammatical treatment of such phenomena is preferable.

Morgan (1977) discussed at length the problems of treating indirect speech acts (and conversational implicature in general) in terms of semantic entailment. He pointed out that while, indeed, (10a) is often used to *convey* (10b), (10a) does not *entail* (10b):

(10) a. *Can you open the door?*
     b. *Open the door*

If the relationship were one of entailment, then there could be no possibility of a co-operative individual ever interpreting (10a) as a questioning of his or her ability to open the door, but this sentence could be interpreted in just such a way. As Morgan concluded: 'the very property of implicature that makes it so useful as a conversational ploy is that it is not entailed, but merely suggested or hinted at' (Morgan 1977: 279–80).

Kempson (1975) carried the attack on grammatical treatments of pragmatics a step farther, arguing that any attempt to include speaker-relative concepts (such as intentions or assumptions) in a grammatical statement is doomed to failure. Focusing on Robin Lakoff's analysis of conjunction (1971), which involves taking 'presupposed common topic' as a grammatical notion, she demonstrated that any mechanism able to predict the required sentence-presupposition pairs would need to be embodied with unconstrainable power. From this, she concluded that speaker assumptions and the like cannot be part of a formal semantic theory.

By around 1973, all of the issues discussed in this section had been debated at conferences, in unpublished (and some published) work, and at a personal level. Generative semantics was on the retreat.

THE COLLAPSE OF GENERATIVE SEMANTICS

In this section, we will probe further the amazingly rapid decline of generative semantics. We still have not arrived at an adequate explanation for the fact that a model whose followers were 'motivated only by personal loyalty to Chomsky' (as popular wisdom had it in 1967) would only twelve years later have become the predominant syntactic theory, with a corresponding decline of its rival.

This is not to say that all generative semanticists abandoned their beliefs, and certainly not to say that all became interpretivists (although some did; examples are Emmon Bach, D. Terence Langendoen, and David Lightfoot). Many adopted newer frameworks of analysis with rather different assumptions from both, like relational grammar, while others ceased altogether to involve themselves in the defence of a particular framework. But most significantly, students entering linguistics from around 1971 or 1972 onwards turned away from generative semantics. And this is the fact that is in need of explanation.

The generative semantic dynamic

It is tempting to think that it was the weight of the interpretivist counterattack that led to the demise of generative semantics. While it played an important role, it was not the deciding factor. For one thing, generative semanticists saw enough defects in the interpretive model for the interpretivist critique to lose some of its force. For another, the majority of the published critiques of generative semantics, including the most comprehensive ones (Brame 1976; Oehrle 1977; Wasow 1976), did not appear until after that model had begun to crumble.

No, the fact is that generative semantics destroyed itself. Its internal dynamic led to a state of affairs in which it could no longer be taken seriously by anyone interested in the scientific study of human language. Generative semantics simply abandoned the attempt to explain grammatical phenomena, leaving the field open to its competitors.

The dynamic that led generative semantics to abandon explanation flowed irrevocably from its practice of regarding any speaker judgement and any fact about morpheme distribution as a *de facto* matter for grammatical analysis. In retrospect, it is easy to appreciate the a priori nature of the practice of reducing all linguistic facts to grammatical facts. It is no more logically necessary that, say, the proper use of *please* in English and the surface order of clitic pronouns in Spanish be treated within the same general framework than it is that any two physical phenomena be necessarily derivable from the same set of equations. Other sciences take a 'modular' approach to their subject matter: they take it for granted that a complex phenomenon is best explained by regarding it as a product of the interaction of a number of autonomously functioning systems, each governed by its own general principles. Generative semantics, on the other hand, attempted to force all phenomena into one and only one system.

Attributing the same theoretical weight to each and every fact about language had disastrous consequences. Since the number of facts is, of course, absolutely overwhelming, simply describing the incredible complexities of language became the all-consuming task, with formal explanation being postponed to some future date. Fillmore explicitly noted the data-collecting consequences of the generative semantic view of language: 'The ordinary working grammarian', he observed, 'finds himself in the age of what we might call the New Taxonomy, an era of a new and exuberant cataloging of the enormous range of facts that linguists need eventually to find theories to deal with' (1972: 16).

This 'exuberant cataloging of . . . facts' became a hallmark of generative semantics, as every counterexample to a claim (real or apparent) was greeted as an excuse to broaden still farther the domain of grammatical analysis. Its data fetishism reached its apogee in 'fuzzy grammar'. Many staunch generative semanticists who had followed every step of Lakoff's and Ross's up to that point, turned away from fuzzy theoretical constructs. 'Of course there's a squish', they objected. 'There's always a squish. It's the nature of data to be squishy. And it's the purpose of a theory to extract order from squishy data.' Generative semantics, it became all too clear, was not such a theory.[3]

The substitution of 'squishy' lists of sentences for rules and derivations took on a life of its own. Generative semanticists squealed with delight at the 'horrors', 'monstrosities', 'mind snappers', and 'wonders' (Postal 1976) which no theory seemed to be able to explain. Darden (1974) captured the nihilistic outlook of the generative semanticists admirably in the following quote (which dealt specifically with natural phonology): 'the multitude of views can be taken as evidence that we have reached that happy state when no one can be sure that he knows anything – except that everyone else is wrong' (n.p.).

It needs to be pointed out that very few interpretivists in the early 1970s were either formalizing rules or presenting grammar fragments. For generative semanticists, however, not doing so became a matter of principle: 'I think that the time has come to return to the tradition of informal descriptions of exotic languages' (G. Lakoff 1974a: 153). To students entering theoretical linguistics in the early 1970s, increasingly trained in the sciences, mathematics, and philosophy, the generative semantics positions on theory construction and formalization were anathema. It is little wonder that they found nothing of interest in this model.[4]

At the same time, generative semantics was being co-opted from the opposite direction by sociolinguistics. Sociolinguists looked with amazement at the generative semantic programme of attempting to treat societal phenomena in a framework originally designed to handle such sentence-level properties as morpheme order and vowel alternations. They found no difficulty in convincing those generative semanticists most committed to studying language in its social context to drop whatever lingering pretence they still might have of doing a grammatical analysis, and to approach the subject matter instead from the traditional perspective of the social sciences.

Not surprisingly, commentators began to see in generative semantics the seeds of a structuralist–empiricist counter-revolution. The first to make this point explicit, Ronat (1972), compared the heavy reliance in Postal (1970) on selectional co-occurrences to the methodology of Zellig Harris and other post-Bloomfieldians, to whom surface distribution of morphemes was also the primary criterion for positing a particular linguistic structure (for a similar critique, see Dougherty 1974). By the time that the consummate critique of the philosophical implications of late generative semantics, Katz and Bever (1976), had been published, even that model had been abandoned by most of its erstwhile supporters. Nevertheless, the following passage from their article is worth quoting, since it was the realization of its point that led many linguists to turn their backs on generative semantics:

> [G]enerative semantics had distorted grammar by including within its goals a complete theory of acceptability. This assimilation of the phenomenon of performance into the domain of grammaticality has come about as a consequence of an empiricist criterion for determining what counts as grammatical. In almost every paper Lakoff makes explicit his assumption that the explanatory goal of a grammar is to state all the factors that influence the distributions of morphemes in speech. On this view, any phenomenon systematically related to cooccurrence is *ipso facto* something to be explained in the grammar. Since in actual speech almost anything can influence cooccurrence relations, it is no wonder that Lakoff repeatedly discovers more and more new kinds of 'grammatical phenomena'. In fact, the generative semanticist program for linguistic theory represents, if anything, a more extreme approach than even Bloomfieldian structuralism, which recognized that a variety of phenomena concerning language are extragrammatical.
>
> (Katz and Bever 1976: 58)

'The best theory'

Probably no metatheoretical statement by a generative semanticist did more to undermine confidence in that model than Paul Postal's paper 'The best theory' (Postal 1972). Interpreted at one level, this paper is no more than a routine plea for a theory without unnecessary apparatus and with as tight constraints as possible on the apparatus which it does have. But that is not how 'The best theory' was generally interpreted. Postal contrasted two hypothetical models, one with just 'A's and another with both 'B's and 'C's, where 'A', 'B', and 'C' are distinct components or rule types. Surely, Postal argued, the first, more 'homogeneous', theory is preferable. Generative semantics would then be preferable to its inter-pretivist competitor, since it is more homogeneous – generative semantics postulates a single mapping from semantic representation to surface structure without the level of deep structure intervening, whereas the latter has (at least) two distinct rule types and an extra level.

If for Postal, 'A', 'B', and 'C' had been constructs of equal complexity and generality, then no one would have objected to his characterization. But for Postal and the other generative semanticists, 'A' came more and more to be nothing but an unconstrained 'rule of grammar', while for the interpretivists, 'B' and 'C' were highly constrained rule types of definite form and specific function. Thus it was the latter alternative that was seen to be preferable, not the former. In the early 1970s, interpretivists were committed to constraining (or at least characterizing) 'B' and 'C', while generative semanticists steadily weakened the content of 'A' by ever increasing the type of data for which it was responsible. Postal's paper was more successful than any interpretivist critique in impressing upon the linguistic community that generative semantics had constructed a more 'homogeneous' theory only by ceasing to make concrete claims about language.

A generative semantic response to such criticism was to deny that the two rival frameworks were even comparable, due to the differing con-ceptual status of their primitives. In generative semantics, such primitives were all 'natural' ones:

> The same considerations of naturalness obtain in syntax [as in phon-ology]. The theory of generative semantics claims that the linguistic elements used in grammar have an independent natural basis in the human conceptual system . . . . In generative semantics, possible gram-mars are limited by the requirement [sic] that the nonphonological elements used have a natural semantic basis, independent of the rules of the grammar of any particular natural language.
>
> (G. Lakoff 1972a: 77–8)

However, such argumentation did not get very far. Many saw through its transparently aprioristic character. Emonds wrote that:

> Lakoff refuses to consider the merits of [the interpretivist] analysis, which employs categories which are well-motivated internal to language (syntactically). This refusal seems to me like requiring that

philosophy define a priori the notions of science, in which case we never would have gotten to gravity, relativity, etc.

(1973: 56)

But even more important, the naturalness 'requirement' was seen as little more than a terminological trick. Taken literally, it embodied the claim that all syntactic behaviour could be expressed in 'natural' semantic terms. Thus stated, however, nobody ever held such a position – how could one possibly explain the radically different syntactic behaviour of the adjective *possible* and the modal *may* on the basis of their meanings, for example? In other words, all of the 'natural' categories of generative semantics would have to be supplemented by a set of 'unnatural' categories, rules or whatever to explain all of the regularities (and irregularities) of language which could not be formulated in strictly semantic terms.

All the appeal to 'naturalness' did, in effect, was to bequeath to the interpretivists the task of searching for syntactic regularity.

Generative semantic style [5]

One last characteristic trait of generative semantics which speeded its downfall was the whimsical style of presentation which pervaded so much written in that framework. This is not to say that all generative semanticists were prone to such practices, nor that partisans of that model alone were, but the free introduction of humour into scholarly writing became more and more identified with generative semantics. The practice manifested itself in the titles of papers and books (12); the names of rules and constraints (13); example sentences (14); and in the prose itself (15):

(12) a. *You Take the High Node and I'll Take the Low Node* (Corum *et al.* 1973)
   b. 'If you hiss or anything, I'll do it back' (Cantrall 1970)
   c. 'Tracking the generic toad' (Lawler 1973)
(13) a. 'Richard' (Rogers 1974)
   b. 'Q-magic' (Carden 1968)
   c. 'Stuffing' (Ross 1972b)
(14) a. *Norbert the narc only reports potheads* (Lawler 1973)
   b. *Tums's taste is wall-to-wall Yucksville* (Ross 1973a)
   c. *Symbolic logic – and, by the way, who invented it? – isn't my cup of Postum* (Sadock 1974)
(15) a. 'The winner gets to say "Nyaah, nyaah!" to the loser'. (G. Lakoff 1973: 286)
   b. 'In summing up this awesome display of cosmic mysteries with scarcely a hint here and there of a denouement, we are reminded of the immortal words of Harry Reasoner'. (Horn 1970: 326)
   c. 'It is no longer necessary to assume that instrumental verb formation applies in one swell foop'. (Green 1972: 84)

Such stylistic traits were undoubtedly grounded in youthful enthusiam (the age of the average generative semanticist in 1970 was well below thirty) and in the rambunctious personalities of several prominent generative semanticists, which served as a role model for their students. Nevertheless, the whimsical style of generative semantic papers served to give extra credibility to the charge of lack of seriousness, to which generative semanticists had opened themselves by downplaying and then abandoning the task of constructing a formalized theory of language. Indeed, it is tempting to regard generative semantic style as a classic example of content both shaping and dominating form. Certainly not all generative semanticists would agree with one ex-partisan that 'we went out of our way to be funny in our papers so that once our ideas were refuted we could get ourselves off the hook by saying, "Oh, did you take us seriously? Couldn't you see that we were just fooling around?"' (personal communication). But most, I suspect, would acknowledge a kernel of truth in it.

In addition to the way this stylistic practice reflected on generative semantics itself, many linguists from outside of American culture found it offensive. Even highly fluent non-native speakers of English found many generative semantic papers impossible to read by virtue of the culture-bound slang and topical examples that permeated them. In at least one instance, even a native speaker was baffled. Stephen Isard, an American linguist resident in Britain, recalls that he had to serve as interpreter for a colleague to help him through Ross's example sentence *It is said that the tacos Judge Bean won't go for* (Ross 1973b: 164). *Tacos, Judge Bean*, and *go for* were all unfamiliar to him. As it turns out, the sentence *It is said that the oranges John won't ask for* would have served just as well to make the relevant theoretical point.

The generative semanticists' organizational problems

Generative semanticists were never able to take full advantage of the numerical and geographical head start which they had over the interpretivists. Of the leading members of that tendency, only James McCawley was able to build a stable base and following. Paul Postal, working for IBM, had no students at all, while John Robert Ross was always very much under Chomsky's shadow at MIT, a fact which for obvious reasons deterred students at that university from becoming generative semanticists. And George Lakoff, by associating himself with four different institutions (Harvard, Michigan, The Center for Advanced Studies in the Behavioral Sciences, and The University of California, Berkeley) during the crucial years of 1969–72, relinquished any possibility of building the kind of programme that Halle and Chomsky had succeeded in building at MIT.

Once at Berkeley, Lakoff did attempt this, but by 1972 it was already too late. Neither the linguistics department there nor the Berkeley Linguistics Society (over which he exerted considerable influence at first) ever became major vehicles for the dissemination of his ideas. And by coming out with a newly named theory almost yearly, from 'fuzzy grammar' (G. Lakoff 1973) to 'global transderivational well-formedness grammar' (G. Lakoff 1974b) to 'cognitive grammar' (G. Lakoff and Thompson 1975) to 'dual-hierarchy grammar' (G. Lakoff 1975) to 'linguistic gestalt theory' and 'experiental linguistics' (G. Lakoff 1977), Lakoff gave the impression of lack of consistency in his approach to theoretical work.

THE LEGACY OF GENERATIVE SEMANTICS

While generative semantics now is regarded as a non-viable model of grammar, there are innumerable ways in which it has left its mark on its successors. Most importantly, its view that sentences must at one level have a representation in a formalism isomorphic to that of symbolic logic is now widely accepted by interpretivists, and in particular by Chomsky. It was the generative semanticists who first undertook an intensive investigation of syntactic phenomena which defied formalization by means of transformational rules as they were then understood, and led to the plethora of mechanisms such as indexing devices, traces, and filters, which are now part of the interpretivists' theoretical store. Even the idea of lexical decomposition, for which generative semanticists were much scorned, has turned up in the syntactic or semantic theories of several interpretivists. Furthermore, many proposals originally mooted by generative semanticists, such as the nonexistence of extrinsic rule ordering, post-cyclic lexical insertion, and treating anaphoric pronouns as bound variables, have since appeared in the interpretivist literature, virtually always without acknowledgment.

While late generative semantics may have proven itself theoretically bankrupt, the important initial studies which it inspired on the logical and sublogical properties of lexical items, on speech acts, both direct and indirect, and on the more general pragmatic aspects of language are becoming more and more appreciated as linguistic theory is finally developing the means to incorporate them. The wealth of information and interesting generalizations they contain have barely begun to be tapped by current researchers.

Chapter 10

Review of Geoffrey J. Huck and John A. Goldsmith, *Ideology and Linguistic Theory: Noam Chomsky and the Deep Structure Debates*

AGAINST THE 'STANDARD STORY'

Geoffrey J. Huck and John A. Goldsmith's (1995) *Ideology and Linguistic Theory* (henceforth *ILT*) defends a revisionist account of the debates between generative and interpretive semanticists of the late 1960s and early 1970s. According to what they call the 'standard story' (1995: 2), told in Jackendoff (1983); Katz and Bever (1976); Newmeyer (1980, 1986); and Riemsdijk and Williams (1986), generative semantics collapsed primarily because it was empirically disconfirmed. Problematically for such a view, however:

> significant chunks of what were evidently standard generative semantics analyses began to reappear in the syntax literature shortly after the movement's demise and are now often regarded as constituting preferred solutions to contemporary problems. Indeed, the picture of grammar presented in much contemporary work, including, for example, Chomsky's *Lectures on Government and Binding* (1981) and *Knowledge of Language: Its Nature, Origin, and Use* (1986), is similar enough in certain crucial respects to that painted by generative semantics in the late 1960s that one who accepts the standard story must be prepared to explain why criticisms of the latter do not also apply to the former.

(Huck and Goldsmith 1995: 2)

The book was begun 'in an effort to resolve a paradox: if the theory of generative semantics had been falsified, why are its central claims by and large still accepted?' (*ibid.*: 92). The answer, according to Huck and Goldsmith, is that the theory was *not* falsified – rather we have to appeal to 'external explanations' (*ibid.*: ix) to account for its demise and for the widespread belief that it was falsified. As for the demise of generative semantics, the primary factor was the inability of its supporters to build the kind of homogeneous programme at any university that could compete with the single-minded efforts of Chomsky and Halle at MIT.

Lacking an adequate programmatic base, generative semantics was no match for the rival interpretivist model, no matter how compatible they may have been at the root. And the claim that its programme was falsified is 'essentially ideological in character and scientifically unjustifiable' (*ibid.*: 93). Hence the title of the book.

I believe that *ILT* contains a fundamental error. While external factors unquestionably played a role in the demise of generative semantics (see Newmeyer 1986: 137–8), the *fundamental* reason why the model was abandoned was because the linguistic community increasingly came to regard it as deficient, both in terms of its empirical claims and its methodology for theory construction. *ILT* greatly exaggerates the similarities between generative semantics and its contemporary interpretivist rival and its government-binding (GB) successor. This exaggeration is fuelled in part by a misconstrual of the defining properties of generative semantics and by an ahistorical view of that model that fails to recognize its changes after 1967.

THE *ILT* VIEW OF GENERATIVE SEMANTICS

What *was* generative semantics? *ILT* follows in a general way the scheme of Lakatos (1970), in which scientific research programmes have two components: the '(protected) core' of the theory, namely strategies for theory construction, which are agreed upon by the community of theoreticians and are not generally subject to empirical tests; and 'auxiliary hypotheses', namely falsifiable propositions, which can be modified or abandoned as the evidence warrants during the life of the theory. *ILT* adds a third component, the 'orientational propositions' of the theory, namely its desiderata, that which it should explain. With this in mind, it presents the 1967 generative semantics programme as follows (*ibid.*: 20):

Orientation: 1. Mediational
2. Distributional
Core: 1. The distribution of linguistic elements is determined by structural properties of the grammatical strings made up of those elements.
2. Structural differences among the grammatical sentences of a language can be accounted for by a set of phrase structure rules and the transformational rules that apply to them.
3. Syntactic and semantic representations are of the same formal nature, i.e., they are labelled trees.
4. Semantic representations resemble the constructions of formal logic, with quantifier scope and anaphor-antecedent relations explicitly expressed.

> 5. Syntactic and semantic representations are related via transformations.

A mediational orientation attempts to discover and explain the relationship between sound and meaning. A distributional orientation presumes that there is a formal structure to language that can be described on its own terms.

For generative semantics the two orientations were linked, given its adoption of what *ILT* calls the 'synthetic conjecture' (*ibid.*: 43) of G. Lakoff (1972d: 551): 'The rules for determining which sentences are grammatical and which are ungrammatical are not distinct from the rules relating logical forms and surface forms'.

Among the auxiliary hypotheses of generative semantics, as put forward in *ILT*, were the absence of a level of syntactic deep structure, the performative hypothesis, and the idea that paraphrases must share the same semantic representation (*ibid.*: 126–7).

In what way, then, can the theory of Chomsky (1981, 1986b) be considered 'similar enough in crucial respects' to generative semantics? The answer that is provided in *ILT* is that, unlike the earliest interpretivist models, Chomsky's theory adopts a strong version of the synthetic conjecture. Its transformational mapping of surface forms on to a level of logical form (LF), where quantifier-variable and antecedent-anaphor relations are represented, mimics the core (and a number of auxiliary) hypotheses of generative semantics and, most crucially, integrates the capturing of grammaticality distinctions with the principles determining semantic well-formedness.

Let us accept for the time being the *ILT* characterization of the essential properties of generative semantics. When all is said and done, this model was not really very similar to current GB. Of the core propositions, only (1) survives and that was inherited from *Syntactic Structures* and *Aspects*, rather than being an innovation of generative semantics. Core principle (2) has been replaced by a view in which (a) phrase structure rules as such do not exist; (b) transformations play a much diminished role; and (c) structural differences are accounted for by a combination of X-bar principles and syntactic constraints that were either rejected by generative semantics (in the former case) or yet to be proposed (in the latter). As for principles (3), (4), and (5), they can hardly be a feature of current GB work, since this model incorporates no level of 'semantic representation'. Chomsky, as is well known, is sceptical about the very existence of such a level (see, for example, Chomsky 1979a: 142). Those advocates of the GB programme who are committed to the existence of semantic representations have a view of their interface with syntactic representations bearing little resemblance to that expressed by the core propositions of generative semantics.

Chomsky's (1971) interpretivist model was actually *closer* to generative semantics than its GB descendent, in that it hypothesized a level of semantic representation. For this reason, Chomsky could speculate that, at a certain level of abstraction, the two models were notational variants. I doubt very strongly that he would regard GB as a notational variant of generative semantics!

As far as the relationship between semantic representation and LF is concerned, LF is regarded as a level that 'interfaces . . . with conceptual-intentional systems' (Chomsky 1993: 2), not as a level representing such systems themselves, or even proper subparts of them. As a consequence, there is no one-to-one correspondence between an element's semantic properties and its LF-structural properties. Indeed, a great part of Hornstein (1984) is devoted to demonstrating that one cannot predict the LF representation of a quantifier on the basis of its meaning.

Conversely, LF is a level at which generalizations of uncontroversial syntacticity are stated. Consider the empty category principle (ECP). Not only is it relevant to quantifier scope, but also to explaining (i) the impossibility in English of finding a complementizer before a tensed verb (e.g., *Who do you think that left?*) (Chomsky and Lasnik 1977; Chomsky 1981); (ii) the order of elements in incorporation structures (Baker 1988); (iii) constraints on the extraction of adjuncts (Rizzi 1991); (iv) the movement of heads (Chomsky 1986a; Travis 1984); and (v) the possibility of extraction over bridge verbs (van Riemsdijk and Williams 1986). A condition like the ECP would seemingly have been unformulable under generative semantics at the level of semantic representation, since it would have violated core principle (4).

But perhaps, one might reply, the mechanics of the two models are so similar that in effect they end up making nearly identical empirical claims. Or similarly, following *ILT*, perhaps the debates of the period, rather than representing a disagreement over the content or the validity of the testable hypotheses that were proposed, were merely empirically unresolvable disputes over what was core and what was auxiliary (*ibid.*: 19). If so, then the fact that their cores are so distinct might be of little real relevance.

I see little merit in either alternative. Once again, the best case imaginable for a core proposition of generative semantics turning into an auxiliary hypothesis for GB involves the representation of quantifier scope. Thus:

> There ended up being very little conceptual difference between the generative semantics rule of quantifier lowering (G. Lakoff 1971a; McCawley 1973b) and, for example, Robert May's (1977, 1985) 'quantifier rule', which had closely related syntactic and semantic effects.
>
> (*ibid.*: 45)

Let me attempt to distill the morass of quantifier scope facts and analyses into a compact presentation, in the course of demonstrating that things are not as simple as *ILT* makes them seem.

It has long been known that sentences whose subjects and objects are each quantified have two potential readings, one with the subject quantifier having wider scope, the other with the object quantifier having wider scope. At the same time, all agree that the subject wide-scope reading seems somewhat more preferred or natural.

During the period of the debate, both sides had analyses that captured the preferred reading at the expense of not characterizing the sentences as ambiguous. Generative semanticists (G. Lakoff 1971a; McCawley 1973b) posited semantic representations in which the wider scope quantifier commanded the narrower scope quantifier, and a rule of quantifier lowering created the superficial monoclausal structure. A global rule relating semantic representation and surface structure (or a level close to it) ensured that if one quantifier had wider scope over another at the former level, it also commanded it at the latter. Interpretivists posited a surface structure rule of semantic interpretation mapping surface structures on to semantic representations on the basis of the positions of the quantifiers at the former level.

Despite their similarities, the interpretivist account was superior for two reasons. First, it had no need for a rule of quantifier lowering, a rule typologically unlike the bulk of others that had been proposed. Hence it allowed for a more constrained syntax. Second, it was embodied in a theory positing that scope is *universally* interpreted at surface structure. Thus the addition of the surface structure rule of interpretation led to no increase in the overall power of the theory; learners would not have to figure out for each language where scope interpretation would apply. However, generative semanticists never undertook a concerted attempt to limit the power of global rules, even to the point of making a universal claim about quantifier scope; their approach allowed global rules, in effect, to link any two arbitrary points in any derivation.[1]

By the mid-1970s, after the debates between generative semanticists and interpretivists had abated, many of the latter opted for an analysis in which multiply quantified sentences were regarded as grammatically ambiguous, that is, they reverted to the position defended by Katz and Postal (1964). May (1977) develops this approach in greatest detail. In May's analysis, the transformation-like rule of quantifier raising moves quantifiers from their surface structure positions, adjoining them to the sentences that contain them. This rule applies at LF to create structures where the structural relation between the quantifiers corresponds to their scope relations, strikingly analogous to the earlier generative semantic treatment. Furthermore, the newly proposed rule of quantifier raising appeared to be the simple inverse of the generative semantics rule of quantifier lowering.

Now then, was a supposedly 'refuted' analysis readopted, without acknowledgement and without the realization that this showed, in effect, that generative semanticists were right all along? Not really. Quantifier raising did not present the typological problems that lowering did. Furthermore, it turned out that the relationship between the moved quantifier and its point of origin was subject to the same kinds of constraints as those between moved elements and their points of origin, i.e., constraints on antecedent-trace configurations. Such constraints were literally inexpressible in generative semantics, which disallowed traces.[2] Also, by maintaining that LF was a syntactic level contributing to semantic interpretation, but not the level of semantic interpretation itself, interpretivists avoided the many well-known problems involved in attempting to represent meaning in predicate calculus form.

Now it may very well be the case that the idea of a quantifier movement rule came into the heads of interpretivists by virtue of earlier work in generative semantics. It is certainly the case that interpretivists should have given generative semantics more credit for mechanical features of their analysis (see Newmeyer 1986a:138). But that is tangential to the issue at hand. The fact that a core hypothesis of generative semantics turned up in a rather different form as an auxiliary hypothesis of GB provides no support for the assertion in *ILT* that generative semantics was not empirically disconfirmed. One compares and evaluates rival theories, not in terms of their mechanics *per se*, but in terms of the theoretical foundations that enable those mechanics.

There are, needless to say, certain auxiliary hypotheses of generative semantics that are, to one degree or another, auxiliary hypotheses of GB. In and of itself, that fact should be of little consequence, since, by definition, auxiliary hypotheses are proposed and dismissed with relative abandon, and can therefore hardly be crucial with respect to comparing the essential content of two theories. In any event, since generative semantics and its rivals share parentage and a host of common assumptions, it is no surprise that, as theoretical work evolved, some auxiliary assumptions of the former turned up (in whatever modified form) as auxiliary hypotheses of the latter.

Take lexical decomposition, for example: it is widely accepted that the strong form of this hypothesis, i.e., one in which morphologically simple words are decomposed in the syntax, has been refuted. We find a weaker version of this hypothesis, i.e., one in which only morphologically complex words are decomposed, in standard GB syntactic analyses. In what sense does that reinforce the *ILT* 'paradox'? Perhaps one could demonstrate that some of the arguments against strong lexical decomposition carry over to refute weak lexical decomposition as well. In that case, advocates of weak lexical decomposition should rationally abandon that hypothesis. Is there any more to be said?

ON THE CORE PROPERTIES OF GENERATIVE SEMANTICS

To this point, I have been granting *ILT* its characterization of the core propositions of generative semantics. But if core propositions are those not subject to empirical test and are held on to at all cost, it cannot possibly be right that propositions (1) to (5) above were *core* propositions. For a few short years after 1967, generative semantics had abandoned each and every one on the basis of empirical evidence. Consider core principle (1), for example. There soon ceased to be the assumption that 'the distribution of linguistic elements is determined by structural properties of the grammatical strings made up of those elements'. In a 1972 interview (published as G. Lakoff 1974a), George Lakoff rejected this assumption explicitly. He wrote that the task of a grammar was to 'specify the conditions under which sentences can be appropriately used . . . . One thing that one might ask is whether there is anything that does *not* enter into rules of grammar'. Or consider McCawley:

> I reject . . . the notion of the 'grammaticality' of a sentence considered apart from its meaning, use and context and take the grammarian's business to be the formulation of rules that specify what devices the language allows for the expression of the various possible meanings, subject to whatever contextual constraints (linguistic or extralinguistic) may be imposed on the use of those devices.
>
> (McCawley 1979: viii)

In other words, in contradiction to (1), the formal structure of language is derivative of extralinguistic context. Lakoff and McCawley were led to this conclusion by what they took to be the empirical evidence, presented in paper after paper from that period (for representative quotations, see G. Lakoff 1971b: 332; McCawley 1973b: 326).

As the above quotes indicate, the abandonment of core principle (1) went hand-in-hand with the abandonment of the idea that there might be principles independent of grammar interacting with it to produce the observed complexity of language. Before Lakoff and McCawley concluded that grammaticality was context-dependent, it was *uncontroversial* that systems outside of grammar proper were involved in determining the acceptability (i.e., the 'distribution') of sentences. Chomsky and Miller (1963), for example, attributed the deviance of multiply centre-embedded sentences to memory limitations and Chomsky (1965) appealed to Gricean implicature to explain why conjoined sentences often convey a temporal reading. Even Ross, at first, was willing to consider a 'pragmatic' alternative to the performative hypothesis (Ross 1970), although he of course did not adopt it.

ILT implies (41–3) that the appeal to extragrammatical principles was a desperate ploy of the interpretivists to avoid dealing with recalcitrant data which were incompatible with a tightly constrained syntax, but for which generative semanticists were providing principled syntactic accounts.[3] A comparison of the entire interpretive and generative semantics 'packages' shows this not to be the case. That is, what must be compared are the interpretivist syntactic theory along with its interacting extragrammatical principles; and generative semantics, which (in its later stages) disallowed extragrammatical principles. By these criteria, interpretivism was the clear winner. Not only was its syntax more constrained, but the principles it appealed to (based on work in the ordinary language tradition, the results of psycholinguistics in memory and processing, etc.) were just those that generative semanticists were attempting, without success, to incorporate into the grammar itself.

The difference in methodologies between the two frameworks is summed up in *ILT*:

> While the interpretivist approach has of course been successful in focusing attention on restrictive syntactic solutions, it needs to be emphasized that generative semanticists were not committed to increasing the power of the grammar so much as they were interested in providing explicit accounts of the syntactic and semantic facts, wherever those accounts happened to lead. From a generative semantics perspective, a more restrictive solution was, all things equal, better than a less restrictive one; but a less restrictive one was better than none at all.
>
> (*ibid.*: 40–2)

But in the early 1970s there were no 'explicit' generative semantic accounts of anything. The choice on the table was an inexplicit generative semantic account of all and sundry versus a fairly explicit and constrained interpretivist theory of syntax, which interacted with pragmatic and psychological principles of varying degrees of explicitness. Surely the rational act was to choose the latter.

Turning to putative core proposition (2) of generative semantics, it was abandoned by 1968 or 1969 with the advent of global rules. In short order, phrase structure rules were identified with the formation rules of predicate logic and transformational rules were rechristened 'local derivational constraints' and accorded considerably diminished importance. Indeed, the very term 'transformational grammar' began to be used by generative semanticists with antipathy (see, for example, G. Lakoff 1972b: i)

The other propositions that *ILT* regards as core were soon abandoned as well. But rather than take my word for it, here is George Lakoff speaking for himself in an interview published in an appendix to *ILT*:[4]

> At the time I proposed generative semantics in 1963, I made a further unstated assumption, namely 'the symbolic semantics hypothesis': all

aspects of meaning that are relevant to grammar can be represented symbolically in logical form. *This was a feature of generative semantics when it was re-adopted [sic] in 1967, and many people incorrectly thought that it was a necessary feature of generative semantics. It was, however, an incidental feature, and it did not last long.* By 1968, it had become clear that the symbolic semantics hypothesis had to be given up . . . . When we adopted possible-world semantics in 1968, we implicitly gave up on the symbolic semantics hypothesis, though we didn't make a big deal of it, since we never saw it as essential at all.

Around the same time, we gave up on the symbolic semantics hypothesis for other reasons . . . . It became clear that grammatical well-formedness was relative to context, and that certain context-based relations . . . could [not] be symbolized as part of logical form without loss of generalization.

(Huck and Goldsmith 1995: 112; emphasis added)

In short, advocates of generative semantics not only regarded *ILT*'s core propositions (1) to (5) as empirically testable and refutable, but they went ahead and tested them empirically and (to their satisfaction) refuted them.

GENERATIVE SEMANTICS AND THE LEVEL OF DEEP STRUCTURE

What were the core principles of generative semantics, then? To me, the answer seems too obvious to belabour: the first, and most important, was the nonexistence of a syntactic level of deep structure, that is, a level segregating the lexical and nonlexical rules. The second core principle was the idea that all profound syntactic generalizations are semantically based. Let us examine them in turn.

If you had asked anybody in 1970 what made generative semantics distinctive, they would have responded: 'it's the version of generative grammar that has no deep structure'. The underground document from 1967 that started generative semantics rolling was entitled 'Is deep structure necessary?' (published in G. Lakoff and Ross 1976). The following year, when McCawley needed a title for a paper illustrating how lexical insertion would be handled in the new theory, he chose 'Lexical insertion in a transformational grammar without deep structure' (McCawley 1968a). And when *ILT* itself presents three generative semantic case studies illustrating rhetorical strategies and linguistic argumentation from the period (Huck and Goldsmith 1995: Ch. 3), two deal primarily with whether or not the level of deep structure exists (G. Lakoff 1972d; McCawley 1968b).[5]

More to the point, however, the nonexistence of deep structure was *never* questioned by generative semanticists during the life of that approach.

ILT considers, but rejects, the possibility that the nonexistence of deep structure might have been a core proposition, with the following comment:

> Clearly, generative semanticists felt that the proposition that there was such a level between semantic representation and surface struc- ture as described in Chomsky's *Aspects* had been empirically refuted; but as regards whether or to what extent there might be syntactic conditions on surface structure which might require mechanisms roughly analogous to postulating such a level, generative semanticists were generally silent.
>
> (*ibid.*: 146; see also pp 29–30)

I find the comment puzzling. Since the key defining feature of the level of deep structure was that it served as *input* to the transformations, how could conditions on surface structure be 'roughly analogous'? A level of deep structure *ipso facto* constrains the transformational component, since only a well-formed deep structure can serve as input to the transformational rules.[6] The more this level is constrained, say by X-bar principles (Chomsky 1970c; Jackendoff 1977), the more movement is constrained, particularly given a theory of structure preservation (Emonds 1976). In the absence of a level of deep structure, such constraints are (by definition) unavailable; at best syntactic conditions on surface structure can filter out sequences of elements whose generation a more constrained approach would have banned in the first place, as critics of the late 1970s proposals for such filters were quick to point out (see, for example, Brame 1981).[7]

As far as the second core principle of generative semantics is concerned, the entire thrust of that approach was to follow Zwicky's call for treatments in which 'natural syntactic classes might be referable to semantic classes in the same way that some phonological classes might be referable to phonetic classes' (Zwicky 1968). As a core principle, the requirement that significant generalizations be semantically based survived the changes in the model. G. Lakoff (1972d) is in large part an extended plea for a theory that grounds form in meaning; as he noted: 'to the extent to which a theory of grammar assigns grammatical form independently of meaning, to that extent that theory will be making the claim that any correspondence between grammatical form and logical form is accidental' (*ibid.*: 547).

ILT remarks that 'the more that surface structure looked like semantic representation, the more natural it was from the point of view of generative semantics' (Huck and Goldsmith 1995: 79). While the evidence presented that generative semanticists really held such a view is weak (see *ibid.*: 151–2), if they did feel this way, they should have pleaded 'guilty' to charges of rampant unnaturalness. Their surface structures could hardly have looked less like their semantic representations. After all, *Floyd broke the glass* does not contain 23 simplex sentences at surface structure; English is not verb initial at that level; nor are adjectives, verbs and nouns represented there by the same category symbol. It took very different syntactic theories interfacing with very different semantic theories before a serious 'fit' between surface structure and semantic representation became a realistic possibility.

In sum, generative semantics was falsified because its core principles were refuted. Phenomenon after phenomenon in the 1970s was uncovered that pointed to nonsemantically based principles applying at the levels of deep or surface structure. Linguists abandoned generative semantics to develop models of grammar which gave prominence to those levels.[8]

CONCLUSION

Because Huck and Goldsmith will not accept the above conclusion, they go overboard in appealing to the external factors that led to the demise of generative semantics. In a chapter written entirely by Huck (Chapter 4), the book discusses the failure of generative semantics to establish a viable institutional base comparable to the way that the MIT department was a base for interpretivism. The University of Chicago was clearly the logical place for such a base; however, in a long and extremely interesting discussion, Huck concludes that the heterogeneity of the Chicago department worked against its playing that role (Huck and Goldsmith 1995: 83–7). But why, one might ask, did so much rest on events in Chicago? After all, in the early 1970s a number of departments had a solid core of generative semanticists that could have played a vanguard role for that theory: Berkeley, Illinois, Michigan, Ohio State, and Texas each had more than one advocate of this approach on their faculty and no rival theory of syntax represented there to act as a counterdraw. No, the obvious conclusion is that people ceased to do generative semantics because they ceased to believe it. Students at the above institutions chose alternative models to work in because they found the core propositions of generative semantics empirically deficient.[9]

Call me a hopeless romantic if you will, but I believe that, in general, scientists can be counted on to make their theoretical choices on rational grounds. The most disturbing aspect, to me, of *Ideology and Linguistic Theory* is its implicit denial that a major turning-point in the development of syntactic theory came about as a product of reasoned debate involving articulately counterposed positions, supported on both sides by the best available evidence. Fortunately, however, I see little in *ILT* to cure me of my romanticism.

Chapter 11

Review of *The Best of CLS: A Selection of Out-of-Print Papers from 1968 to 1975*, edited by Eric Schiller, Barbara Need, Douglas Varley, and William H. Eilfort

This useful anthology (henceforth *BCLS*) assembles twenty-nine out-of-print papers presented at Chicago Linguistic Society (CLS) meetings in the late 1960s and early 1970s.[1] These were the glory years of the Society, when generative semantics and natural phonology dominated theoretical linguistics in the United States, and the CLS was the principal forum for the exchange of the latest ideas in these kindred frameworks.[2]

BCLS is divided into four sections: 'Syntax'; 'Semantics and Pragmatics'; 'Phonology'; and 'Other'. The syntax section contains an introduction by James D. McCawley followed by Arlene Berman's 'A constraint on tough movement'; Georgia Green's 'On the notion "related lexical entry"'; George Lakoff's 'Syntactic amalgams'; Judith Levi's 'Where do all those other adjectives come from?'; Noriko McCawley's 'Boy! Is syntax easy!'; Paul M. Postal's 'Anaphoric islands'; Quang Phuc Dong's (i.e., James McCawley's) 'The applicability of transformations to idioms'; and John R. Ross's 'Guess who?'.

The semantics and pragmatics section begins with an introduction by Jerrold M. Sadock and includes the following papers: 'The speaker knows best principle' by Donald Forman; 'Conversational postulates' by David Gordon and George Lakoff; 'A presuppositional analysis of only and even' by Laurence R. Horn; 'Tracking the generic toad' by John M. Lawler; 'AND and OR; some SOMEs and all ANYs' by Jean E. LeGrand; 'On the treatment of presupposition in transformational grammar' by Jerry L. Morgan; 'Read at your own risk: Syntactic and semantic horrors you can find in your medicine chest' by Jerrold M. Sadock; and 'Deliberate ambiguity' by Ann Weiser.

The papers in the phonology section are introduced by Bill J. Darden. This section contains Lloyd Anderson's 'The left-to-right syllabic cycle'; Robert Bley-Vroman's 'Opacity and interrupted rule schemata'; Michael Kenstowicz and Charles Kisseberth's 'Rule ordering and the asymmetry hypothesis'; James D. McCawley's 'Can you count pluses and minuses before you can count?'; Patricia D. Miller's 'Bleaching and coloring'; Theo Venneman's 'Words and syllables in natural generative grammar'; and

Arnold M. Zwicky's 'The free ride principle and two rules of complete assimilation in English'.

The last section is introduced by Barbara Need and contains papers on a diverse assortment of topics: 'Notes on expressive meaning' by Gerard Diffloth; 'The muzzy theory' by Lyn Haber; 'Morpho-syntax as proof in etymology' by Eric Hamp; 'Sunday Greek' by Kostas Kazazis; and 'I forgot what I was going to say' by Victor Yngve.

Finally, several of the papers are followed by fascinating retrospectives written specifically for the volume, in which the authors place their work in historical perspective and comment on how they would treat the same problems today.

The papers date from a period in which an almost universal conviction had arisen that there were serious inadequacies in the programme for syntax put forward in Chomsky's 1965 book *Aspects of the Theory of Syntax* and in the programme for phonology in Chomsky and Halle's (1968) *Sound Pattern of English* (*SPE*). The alternative conception that prevailed at the University of Chicago, and which, therefore, provided the principal animus for the CLS, was to overcome these inadequacies by attempting to provide syntax and phonology with a 'natural' basis, i.e., one whose primitive terms are independently necessary for the description of natural language phenomena.[3] Thus the goal of generative semantics was to ground syntax (and ultimately pragmatics as well) in semantics, and the goal of natural phonology was (to a great extent) to separate those processes that could not be supplied with phonetic motivation from those that could, and to focus research on the latter. Well over half the papers in *BCLS*, then, are devoted either to demonstrating the seemingly inextricable intertwining of syntactic, semantic, and pragmatic facts or to challenging the nonphonetically motivated phonological representations of *SPE*.

For reasons that would take us beyond the scope of this review, the agenda set by generative semantics and natural phonology has been shelved and replaced by one willing to countenance a wide variety of abstract theoretical devices in both the syntactic and phonological components.[4] Thus we might be tempted to greet the publication of *BCLS* with the same degree of enthusiasm that we would exhibit after discovering on the library shelf a Festschrift published a generation ago honouring a once-prominent proponent of some superseded theory of language.

It would be a mistake for several reasons, however, to consign *The Best of CLS* to the status of an unmovable fixture on the shelf of the university library. For one thing, the heyday of generative semantics and natural phonology was recent enough that a careful study of its claims and methodology affords us an understanding of why we have come to believe what we do today. Take, for example, the Gordon and Lakoff paper, by far the most influential contribution in *BCLS* and possibly the most important ever read at a CLS meeting. I strongly recommend study-ing its clearly delineated programme for reducing pragmatics to semantics, and then reading some of the subsequent refutations, such as Gazdar (1979) and Morgan (1977). I can guarantee that after doing so, one will have arrived at a far greater appreciation of why the current consensus favours a 'modular' conception of language, in which there exist distinct, though interacting, principles from syntax, semantics, and pragmatics, than one would have simply by reading the current literature.[5] One's understanding of current phonological theory will be similarly enhanced by reading the Darden, Miller, or Venneman papers in conjunction with Anderson (1981), Kiparsky and Menn (1977), or some other critique of 'naturalness' as the principal motivating force in phonology.

Second, many of the contributions are worthy of reading in their own right, independently of any historical considerations. One would think less of any current paper on the general nature of syntactic deletion rules that failed to cite Ross's contribution or of one on local ordering that ignored Bley-Vroman's. Likewise, the treatment of lexical presuppo-sitions in the contributions by Horn and Lawler seems very 'modern' to us for the simple reason that the formal study of this topic was initiated and given its shape by these papers, along with others that were first presented at CLS meetings in the late 1960s and early 1970s.

Finally, while many of the contributions present data that are adequately treated in current work (the generalizations in the Postal and Levi papers can be handled nicely, for example, given most current approaches to lexical and morphological structure), the facts presented in others still defy adequate analysis. Theories of indirect speech acts have not advanced to the point where the data put forward by N. McCawley and Forman fall out as special cases, nor have the particular examples that Kenstowicz and Kisseberth adduced in their critique of rule ordering ever been treated within lexical phonology. Thus BCLS contains a repository of linguistic generalizations to challenge a generation of theoreticians yet to come.

Unfortunately, the organization of BCLS serves to undermine seriously its potential usefulness. Given that the moral of so many of the contri-butions is that syntax is inseparable from semantics and pragmatics, I cannot imagine what persuaded the editors to attempt to categorize particular contributions as 'syntactic' or 'semantic/pragmatic', and then to pigeon-hole them into sections with analogous labels. I doubt that George Lakoff or Noriko Akatsuka McCawley, for example, would have regarded (or would now regard, for that matter) their contributions as something apart from semantics and pragmatics, nor would Jerrold Sadock have felt that his study of the language of labels is not in equal parts a syntactic, a semantic, and a pragmatic one.

More seriously, it is not easy to extract from BCLS an indication of the year that any particular contribution was published, a problem that is aggravated by the fact that, within each section, the papers are arranged alphabetically by author, rather than chronologically.[6] Now for most anthologies, this fact would be of little consequence, since there is rarely an iconic relationship between the organization of a collection of reprinted papers and its usefulness to a reader. For *BCLS*, however, the organizational format renders it not only cumbersome but also impractical for what is clearly its most important function: to help the interested reader understand how a central conception about the nature of linguistic constructs (their 'naturalness') progressed in its instantiation over a decade of the recent history of linguistics.

So, for example, a rational organization of *BCLS* would have placed Berman's 1973 global rule treatment of a syntactic process after Ross's 1969 paper, since the latter appealed to 'doom markers' which global rules would come to replace. But alphabetical order demanded otherwise.[7] A chronological organization would also help the reader to place the rhetorical style of so many of these contributions in a better historical context. For example, both the Green and Morgan papers from 1969 and George Lakoff's paper from 1974 are full of what a current reader would take to be a harping-toned self-congratulatory gloating at having uncovered linguistic problems that no theory yet devised had succeeded in treating adequately. But what that reader could never guess, given the organization of *BCLS*, is that at the root of the former was the joy of new discovery powered by youthful enthusiasm (and was taken as such by the audience at the conference at which the papers were presented), whereas the latter seemed then, as now, to be nothing but tendentious.

It is easy to sympathize with the editors' dilemma at having to choose which of the hundreds of papers presented at CLS meetings were the 'best', and one is not surprised to learn in the Preface of the 'riotous conditions' that attended the selection process. While I feel that their final selection is not unreasonable, I would suggest that the following papers from the 1967–75 period have been at least as important historically (not to mention equal quality) as most of those that were selected: James McCawley's 'Lexical insertion in a transformational grammar without deep structure' (*CLS* 4, 1968: 71–80); David Stampe's 'The acquisition of phonetic representation' (*CLS* 5, 1969: 443–54); John Kimball's 'Super-equi-NP deletion as dative seletion' (*CLS* 7, 1971: 142–8); James Foley's 'Phonological change by rule repetition' (*CLS* 7, 1971: 376–84); Charles Pyle's 'On eliminating BM's' (*CLS* 8, 1972: 516–32); David Dowty's 'On the syntax and semantics of the atomic predicate CAUSE' (*CLS* 8, 1972: 62–74); Jorge Hankamer's 'Analogical rules in syntax' (*CLS* 8, 1972: 111–23); Robin Lakoff's 'The pragmatics of modality' (*CLS* 8, 1972: 229–46) and her 'Logic of politeness' (*CLS* 9, 1973: 292–305); Arnold Zwicky's 'On casual speech' (*CLS* 8, 1972: 607–15); and James Fidelholtz's 'Word frequency and vowel reduction in English' (*CLS* 11, 1975: 200–13).

Perhaps the editors would consider publishing a follow-up volume featuring these papers. A natural title suggests itself: *The Second-Best of CLS*!

As a final point, while the issue of whether this collection represents the 'best' of CLS may never be resolved, there is no questioning that it is not (nor does it claim to be) *representative* of CLS. Almost every CLS meeting, for example, included papers written in the lexicalist framework. Not one appears in *BCLS*. Furthermore, through design or happenstance, the University of Chicago is vastly overrepresented in *BCLS*. Fifteen of the twenty-nine papers (52 per cent) are by scholars who were affiliated with that university in the late 1960s or early 1970s. Seven more are by individuals from Ohio State, Michigan, or Illinois, midwestern universities that then had theoretically congenial departments. Thus the total percentage of papers from linguists affiliated to one (or more) of these four universities is a whopping 76 per cent. By contrast, in 1972, a typical CLS year, the corresponding percentages were a more modest 25 per cent and 62 per cent respectively.[8]

To conclude, then, despite the book's faulty organization and arguably imperfect selection of contributions, *BCLS* is a worthy resource, containing material relevant both for linguistic problems that are currently under investigation and for helping to provide a clearer understanding of why work in the field is at the point it is today.

Part III

Grammatical theory and second language learning

Chapter 12

The ontogenesis of the field of second language learning research

Co-authored with Steven H. Weinberger

The question of how a second language is acquired has occupied the interest of scholars for millenniums.[1] Nevertheless it seems fair to say that throughout most of history, the question of second language *learning* has been inextricably bound up with that of second language *teaching*. Indeed, until very recently, second language learning as an intellectual discipline was simply nonexistent: even the principal theoretical proposals addressing the acquisition of a second language have typically been embedded in works whose main goal is wholly practical, namely, how most effectively to teach that language.

Over the past fifteen or so years, however, the situation has begun to change. There are unmistakable signs that second language learning research has begun to mould itself into a distinct field, with its own goals, methodology, and research programme. And most significantly, it has begun to break away from the position of being no more than an ancillary to the concerns of the pedagogue. Journal articles, research monographs, anthologies, and conferences now address the question of the intrinsic human capacity to acquire a second language and the cognitive faculties governing such acquisition, without necessarily drawing lessons for effective classroom teaching. And there is a small but growing body of scholars whose interest in second language learning is not primarily a result of their desire to improve instruction, but rather stems from the intellectual challenge posed by an attempt to explain the phenomenon.

In this paper, we will describe the circumstances surrounding the birth of the field of second language learning research. We will furthermore place the relationship between this field and that of theoretical linguistics in historical perspective and discuss the relative maturity of the field of second language learning research as compared with other disciplines.

The field of second language learning research has its modern roots in the programme of 'contrastive analysis', which, although it has a long history in Europe (see Fisiak 1980), arose in North America only in the 1940s, and primarily as a means of bridging the gap between the theory of structural linguistics and the classroom teaching of foreign languages.

In America, the pedogogically orientated contrastive analysis used the behaviourist terminology of the times to codify the age-old observation that the properties of one's native language tend to influence one's performance in a second language. Thus, contrastive analysis was in no sense an independent intellectual discipline – its advocates were clear that it was to be evaluated not so much on the basis of its ability to provide a theoretical explanation of second language learning as on its usefulness as a tool in preparing language teaching curricula. There is no question that structural linguists believed that it was useful. Most agreed that 'the most effective [teaching] materials are those that are based upon a scientific description of the language to be learned, carefully compared with a parallel description of the native language of the learner' (Fries 1945: 9). Utilizing such contemporary behaviourist notions as 'imitation', 'positive transfer', 'negative transfer', and so on, the linguists and applied linguists of the day formulated an extremely strong relationship between the structural properties of the L1 and the L2 and the degree of difficulty of learning. According to this 'contrastive analysis hypothesis', 'the student who comes in contact with a foreign language [will find that] those elements that are similar to his native language will be simple for him, and those elements that are different will be difficult' (Lado 1957: 2).

Contrastive analysis was in its heyday in the 1950s and 1960s as the pages of *Language Learning* were filled with detailed comparisons of English with a multitude of foreign languages and major contrastive studies were undertaken at the Center for Applied Linguistics under contract with the Office of Education. By 1965, almost 500 contrastive analyses had been published, which dealt with more than eighty-four languages, from Afrikaans to Zulu (Hammer and Rice 1965). The implicit expectation of all of these studies was of course to 'provide the basis for more effective classroom practices by systematically revealing those aspects of the target language which needed particular emphasis through carefully constructed drill' (Alatis 1968: 1).

Nevertheless the contrastive analysis hypothesis, once believed to be a prerequisite for every language teacher, rapidly fell into disrepute. Its fall was so abrupt that by the end of the 1970s it had become a theoretical nonentity: the term 'constrastive analysis' received not a single mention in the 1979 TESOL convention *Advance Program*.

A number of factors helped simultaneously to seal the fate of contrastive analysis and to lay the basis for the modern field of second language learning research. To begin with, it simply proved inadequate empirically. The initial appeal of the contrastive analysis hypothesis lay in its apparent success in handling cases of 'phonological interference', for example, facts such as the difficulty that Japanese speakers tend to have in distinguishing English /r/ and /l/. But as more and more careful research was undertaken in second language learning, particularly in the realm of syntax (a neglected area within structural linguistics), it became clear that the hypothesis could not be empirically validated. Not only did learners fail to exhibit the errors predicted by negative transfer, but many cases of positive transfer did not materialize. Moreover, as syntactic investigations increased, it was found that interference errors accounted for only a minority of those reported. As it turned out, developmental errors such as overgeneralization and simplification constituted the majority of second language errors. Such facts posed an intractable problem for contrastive analysis, while at the same time pointing to the need for a more sophisticated theory placing more emphasis on the relationship between transfer and developmental processes.

Second, as time went on, structural linguists came to realize that their programme of contrastive analysis suffered from profound internal contradictions. A basic tenet of the form of structuralism practised by American linguists was that languages could be described adequately only on their own terms, not by recourse to a universal framework of reference which encompassed all languages. But, as pointed out by Ferguson (1963), contrastive analysis demands the latter – in order to compare and contrast two grammars, one must make the assumption that their properties can be phrased within the same universal terminology and with recourse to the same theoretical apparatus. Since the American structuralists rejected in principle a universalist approach, the more astute of them came to realize that any attempt on their part to do contrastive studies was to cause them to violate their basic philosophy. Thus those who aspired to do contrastive studies were put on the horns of a dilemma; either they could carry out the studies (and violate the principles of post-Bloomfieldian linguistics) or abandon contrastive studies (and remain true to contemporary theoretical principles). For a time, at least, many chose the latter alternative.

But by the 1960s, many others had chosen the former. The new theory of transformational generative grammar rejected the anti-universalism of structural linguistics, and thus provided no obstacle to contrastive studies. Moreover, its extensive theoretical apparatus provided contrastive analysis with many different structural properties of the language for comparison. Hence, during the mid- and late 1960s, not just the superficial aspects of syntax and phonology were subject to contrastive analysis, but also the abstract elements, such as their deep structures and transformational rules (see, for example, Di Pietro 1968; Dingwall 1964; James 1969; Stockwell, Bowen and Martin 1965). This period of generativist-orientated contrastive studies was, however, short lived. It was soon realized that as a pedagogical tool, these studies were as inadequate as the structuralist ones that preceded them, if not more so. What use could it possibly be to the teacher to know that the rule of passive, say, preceded the rule of relative clause formation in the grammar of the native language, but followed it in that of the target language? Moreover, the rapidity of the changes of theory (and analyses based on it) in this period seemed to shatter any hope of the pedagogue seizing on contrastive studies for classroom application. Not surprisingly, the linguists' own doubts about contrastive analysis helped to fuel the growing feeling among language teachers that it might be of no use to them in the classroom, and, by extension, that the results of linguistics might not be of any relevance to them. Many teachers reasoned that if contrastive analysis was a misguided enterprise, then it naturally could be disregarded. Some went farther and wondered whether even if it were right, it would necessarily follow that it could be utilized in teaching. William Mackey, speaking for a growing number of language teachers frustrated with the linguists' seeming lack of ability to provide them with effective teaching tools, asked: 'What is the use of predicting mistakes already heard?' (Mackey 1973: 8).

The Chomskyan revolution may have sounded the death knell of the structuralist-derived approach to contrastive analysis and ushered in the short period of generativist-orientated contrastive studies described above, but it in fact was responsible for the collapse of contrastive analysis in general in the 1970s. Just as Chomsky's 1959 review of B. F. Skinner's *Verbal Behavior* (1957) knocked out the underpinnings from the behaviourist psychology to which early contrastive analysis owed its theoretical rat- ionalization, the first chapter of his 1965 book *Aspects of the Theory of Syntax*, by outlining a theory of language acquisition in terms of an innate 'language acquisition device' that facilitated the learning of abstract grammatical rules, made any sort of contrastive analysis seem theoretically suspect. Since children were now regarded as 'little linguists', constantly forming and testing hypotheses about the native language that they were learning, it made sense, as was pointed out in a very influential paper (Corder 1967), to think of second language learners in the same way. Now the errors made by the learner took on a particularly central status. They were no longer 'habits' to be eradicated, nor an inevitable by-product of the conflict resulting from the distinct structures, levels, and rules of two gram- mars; they were now evidence to support the constructive hypotheses of the learner – evidence which was of profound intellectual interest, since the discovery that learning takes place to an extent independent of teaching implied that research in second language was no longer necessarily tied to pedagogical concerns.

Contrastive linguistics thus gave way to a new field of 'error analysis', which gathered, organized, and tabulated the errors of the second language learner. Despite its origins in the replacement of structural linguistics by generative grammar, very few papers in error analysis went beyond such a taxonomy to draw interesting theoretical conclusions about the mechanisms governing acquisition. And, as one might expect with a taxonomic approach, error analysis embodied a large amount of pure arbitrariness. For example, when Russian or German learners of English devoice their final English obstruents, are they committing a developmental error or a transfer error? Error analysis provided no principled way of deciding. In an early critique of error analysis, Eric Hamp noted that while it might prove useful to compile the errors likely to be made by learners in particular situations, here, 'as we have discovered in the case of generative grammar for other matters, we wish not simply to categorize or taxonomize existing cases' (Hamp 1968: 146). What an interesting irony it is that the taxonomic theory of structural linguistics spawned the theory-driven second language research programme of contrastive analysis, while generative grammar, committed to deep explanation, gave birth to the data-driven, taxonomic programme of error analysis!

Why was this early attempt at second language learning research under the umbrella of generative grammar carried out in such a theoretical vacuum? The answer is based in part on the predominant late 1960s and early 1970s climate of opinion in linguistics and in part on contemporary attitudes to the human capacity for language acquisition. In this period, theoretical linguistics was dominated by the framework of 'generative semantics'. Generative semantics gradually withdrew from the programme of formal explanation to one in which simply noting interesting facts about a variety of languages became the general practice. As George Lakoff, the framework's foremost practitioner, put it, 'I think that the time has come to return to the tradition of informal descriptions of exotic languages' (G. Lakoff 1974a: 153). It is not surprising that since linguistic theory found itself in 'the age of what we might call the New Taxonomy, an era of new and exuberant cataloguing of the enormous range of facts that linguists need eventually to find theories to deal with' (Fillmore 1972: 6), the field of second language learning research also took a taxonomic direction.

But attitudes towards language acquisition itself were partly to blame for the nihilistic state of affairs in the field. In this period, a biological explanation of the fact that most adults fail to achieve a native-like proficiency in their second language gained wide acceptance – particularly among generative grammarians. Based in part upon the suggestion of Penfield and Roberts (1959) that physiological changes in the brain may account for the lack of second language proficiency in adults, Lenneberg (1967) proposed his critical period hypothesis, which equated the inability to fully acquire a language with the completion of brain lateralization. Put simply, Lenneberg believed that the language acquisition device shuts off at puberty, thereby preventing an adult from ever acquiring an accent-free second language. But a consequence of such a belief is that studies of adult second-language acquisition can, in principle, shed no light on the nature of the language acquisition device. Thus the promise of a fruitful generativist field of second language learning research was nipped early in the bud; the Lenneberg hypothesis seemed to leave researchers no avenue of research more fruitful than that devoted to the compiling of errors.

If Lenneberg's views had withstood the test of time, it is unlikely that there would now be a field of second language learning research that derived its conceptions in any sense from linguistic theory. But the barrier such views imposed between second language researchers and theoretical linguists gave way with the increasing calling into question of Lenneberg's hypothesis. Krashen (1973), for example, challenged the idea that the completion of brain lateralization coincided with puberty by pointing to evidence that indicated brain lateralization at age five or earlier. Yet children between that age and puberty clearly have the ability to acquire a language fluently. The idea that universal grammar (or 'UG' – the term that had replaced 'language acquisition device' by the mid-1970s) ever becomes inoperative was challenged in the 1970s by evidence from second language data itself. Put simply, Bailey *et al.* (1974), d'Anglejan and Tucker (1975), Dulay and Burt (1974), and others found that second language acquisition *is*, in crucial respects, like first language acquisition, and the same theoretical constructs can be invoked to explain both. As they showed, developmental L2 errors tend to mimic those committed by the L1 learner, and, with respect to the morpheme studies, the order of acquisition of certain morphemes in L2 mirrors that in L1 (for L1 order of acquisition studies, see R. Brown 1973; De Villiers and De Villiers 1973). Although the L2 morpheme acquisition studies are not unproblematic (see Rosansky 1976), they, along with other evidence, resulted in a new consensus about L2 acquisition, namely that UG does not shut off at puberty. At the same time, evidence mounted that an L2 learner's grammar, far from being a mere hodge-podge of deviant forms, itself obeys the crucial properties of naturally occurring human languages, subject to the same principles of organization and constraints (for evidence to this effect from syntax, see Adjémian 1976 and Ritchie 1978; from phonology, see Eckman 1981).

Such findings signalled the birth of the contemporary field of second language learning research, a field both in principle independent of pedagogy and with the promise to stand in the same interdependent relationship with linguistic theory as do the fields of aphasiology, speech error studies, and first language acquisition research. Now, the properties of UG could be probed in L2 research, and theories of L2 acquisition would necessarily be sensitive to the best available theories about the nature of UG. And at the same time, the goals and methodology of the fields of first and second language acquisition were placed on parallel tracks: L2 acquisition studies too became studies of the universally constrained development of grammars (for discussion, see Hakuta and Cancino 1977).

Recent second language acquisition studies have paralleled those of first language acquisition studies in an important way – they have tended to focus more on the acquisition of syntax than on the acquisition of phonology. Studies of the acquisition of L2 syntax outnumber those of phonology by about five to one; indeed, at the three-day Linguistic Theory and Second Language Acquisition Conference, held at MIT in October 1985, only one paper was devoted to phonology. There are a number of reasons for the priority granted to syntax. First, this state of affairs simply reflects that of theoretical linguistics as a whole. Rightly or wrongly, a widespread opinion holds that the frontiers of linguistic knowledge will be pushed back primarily through the investigation of syntax. Not surprisingly, then, L2 researchers have also focused on syntax. It should be recalled by way of comparison that structural linguists, who granted theoretical priority to the study of phonology, dealt primarily with that area in their applied work as well.

Indeed, the structuralists' obsession with phonological interference in their L2 research might be a second reason for the unpopularity of its study by generativist-orientated L2 researchers. Contrastive analysis did, after all, achieve a limited measure of success in the realm of phonology. Perhaps this fact has led some current researchers to conclude that the problems of the acquisition of phonology really *are* trivial and attributable to transfer. With developmental universals, overwhelmingly gleaned from the study of syntactic acquisition, in the spotlight, it is hardly surprising that L2 phonological studies have tended to remain in the shadows.

Finally, the scant attention paid to L2 phonology might be a consequence of the popular idea that a foreign accent is biologically inevitable for adults (Scovel 1969), and thus the attainment of native-like pronunciation is a hopeless pursuit. If such were indeed the case, then there would be little point for linguists in devoting time to the acquisition of phonology. Even if a weaker hypothesis is adopted – for example, one that related L2 phonological development to non-linguistic affective factors, linguists would still have very little to contribute to the understanding of L2 phonology.

In fact, however, the long avoidance of phonology by theoretical L2 researchers has begun to reverse itself. Just as the interaction of transfer and language universals in L2 syntax has shown itself to be theoretically interesting (see Gass 1984; Gass and Selinker 1983; Scovel 1969), a similarly interesting interaction appears to be at work in L2 phonology. Indeed, research conducted by Eckman (1977), Flege and Hillenbrand (1984), and Tarone (1980) has shown that transfer in phonology, whether negative or positive, is not sufficient to determine a learner's errors.

Furthermore, the new and exciting theories of phonological structure within linguistic theory have been productively adopted by L2 researchers. For example, Broselow (1984) has demonstrated that non-linear approaches to syllable structure can be invoked to explain data from Arabic-speaking learners of English. Likewise, Rubach (1984), using a lexical phonology model, has accounted for the relative transferability of cyclic and post-cyclic phonological rules in Polish.

Perhaps the most important reason why phonology is gaining ground in L2 research is due to a re-evaluation and renewed acceptance of contrastive analysis. The past association of this approach with behaviourism and descriptivism left a bad taste in the mouth of generativist L2 researchers, which tended to discredit any sort of contrastive studies, but many now have come to realize that there is nothing intrinsically wrong with 'contrasting' the grammars of two languages for the purpose of understanding better the acquisition of one by a native speaker of the other. As a consequence, contrastive analysis has been reconstituted on a higher theoretical plane, in which theoretically significant features of the languages involved are contrasted and not, as in much past work, only the superficial and readily observable ones. Thus, for example, Eckman (1977) predicts errors in L2 phonology by means of his 'markedness differential hypothesis', which is essentially an updated version of contrastive analysis utilizing the theoretical notion of 'markedness'.

Contrastive analysis has been reborn in studies of L2 syntax as well. Flynn (1984), for example, predicts aspects of L2 acquisition on the basis of the similarity or differences involved in the relevant languages' principal phrase-structural branching direction, and she and a number of others have attempted to explain learners' errors in terms of the differences in the syntactic parameters (Chomsky 1981) between the L1 and the L2.

Studies of second language learning have progressed impressively over the past fifty years. One should not denigrate the impressive feat of a field which rose from total nonexistence to become the pedagogical wing of structural linguistics and from there to achieve relative independence in the space of only two generations. At the same time, however, it is important to keep these achievements in proper perspective. The field of second language learning still shows all the signs of being an immature discipline. In particular, it has the tripartite character inherent in all immature disciplines: first, it is a domain of scientific investigation and, as such, seeks to develop theories specifically within its domain; second, it is an applied science, in that it takes theories developed in other domains – in particular, linguistics and psychology – and investigates how they might be applicable to practical problems; third, it is a field of 'engineering', so to speak, in that it is committed to a practical goal, namely how best to teach languages.

While it is not the case that every member of the discipline is engaged in all three activities, there is no incongruity seen in being so. Quite the contrary, in fact – some of the most highly regarded contributions to the field combine science, applied science, and engineering in one big package. Take Stephen Krashen's work as an example (see especially Krashen 1982). On the one hand, his 'input hypothesis' is a theory whose domain is specifically limited to (second) language acquisition – certainly there is no implication that it follows as a consequence of independently motivated psychological or linguistic principles. On the other hand, his 'affective filter hypothesis', as we understand it, is (or can be shown to be) wholly derivative of principles governing learning in general. And finally, Krashen peppers his work (his 1982 book *Principles and Practice in Second Language Acquisition* is a typical example) with hints on how conversation groups, pleasure reading, and so on can speed second language learning.

By combining science, applied science, and engineering, second language learning stands in stark contrast to intellectually more mature disciplines. It is taken for granted in the 'hard' sciences that the three are distinct. Da Vinci might have drafted plans for flying machines and Galileo might have designed scientific equipment, but in the physical sciences, the scientist–applied scientist–engineer has long passed from the scene. Physics is not atypical: as fields develop distinct explanatory principles, the principles themselves become the basis for an autonomous discipline. Linguistics itself furnishes an historical example of this process: despite the fact that language had been an object of intellectual investigation for millenniums, it took the success of the comparative method to separate it from philosophy and classical philology.

The struggle of the field to free itself from ties to pedagogy has been slow and arduous, and is still a long way from being totally achieved. But interestingly, the impetus needed to begin the severance of these ties was provided by the same set of circumstances that made L2 acquisition by adults such a productive research topic – the abandonment of Lenneberg's critical period hypothesis. This hypothesis explains why children don't have to be literally 'taught' the grammar of their first language –uncontroversially, UG is operative in this period. But, one might reasonably ask, if UG governs L2 as well, then why should L2 grammar have to be taught either? Why, as a theoretician, should one involve oneself with questions of pedagogy? (Even before Lenneberg's downfall, Leonard Newmark made this point in an article entitled 'How not to interfere with language learning' (Newmark 1966).) Given such a conclusion, the door was open to the study of L2 acquisition without concomitant concern for its effective teaching. Needless to say, no one ever took the position that there is no difference between L1 and L2 acquisition – obviously, the conditions surrounding the latter are different from those surrounding the former. But since the differences (some of which have been characterized by constructs such as 'competing cognitive structures' (Felix 1985) and the 'monitor' (Krashen 1978b)) seem not to involve UG, they could be left to the educational psychologist to study, rather than to the linguist or linguistically orientated L2 researcher.

But the links between research and pedagogy are still not fully severed. Even many of the most theoretically orientated papers in second language learning devote space to the presumed pedagogical implications and applications of the proposal discussed (see, for example, the papers by Eckman and White in Wheatley *et al.* 1985). Part of the continued attention to pedagogy by theoreticians is due without doubt to pressure from publishers, who wish to exploit the vast market of language teachers in any publication dealing with L2 acquisition. Thus the editors of an anthology devoted to interlanguage phonology (Ioup and Weinberger 1987) were put under pressure by Newbury House to devote space to the pedagogical implications of the theoretical proposals therein. It does not seem unreasonable to speculate that such economic pressure has slowed down the development of second language learning research as an independent discipline and will continue to do so in the future.

Nevertheless, the field of second language learning research shows every sign of shedding its legacy of direct involvement in pedagogical questions, however gradually this process might be taking place. We feel that the next ten years will see the field further strengthen its relative position among the academic disciplines as it gains in maturity. One sign that this will happen is the growing respect accorded to the field by theoretical linguists. Ten years or so ago, second language learning was a topic about which most theoreticians were proud to exhibit full ignorance, but today many follow with interest the progress of L2 research. And it stands to reason that they should. If such notions as 'markedness', 'the sonority hierarchy', 'parameterized grammars', and so on can be shown to be necessitated by the facts of second language acquisition, then their incorporation into UG is *ipso facto* supported. The symbiotic relationship between second language learning research and linguistic theory is a healthy sign that the former field is on the brink of achieving the stature it deserves.

Chapter 13

The current convergence in linguistic theory

Some implications for second language acquisition research

INTRODUCTION[1]

Noam Chomsky, in his most extensive published remarks on the topic of second language acquisition (a 1970 paper based on a lecture presented in 1966), called attention to those findings of linguistic theory that might be expected to have the greatest potential impact for acquisition research.[2] First, and most importantly, he singled out the 'creative' aspect of language, the fact that normal linguistic behaviour is stimulus-free and innovative. He pointed also to three properties of grammatical principles themselves: first, that they are abstract, in the sense that they interact in a complex web to determine the surface form of sentences; second, that their essential properties are universal and innately specified; and third, that they come directly into play in a variety of cognitive processes, for example, syntactic rules are involved in the analysis of the signal in perception.

The findings to which Chomsky alluded are today taken for granted as truisms within the field of second language research. Indeed, they collectively define the research programme of the field.[3] The realization of the stimulus-free nature of linguistic behaviour, for example, provided an explanation of the failure of the research programme of contrastive analysis (and the pedagogical approaches that accompanied it) and led directly to a view of acquisition that accorded a greater role to the learner's own contribution to the process. Likewise, a central place on the research agenda of the past twenty-five years has been granted to the investigation of how the clash between the abstract rules and structural principles of the L1 and those of the L2 manifest themselves in the 'interlanguage' (Selinker 1972) of the learner. A major point of controversy in the field centres on the extent to which the principles of universal grammar (UG) shape the course of second language acquisition. While the great majority of researchers agree that UG does play a role, unanimity on this point has not been achieved.[4]

The fact that the results to which Chomsky pointed are truisms means that they are all but useless in guiding research at any but the most general level. Clearly, if one is interested in the explanation of some concrete phenomenon, such as why learners of a particular language systematically make one set of errors but not another, then the simple knowledge that the grammars of the native and target languages embody abstract principles is not going to be a great deal of use. The question that second language learning researchers need answered, then, is whether linguistic theory has produced more *concrete* results that they can take for granted in their accounts of the acquisition process.

The first thought of anyone who has some acquaintance with the course of linguistic theory in the last generation is undoubtedly that this question has a negative answer. As it turns out, 1966, the year of Chomsky's presentation, was the last year in which there was anything resembling unanimity among theoretical linguists about the organization of UG and the nature of its rules and principles. That year saw the birth of the framework of 'generative semantics', which in its later stages had come to challenge virtually every assumption about the workings of UG that had been put forward in Chomsky's 1965 book *Aspects of the Theory of Syntax*. At the same time, Chomsky himself dramatically altered his own previous views, arguing in turn that deep structures are much closer to surface structures than had been previously imagined (Chomsky 1970c), that surface structure plays a major role in semantic interpretation (Chomsky 1971), and that derivations embody a set of principles hitherto unrecognized, including the idea that movement rules leave behind traces at the site of extraction (Chomsky 1973).

The collapse of generative semantics in the mid-1970s did little to alter the fragmented state of linguistic theory. By this time, a sizeable number of grammarians had begun to express reservations about the direction in which Chomsky's 'extended standard theory' (EST) was headed, and began to develop a number of alternative models whose common feature was an even further diminished role for transformational rules. By the mid-1980s, a veritable alphabet soup of competing frameworks had come into being, including, most importantly, Chomsky's own government-binding theory (GB), itself a major modification of the 1970s EST, and the more surface-orientated frameworks of generalized phrase structure grammar (GPSG) and lexical-functional grammar (LFG).

The plethora of approaches poses a dilemma for second language learning researchers, many of whom must feel as Roger Brown did when he observed that:

> the fact that linguistic theory changes, and does so at a rapid clip, poses real difficulties for the psychologist who wants to use linguistic theory in his own work. What one discipline wants from another – in inter-disciplinary work – is always The Word. 'Don't tell me your troubles,

tell me your results', is the borrower's real attitude. It is not a possible attitude for the psycholinguist in 1969.

(Brown 1970: ix)

Almost twenty years later, second language acquisition researchers seem to be no better off than Brown. Which framework should they adopt? What, if anything, do the competing frameworks have in common that can be taken as uncontroversial and definitively established? The dominant trend has been to adopt the assumptions of GB, paralleling the fact that within linguistic theory itself, GB has considerably more supporters than the other models. Still, however, a lingering, and entirely understandable, feeling persists that if so many questions about linguistic theory are still up for grabs, then the results of an allied field which are based on a specific set of assumptions internal to one particular theoretical framework can hardly be secure.

It is my purpose in this chapter to argue that there is no need for pessimistic conclusions. After a period of fifteen or so years in which approaches to grammatical analysis diverged more with each passing year, the tide has turned in the opposite direction. In the past few years, there has been a surprising (and welcome!) convergence among the leading frameworks on a wide variety of issues, some of them at a rather detailed level. This convergence bodes well for second language learning researchers and others who wish to apply the results of linguistic theory to their own domain of investigation. Since, given both human nature and the sociopolitical organization of academia, the normal tendency is for differing frameworks ever to increase their differences from each other, the fact that the opposite is happening suggests that a set of incontrovertible results is being attained independently, results that are unlikely (as has frequently been the case) to be abandoned even before they have a chance to be applied.

I will outline below the major points of convergence among the principal frameworks, giving, where it seems appropriate to do so, some (admittedly nonspecialist) views on how they might pertain to second language learning research. I will also call attention to the major points of controversy that still remain, both methodological and substantive.

POINTS OF CONVERGENCE WITHIN LINGUISTIC THEORY

I will assume in the following subsections a basic acquaintance with the three leading approaches to syntax in their broad outline. Overviews of GB can be found in Chomsky (1981) and Riemsdijk and Williams (1986); GPSG in Gazdar *et al.* (1985); and LFG in Bresnan (1982a). For discussion that treats the frameworks from the point of view of comparing their similarities and differences in more detail than can be achieved here, see McCloskey (1988), Newmeyer (1986a), and Sells (1985).

The major points of convergence can be assimilated to two leading ideas: first, that linguistic phenomena are best explained through the modular interaction of autonomously functioning systems (see below); and second, that relations between grammatical elements meet strict locality conditions (see p. 162).

Modularity

It is now taken for granted by every generative framework that there exists an autonomous linguistic competence, that is, at the heart of language lies a grammatical system whose primitive terms and principles are not artefacts of a system that encompasses both human language and other human faculties or abilities.

The general adoption of the idea of an autonomous competence has come about primarily with the increased realization of the great disparity between linguistic form and communicative function, a disparity that appears to be the general rule rather than the exception. In other words, there are principles governing structural regularity in language that are not by-products of principles external to it, i.e., competence demands a characterization in its own terms.

The discovery (and increased acceptance) of the idea of the autonomy of formal grammar is of profound importance in and of itself. The broader implications of this concept follow from the current conception of the relationship between the grammar and the other faculties involved in language. It is now well accepted that complex linguistic phenomena are best explained in terms of the *interaction* of these diverse systems. This so-called *modular* approach to linguistic complexity can be represented schematically (following Anderson 1981: 494) as in Figure 13.1.

The appeal of modular explanations is, in essence, that they allow order to be extracted from chaos. In the typical case, if one system alone (whether linguistic, perceptual, or whatever) were forced to deal with some set of complex facts, then no elegant account of them emerges; but such an account is the natural result of regarding superficial complexity as the product of simple principles, each from a distinct domain. Modular explanations have been invoked to handle a wide variety of disparate data in recent years, and in many cases dramatic results have been obtained. These results have been instrumental in kindling the resurgence of interest in generative grammar after its eclipse in the 1970s.[5]

The idea that the principles of grammatical patterning are independent of principles of language use should come as no surprise to those whose goal is to understand the process of acquiring a second language. It has long been a commonplace observation that a learner's mastery of the grammatical structure of a language is typically out of step with his or her ability to communicate or process information in that language. Indeed,

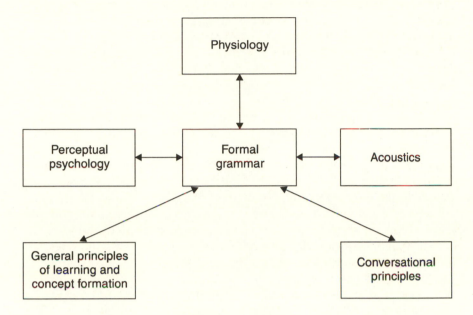

Figure 13.1 The modular conception of language

the conception that a full account of language must appeal to the interaction of grammatical and other faculties has developed independently
within second language acquisition research. Such constructs as the
'monitor' (Krashen 1978b) and 'competing cognitive structures' (Felix
1985), with their recognition that the acquisition process involves a welter
of interacting (and interfering) principles and strategies, grant central
recognition to the idea of modularity in language.[6]

The modular conception of language undermines the conclusion that
the search for strictly structural principles of acquisition should be abandoned in favour of pragmatically based ones, on the basis of the idea that
the primary function of language is communication (for this point of
view, see Oller 1973). Given modularity, there is no incompatibility
between principles from these two domains; indeed, a full account of
acquisition must appeal to both.

It is now uncontroversial among generative grammarians that the
complexity of language can be explained by recourse to the modular
interaction of formal grammar with principles from physiology, cognition, sociology, and so on. An important development during the past ten
years has been to carry modular explanations to progressively 'lower'
levels of linguistic structure. For example, practitioners of all generative
frameworks now agree that there are principles governing meaning which

are to one degree or another independent of principles governing form, that is, that linguistic theory cannot conflate syntax and semantics. Generative semantics *did* attempt such a conflation, and foundered on it. Now, GB, GPSG, and LFG all propose specifically syntactic principles to handle the linear ordering of elements within the phrase and clause and the hierarchization of structure, though, of course, these principles differ markedly from framework to framework. Analogously, the three frameworks each admit specifically semantic notions (such as thematic roles) into their conception of language. Complex phenomena are derived from the interaction of principles from the two domains: two examples that might be cited are the GB account of the passive construction, which involves both syntactic (or morphological) Case theory and the theory of thematic relations, and the GPSG treatment of variable binding in unbounded dependency constructions, which appeals to a variety of syntactic feature transmission mechanisms and to principles of predicate logic.[7]

The independence of formal generalizations and semantic ones has implications for second language learning research. First, it demonstrates the misguided nature of the late 1960s and early 1970s calls for approaches to second language learning that attempt to bypass syntactic principles in place of those based on meaning (H. D. Brown 1972b; Lamendella 1969). It is not surprising, then, that research continues to reveal examples of learners who have mastered the syntactic principles governing some construction, yet do not assign the proper meaning to that construction, and vice versa (for examples and discussion, see Berent 1985 and Rutherford 1982: 103).

The central guiding principle of much current work within grammatical theory is that the internal structure of the grammar is modular as well. That is, syntactic complexity results from the interaction of grammatical subsystems, each characterizable in terms of its own set of general principles. Identifying such systems and deriving the effects of their interaction thus becomes a central goal of syntactic theory.

Most early work in generative grammar was rather nonmodular in character. Essentially, each construction had its own associated rule: passives were derived by the passive transformation, subject-raised sentences by the raising transformation, and so on. It seems fair to say that a great deal of the ultimate failure of the generative grammar-based conceptions in psycholinguistics in the 1960s was a direct result of their carrying over to their research this view of grammatical organization. But as the work on constraints on rules accelerated throughout the 1970s, it became clear that at least some of the complexities of particular constructions could be attributed to general principles, rather than having to be stated *ad hoc* as particular rules. In GB, grammar-internal modularity is carried as far as it can go; with some minor exceptions, syntactic complexity results from the interaction of general grammatical principles.

It is important to point out that GB does not have a monopoly on grammar-internal modularity. Here the convergence between GB, which pioneered such an approach, and its competitors is remarkable. All of them have increased their degree of modularity in recent years. Take the development of GPSG, for example. In its early stages, it essentially recapitulated the rule/construction homomorphism of early generative grammar: for the most part, each phrase structure rule or metarule served to characterize a particular construction in the language. But this is not true today; now a wide variety of interacting principles must be appealed to in order to derive any single construction (see, for example, the discussion of the English 'fronted auxiliary' construction in Gazdar *et al.* 1985: 60–5, in which four separate principles interact to yield the surface forms, only two of which are particular to the construction).[8] While of the three frameworks under discussion, LFG is the most conservative with respect to the degree of grammar-internal modularity, the treatment of control in Bresnan (1982b) readily illustrates that the idea of deriving grammatical regularity from interacting principles is not incompatible with that framework.

The shift from construction-specific rules to more general principles has profound implications for L2 research. Since given grammar-internal modularity, 'grammatical construction' is a derivative notion, acquisition research that has centrally embodied such a notion must be rethought. For example, consider studies such as Eckman (1985), Gass (1979), and Ioup and Kruse (1977) that have appealed to the learner's being able to draw upon the 'accessibility hierarchy' for relative clause formation (Keenan and Comrie 1977). These are clearly in need of reinterpretation (as pointed out in White 1985b), since in most current work, the notion 'relative clause' is an epiphenomenon, a chance by-product of the interaction of a set of structural principles. Thus the hierarchy, which centrally incorporates the notion 'relative clause', has no theoretical status.

Analogous remarks can be made about the dozens of studies that have appealed to 'markedness' in an attempt to explain why some structures are typically acquired before others (for a recent example pertaining to the English indirect-object construction, see Mazurkewich 1984). Typically, such studies have attributed the difficulty of acquiring some particular structure or construction to its 'marked' character with respect to another. But again, learners do not acquire structures or constructions; they acquire rules and principles through whose interactions the former are derived. To the extent that markedness is a valid theoretical concept at all for acquisition research, it must therefore be one whose domain is these rules and principles (for an example of an acquisition study that applies markedness in such a way, see Zobl 1986).

What many have found most appealing about a modular approach to the internal structure of the grammar is that it provides a theoretical foundation for linguistic typology. In this view, what appear, on the surface, to be major structural differences among languages result from each language setting slightly different values ('parameters') for each of the various grammatical subsystems. Thus, just as we have seen to be the case with a modular approach to language as a whole, a modular approach to grammar allows, to a significant degree, apparently complex and recalcitrant data to be derived from an elegant set of basic principles – principles that vary, but within circumscribed limits, from language to language. While it is the case that such a parametric approach to variation has been exploited in GB, rather than in other frameworks, there is nothing intrinsic to GPSG and LFG that would prevent them from adopting the same strategy for characterizing language-particular differences. One may assume that as work progresses in these frameworks, we will see explicit references to particular parameters of variation from language to language.

The acquisition of parameterized principles is now a major topic of second language acquisition research, and has been applied to such diverse topics as pidgin development (Macedo 1986), pronominal anaphora (Flynn 1987), reflexive binding (Finer and Broselow 1986) and null subjects (White 1985a) (for general discussion of the role of parameters in second language acquisition, see Flynn 1983 and White 1985b).

Locality

The second major point of convergence among the various generative frameworks centres around their increasing adoption of a local, rather than a global, view of syntactic processes. Locality manifests itself in several (interconnected) ways, each of which will be discussed in turn: syntactic structure is, to a great extent, a projection of lexical structure, with a concomitant decrease in the degree to which levels of syntactic structure may differ; more and more grammatical principles are stated directly on static configurational representations, rather than as conditions that successive stages of a derivation must meet; and the principles themselves obey constraints that limit the 'distance' from each other that their terms may lie within the representation.

In early generative grammar there were essentially no constraints on the distance that the deep structure of a sentence might be from its surface structure, nor was there any reason to expect that the two levels would share any particular principles of organization. Indeed, the 'universal base hypothesis' of generative semantics (Bach 1968) represented the explicit disavowal of the existence of an interesting set of shared properties between the two levels; since the deep structures (i.e., semantic representations) of all languages were hypothesized to be identical, the mapping from that level to the surface had to be essentially arbitrarily idiosyncratic from language to language.

The EST incorporated two proposals that served to constrain the degree to which the two levels could differ. First, the 'lexicalist hypothesis' (Chomsky 1970c) ensured that, details of inflectional morphology aside, lexical items could undergo no internal distortion in the course of a derivation. The hypothesis also embodied the possibility of relating lexical items in the lexicon itself, rather than by transformation, as had previously been the case. Thus a large set of previously accepted rules of nominalization, incorporation, and so on were removed in principle from the transformational component, with the resultant 'shallowing' of the level of deep structure. Second, the structure-preserving constraint (Emonds 1976) demanded an even stronger homomorphism between the two levels: aside from two formally identifiable classes of rules, no transformation had the ability to change the phrase structure configuration that it took as its input. Transformations such as passive and *wh*-movement, for example, which had previously been posited to wreak structural havoc with phrase structure, were reanalysed as having next to no effect at all on the configurational relations in the phrase marker.

The parting of the ways between Chomsky's EST and what would become LFG was triggered in great part by the observation by Brame, Bresnan, and others that the conjunction of highly structured lexical entries and lexical rules and the structure-preserving constraint seemed to make transformations unnecessary. Since the latter entailed that such rules could play no role in simplifying the grammar – their operation merely echoed the effects of independently necessary phrase structure rules – it was reasoned that they could be eliminated entirely and their effects be taken over by rules applying in the lexicon. LFG thus generates surface structures directly and captures lexically relations such as that between actives and passives. GPSG also, of course, generates surface representations of sentences, although it relies more heavily than does LFG on semantic rules, rather than lexical ones, to assume many of the functions that had been accorded to transformations. Nevertheless, the GPSG constraint proposed by Flickinger (1983) that allows metarules to map only from one rule that introduces lexical nodes to another converges with the LFG position that syntactic structure is to a significant degree a projection of lexical structure.[9]

For years, Chomsky's work stood in stark contrast with the surfacist approaches, as it continued to maintain the levels of both deep (or D-) structure and surface or (S-) structure. But more and more, GB has diminished the degree to which these levels may differ, to the point where the properties of the latter are largely determinable directly from the information encoded in the lexicon. A major move in this direction was the projection principle, proposed in Chomsky's 1981 book *Lectures on Government and Binding*. The principle can be thought of as a vastly strengthened structure preserving constraint. The latter is a constraint on rules alone, i.e., on successive stages of a derivation. But the projection principle is a constraint on the entire mapping from D-structure to S-structure, and demands that no structure be gained, lost, or altered in the course of this mapping. In effect, then, it demands that the sub-categorizational properties of particular lexical items be maintained throughout the derivation. Thus the projection principle sets the stage in GB for an even greater convergence with GPSG and LFG by diminishing the implausibility of the direct generation of S-structures (for further remarks on this point, see below).

Another interesting convergence that relates to the role of the lexicon is worth pointing out. In his 1986 book, *Knowledge of Language*, Chomsky adopted and developed Stowell's idea (1981) that phrase structure rules could largely be dispensed with in favour of projecting syntactic structure directly from the subcategorizational frames of lexical items, an idea that has also been put forward within a version of GPSG (see n. 9, p. 189). And paralleling LFG, though not GPSG, Chomsky also suggested that this subcategorizational information might be predictable directly from the thematic roles associated with the particular predicate.

The frameworks are also converging in their approach to the notion 'derivation of a sentence'. At first thought, this claim seems implausible; GB appears to differ drastically in this regard from GPSG and LFG. In GPSG, for example, sentences have single syntactic representations, rather than step-by-step derivations yielding successively distinct represent-ations. These representations result from the interaction of a set of rule-like grammatical statements and a set of universal principles governing the way in which they define structure. In LFG, one can speak of a derivation of a sentence, though the bulk of the work of the syntax is accomplished by a set of principles that apply to a single level of syntactic structure (F-structure), itself derived by a trivial algorithm from surface constituent structure.

In 'classical' GB, by contrast, derivations are intricate and involve many different rule types applying at a variety of levels. *Lectures on Government and Binding*, for example, adopts without essential alteration the highly articulated model of grammatical organization depicted in Figure 13.2, which had been assumed within the EST for several years.

Thus, the derivation of a single sentence might involve one or more applications of Move-α in the mapping between D-structure and S-structure; any number of deletions, filters, and stylistic rules in the determination of its surface form; and a set of rules in the LF component, some of which might serve only to limit its range of interpretations, but others (such as the ECP) having the ability to act as post-S-structure

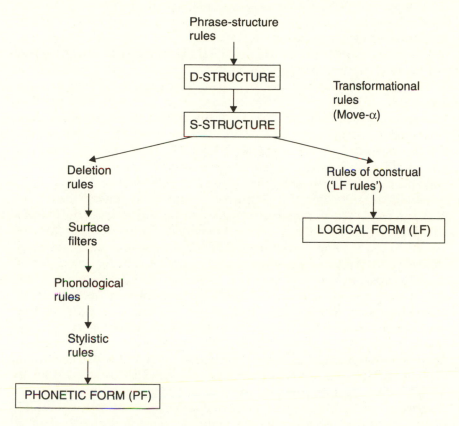

Figure 13.2 Grammatical organization in the government-binding framework

conditions on well-formedness (i.e., there is no guarantee that a sentence that survives the D-structure to PF mapping will necessarily be grammatical).

Clearly, this model is far removed from the representational theories of GPSG and LFG.

One of the most significant developments in GB in recent years has been a slow but steady erosion of the classical model, an erosion that has significantly reduced the need for the wide variety of rule types which it embodies, and has brought GB ever closer to being a representational, rather than a derivational, model of language.

As noted above, the projection principle has robbed transformational rules (i.e., Move-α) of the lion's share of their motivation. Few obstacles remain now to the direct generation of S-structures, complete with the trace-antecedent pairings that would have previously resulted from movement. Admittedly, Chomsky and most other GB practitioners continue to refer to 'movement' (see, for example Chomsky 1986a), but the term now seems wholly metaphorical in its usage; there appear to be few processes described in terms of movement that could not be handled just as elegantly through base generation.[10]

What about the variety of rules posited to apply in the PF component (i.e., between S-structure and PF)? Recent work has called into question the idea that any truly syntactic rules apply in this component at all. Case and binding theories have eliminated the need for most, if not all, of the filters posited to apply by Chomsky and Lasnik (1977) and others to the output of S-structure. As far as deletion rules are concerned, while they have been granted little attention recently, it appears that they all could be reanalysed in favour of base-generated empty categories without repercussions for established analyses of other phenomena. Also, virtually all of the stylistic rules have been shown to produce outputs that are subject to the binding theory or the ECP, a fact that suggests that they should apply in the syntax, rather than post-S-structure (for discussion of specific cases, see Culicover 1981 and Newmeyer 1988b).

It is only the mainstream GB insistence that there exists a syntactic level of LF (and a set of rules mapping from S-structure to that level) that seems to present an insurmountable obstacle to its becoming a representational, rather than a derivational, theory of grammar. Yet there is no unanimity among GB practitioners that such a level is necessary. Williams (1986), for example, argues that LF can be dispensed with, given the algorithm for scope assignment that he proposes applies directly to S-structure. Indeed, Williams provides compelling evidence that a distinct level of LF actually complicates a number of aspects of grammatical description. While it must be admitted that only a minority of workers in GB support Williams's position, there is nevertheless a new openness to the idea that the functions of that level can be reassigned. If Williams is correct, then his hypothesis, in conjunction with the conclusions outlined in the above paragraphs, leads to the possibility of GB being, like GPSG, a wholly representational theory (for an attempt to outline the structure of such a theory, see Koster 1986).

Finally, there has been a general trend, shared by all three frameworks under discussion, towards viewing grammatically significant relationships *within* a particular configurational structure as being subject to strict locality conditions. Such conditions are built directly into the structure of GPSG and LFG. In the former theory, for example, there is no alternative to analysing the relationship between the *wh*-phrase *which book* and its associated gap as resulting from a series of linked mother–daughter dependencies in sentences like *Which book do you think that Bill asked Mary to tell Tom to buy* ——? But again, GB has been developing in the direction of the more surface-orientated frameworks. Early transformational grammar had no locality conditions at all: the seemingly unbounded dependency illustrated above was analysed as resulting from the one-step movement of *what* to its surface position at the front of the sentence. Chomsky (1973) proposed the first major locality condition: the subjacency constraint, which (oversimplifying somewhat) prevents any rule from relating two positions separated by more than one clause boundary. This constraint has been carried forth into current GB and supplemented with even stronger locality conditions (such as the one that demands that the central 'government' relation be confined, essentially, to elements *within* one maximal projection). Other approaches within GB take an even stronger position with respect to locality than Chomsky: the approach of Kayne (1984), for example, mimics GPSG to the extent that it demands that all long distance dependencies be broken down into a series of linked mother–daughter pairs.

The implications of the various aspects of locality for second language acquisition research remain to be explored. In particular, few studies have placed the acquisition of the lexicon in any current theoretical context nor have they probed the extent to which the learning of a lexical item triggers the acquisition of syntactic structure. It would be interesting to examine and, perhaps, rework the many contrastive studies that have focused on differences in meaning and use of roughly analogous lexical items in two particular languages. It is not inconceivable that such studies contain data relevant to currently debated questions about the relationship between lexical and syntactic structure.

Along the same lines, if the structural principles of language are essentially representational rather than derivational, then the many studies that have assumed that learning a second language involves the acquisition of a set of sequentially applying rules need to be re-evaluated (for an example of such a study, see Perkins *et al.* 1986). Rather, investigations need to be undertaken of how the binding relations, feature transmission conventions, and so on of the L1 predispose the learner to approach the L2 and the extent to which their differences are likely to pose difficulties.

Finally, it seems likely that the now widely accepted conclusion that grammatically significant configurations are local ones has implications for second language learning. As it turns out, first language acquisition research has produced results that have dovetailed with conclusions arrived at through strictly grammatical argumentation: Wexler and Culicover (1980) have shown that the child must, in principle, be able to construct a complete grammar with input sentences whose depth of embedding is no greater than one. While certain of the assumptions upon which their conclusions were based are clearly inapplicable to second language acquisition (such as, for example, the nonexistence of negative evidence presented to the learner), there is no reason to believe that the acquisition of an L2 requires input strings of any greater complexity than that of an L1; indeed, it seems intuitively reasonable that the reverse is true. This question seems like a fruitful one for empirical investigation (for remarks on L2 learnability, see Cook 1985; Liceras 1987; and Sharwood Smith 1982).

CONCLUSION

The amount that can be taken for granted as established results within linguistic theory has increased dramatically in recent years. In 1966, Chomsky could point to little more than the stimulus-free nature of verbal behaviour, and the abstractness, universality, and complex organization of grammatical principles as definitive results upon which the great body of generative grammarians were united. Today, a consensus has emerged on a wide variety of specific aspects of grammatical organization. In particular, virtually all grammarians take a modular approach to the interaction of grammatical principles and view these principles as constrained by locality restrictions of various sorts.

This convergence of opinion should be heartening to second language learning researchers and others who wish to apply the results of linguistic theory to the understanding of the workings of some concrete domain. It can lead only to the possibility of more rapid and fruitful development of their areas of enquiry.

Chapter 14

Competence vs. performance; theoretical vs. applied

The development and interplay of two dichotomies in modern linguistics

Many language teachers, or – more properly – many of those whose goal is to *inform* language teachers, have attempted to draw pedagogical conclusions from contemporary views about the nature and structure of language.[1] Since around 1960, the most visible theory of language has been transformational generative grammar, which, naturally, has formed a pole of attraction for language teachers. Some have looked for pedagogical inspiration from that theory's central conception, namely, that at the heart of language lies an autonomous linguistic competence that represents the speaker's tacit knowledge of the structure of his or her language.

In this paper, I will attempt to establish two central points. First, as theories of the nature of competence have changed, so have the attempted applications. Indeed, we can point to a quite marked 'mirroring effect'. Every significant change in the theoreticians' views about the structure of the competence model has been accompanied – normally after a short time lag – by a revised view of how the theory might be applied to second language teaching. Second, throughout the past three decades, there have been three different competing strategies for applying the theory – the 'mechanical', the 'terminological', and the 'implicational' – each of which I will discuss in turn.

After documenting the recent history of the pedagogical applications of generative syntax, I will make some somewhat speculative remarks about the field of applied linguistics and contrast it with other attempts to apply the conceptions of basic science to practical domains.

It seems reasonable to begin by pointing to the origins of the notion 'linguistic competence', and its companion notion 'linguistic performance'. Their roots, of course, lie in the celebrated dichotomy between *langue* and *parole* (Saussure 1966). American structural linguists adopted the dichotomy implicitly, but attempted to recast it in terms more congenial to their (empiricist) view of language. Zellig Harris, for example, characterized *langue* as 'merely the scientific arrangement of [*parole*]' (Harris 1941: 346). Charles Hockett, taking, as always, one of the more 'realist' stances of the post-Bloomfieldians, compared the relation between *langue* and *parole* to that between habits and behaviour (Hockett 1952).

Neither the terms '*langue*' nor 'competence' can be found in Chomsky's 1957 book *Syntactic Structures*. The *langue/parole* dichotomy manifests itself in that book in a curious way – as that between grammar and meaning. Chomsky, at that time still under the influence of the Oxford philosophers, equated 'meaning' with 'use'. Indeed, as I have argued (Newmeyer 1986: 27), Chomsky's many arguments in that book for the autonomy of grammar with respect to meaning, are, in essence, arguments for the dichotomy between *langue* and *parole*.

Chomsky introduced the terms 'competence' and 'performance' in his 1962 plenary session address to the Ninth International Congress of Linguists (see Chomsky 1964b). While not denying that they were in essence parallel to *langue* and *parole*, he chose to coin new terms in order to stress the differences between *langue* and competence. In particular, Chomsky called attention to the idea of competence as a generative grammar expressing rule-governed creativity, contrasting it with Saussure's notion of *langue* as an inventory of elements.

One can point to four distinct periods in the development of the theory of competence, each of which can be characterized in terms of whether rules or principles have formed its principal research focus.[2] Figure 14.1 lists the periods, the years when they have been predominant in generative studies, and the published work that provided their principal inspiration.

The first period, that of Early Transformational Grammar, lasted from 1957 to about 1967. In this period, competence was viewed essentially as a set of rules, each of which was homologous to a particular construction in the language. Both phrase-structure and transformational rules were

Period	Nature	Years predominant	Principal inspiration
Early Transformational Grammar	Rule-orientated	1957–67	Chomsky, *Syntactic Structures* (1957)
Generative Semantics	Principle-orientated	1967–72	Katz and Postal, *An Integrated Theory of Linguistic Descriptions* (1964)
Lexicalism	Rule-orientated	1972–80	Chomsky, 'Remarks on nominalization' (1970)
Government-Binding	Principle-orientated	1980–	Chomsky, 'Conditions on transformations' (1973)

Figure 14.1 Four periods in the development of generative grammar

accorded importance, though the general thrust was to argue that the former should, in many cases, be dispensed with in favour of the latter.

It was in large part dissatisfaction with the increasingly rule-centred nature of the first period that led to the second period, that of Generative Semantics, which lasted from about 1967 to 1974. This period, in which Chomsky and his co-thinkers formed a small minority of generative syntacticians, was dominated by the view that the boundary between syntax and semantics (and ultimately pragmatics as well) was illusory. The principal object of study, then, was semantic representation and the semantic basis of both syntax and pragmatics.

Generative semantics was, first and foremost, a *principle-orientated* approach to grammar. Virtually every paper written in that framework put forward some novel principle governing universal grammar or sought to provide evidence for some already proposed one. At the same time, language-particular rules were downplayed to the point where, in most generative semantic work, not a single one was formalized.

The rapid decline in the fortunes of generative semantics in the early 1970s was in part a consequence of the vagueness with which its proposals were formulated and in part a consequence of the fact that many of its specific empirical claims about the syntax–semantics interface were disconfirmed. As a consequence, many linguists turned to a model that Chomsky and his students had been developing since the late 1960s. In this third, 'Lexicalist', period, which lasted from about 1974 to 1981, the *non*-transformational nature of many processes was stressed, and much attention was paid to lexical rules and rules of semantic interpretation.

Finally, since around 1981 we have been in the Government-Binding period, in which the model of Chomsky 1981 has inspired a high percentage of the research in syntactic theory. Virtually no syntacticians today view the competence model as containing a list of construction-specific rules. Rather, syntactic complexity is derived from a set of interacting principles that are parameterized within specific limits from language to language. These principles define 'core grammar' – the central feature of competence. Lying outside the core is a 'periphery' of processes that are presumably characterized and learned on an individual basis.[3]

Now I will outline in somewhat more detail the three strategies for applying competence conceptions to language teaching, after which I will show how each has been utilized in each period of the development of generative syntax.

The *mechanical* strategy is to take theory-internal conceptions from generative syntax and to provide them with direct pedagogical interpretations. That is, it assumes that theoretical constructs lend themselves mechanically to classroom implementation.

The *terminological* approach does not involve any real change in pedagogical practice. Rather, it invokes currently predominant conceptions from generative grammar to justify, motivate, or reinforce *pre-existing* approaches to the teaching of foreign languages.

Finally, those advocating the *implicational* strategy reject both the mechanical and the terminological approaches, the former for being ill-conceived theoretically and the latter for failing to make an original contribution to language teaching. The essential idea of this strategy is that competence theory taken *as a whole* has profound implications for language teaching.

Let us begin with a discussion of the mechanical strategy. During the Early Transformational Grammar period, transformational rules and their ordering were central to competence. As it turns out, we find in the applied literature of this period proposals for teaching transformational rules to the second-language learner in the order that the generativist posited that they applied in the grammar: Banathy *et al.* (1966) and Lado (1968) are two examples. The ensuing Generative Semantics period produced its own mechanical applications, in particular in its variant known as 'case grammar'. For example, both T. G. Brown (1971) and Nilsen (1971) advocated taking the abstract case frames posited by this framework and building them directly into the programme for instruction. Interestingly, the third, Lexicalist, period produced no mechanical application proposals that I am aware of. This is surely a consequence of the decline in popularity of generative grammar in general in this period, to which I alluded earlier. However, the resurgence of the generativist model in the present decade has, inevitably, brought with it renewed suggestions for basing pedagogical materials directly on some structural property of competence. Hence we find Belasco (1985) prioritizing 'core' over 'periphery' in second language instruction, with the strong implication that the former should be stressed in the classroom at the expense of the latter.

Such direct mechanical application proposals, however, have been the exception, rather than the rule, throughout the history of applied generative grammar. A far more common practice has been to take some time-honoured method of language teaching and assert that it is justified on the basis of some current conception within generative grammar. Since this approach typically has involved little or no actual change in classroom practice, I refer to it as the 'terminological' strategy. The stage for this strategy was set in Saporta *et al.* (1963). The authors described three established types of grammar drill – sentence completion, pattern substitution, and pattern alternation – and asserted categorically that each could be justified theoretically on the basis of a different model of grammar: finite-state, phrase-structure, and transformational respectively (see also Gefen 1966). In the period of Early Transformational Grammar, it was common to see publications that did little more than adopt the technical vocabulary of generative theory in the name of 'applying' that theory to some practical end. Literally dozens of papers and books, for example, Gefen (1967), Hunt (1970), Ohmann (1964), and Rutherford (1968), spoke of applying 'transformations' and 'transformational grammar' simply by exploiting the fact that in every language there are classes of sentences that share syntactic properties. Others, such as Di Pietro (1968) and Jacobson (1966) wrote of applying deep structures in the classroom, when it is clear that they meant no more than that students should understand the meanings of the sentences they learn.

This practice continued in the Generative Semantics period. Long before 1967, many language pedagogues had advocated placing an emphasis on meaning and communicative skills over mastery of grammar. But now, such approaches were often claimed to be 'based' on the generative semantic approach to linguistic competence (see, for example, H. D. Brown 1972a; Dirven 1974; R. Lakoff 1975b). And today, the terminology of the government-binding approach to competence finds its way into the pedagogical literature. In Rutherford (1987) and Rutherford and Sharwood Smith (1988), for example, we find much discussion of such notions as 'parametric settings' and 'negative evidence', though it is not clear that any real change in pedagogical practice is involved as a consequence of their adoption.

A reaction to both the mechanical and terminological strategies had begun to appear even in the 1960s (see, for example, R. Lakoff 1969). Some, such as Lamendella (1969) concluded that generative grammar itself had nothing to offer the language teacher, a view that gained adherents throughout the 1970s. But many others simply rejected the idea that one could profitably take a theory-internal construct and implement it directly in pedagogy. A consensus began to form that the theory has profound *implications*, though probably few if any direct *applications* (the application/implication distinction was first elaborated in Spolsky 1970). James Harris (1973), for example, demonstrated the hopelessness of teaching directly the generative rule governing a particular vowel alternation in Spanish; the rule might be good linguistics, he concluded, but good linguistics can be bad pedagogy. Nevertheless, Harris and many other second language specialists with a commitment to generative grammar – Newmark and Reibel (1970) and Spolsky (1970) are examples – remained convinced that the theory has important implications for the language teacher.[4] In particular, they asserted that its rationalist philosophical basis is incompatible with the audio-lingual method and suggested instead an approach drawing heavily on the learner's internal resources, including the ability to use language creatively.

This implicational strategy is developed most thoroughly in Diller (1971). Diller contrasts two camps of language teaching specialists: the 'empiricist' and the 'rationalist'. In the empiricist camp he places Otto

Jespersen and Harold Palmer, along with the post-Bloomfieldian structuralists. Diller's rationalists include James Asher, M. D. Berlitz, Emile de
Sauzé, and François Gouin. According to Diller, their work is guided by
the following four principles: first, 'A living language is characterized by
rule-governed creativity'; second, 'The rules of grammar are psycho-
logically real'; third, 'Man is specially equipped to learn languages'; and
fourth, 'A living language is a language in which we can think' (1971: 23).
Diller argues at length that the rejection of these points by empiricists
would naturally lead them to favour the audio-lingual approach, while
their acceptance would lead rationalists to favour the (presumably more
successful) innovative methods.

Interestingly, Chomsky appears to be in agreement with Diller's position.
In one of his rare published remarks on second language teaching,
Chomsky asserted that his rationalist view of language has implications
for the teaching of languages which are:

> of a rather negative sort . . . . The assumption that language really is a
> habit structure . . . is entirely erroneous, and drills to form stimulus–
> response associations is a very bad way . . . to teach language . . . . All
> we can suggest . . . is that a teaching program be designed in such a
> way as to give free play to those creative principles that humans bring
> to the process of language learning . . . . I think that we should prob-
> ably create a rich linguistic environment for the intuitive heuristics that
> the normal human automatically possesses.
>
> (Chomsky 1970b: 107–8)

In short, the implicational strategy entails the proportion: empiricism is
to the audio-lingual approach as rationalism is to naturalistic teaching
methods.

As we have seen, there have been profound differences of opinion in
recent history on the proper method of applying the competence model
to language teaching. Many would agree, I am sure, that the theory has
never been applied successfully. In the remainder of this chapter, I would
like to speculate on the reasons for these problems and offer the opinion
that there are serious difficulties inherent in *any* attempt to apply a
cognitively based theory to teaching.

Let us pose the question: 'What is applied science?'. Typically, it has
involved taking some scientific principle and putting it into practice, say,
in a useful device. Thus soon after Faraday discovered, in 1831, the
principle of electro-magnetic induction, he utilized that principle in the
construction of the first dynamo. Similar direct applications *have* occurred
in linguistics, as, for example, in the incorporation of models of grammar
into language processing systems. Computational linguistics is – or can
be – true applied linguistics.

But a very different situation obtains with language pedagogy. Principles of linguistic competence are principles of *knowledge*. But the goal of the language teacher is not to create some practical device embodying these principles. Rather it is to *transfer* those principles to the learner. Since there is no reason to think that principles of imparting knowledge have any direct relationship to the principles of knowledge themselves, it is difficult to see how the language teacher might apply linguistic competence at all; one suspects that the term 'applied linguistics', when used to refer to strategies for language teaching, is a misnomer.

As I see it, the implicational strategy's linking of empiricism with the audio-lingual method and rationalism with natural, direct, or other 'innovative' methods of language teaching is highly suspect. For one thing, most rationalists, Chomsky included, would agree that conditioning plays *some* role in language learning. But conditioning aside, it is by no means obvious that the kind of orderly presentation of contrasting structures inherent in the audio-lingual method might not be a suitable device for allowing the learner to induce the grammatical principles governing the target language. Indeed, both Jakobovits (1970) and Rutherford (1968) have devised pattern practice drills with just such an idea in mind.

Likewise, there's no logical reason why an empiricist should not favour any one of the various innovative approaches to language teaching. To take the position that language is acquired through conditioning is not automatically to embrace a particular *form* of conditioning: an empiricist might well argue that approaches to language teaching that simulate the 'natural' environment of learning are best suited for the formation of the stimulus–response–reinforcement chains presumed to be at work.

Returning to Diller, I feel that he has failed to make a convincing case that a *historical* connection has in general existed between one's approach to the source of knowledge (i.e., whether one is an empiricist or a rationalist) and one's general approach to language teaching. It seems unfair of him, for example, to characterize Otto Jespersen as an 'empiricist'. Jespersen's work is peppered with observations about universal grammatical categories and the relationship between language and thought that place him squarely in the rationalist camp (see, for example, Jespersen 1924). Yet, indisputably, he saw a place for pattern drills in a language teaching programme. The same point could be made about Palmer, who, far from being an empiricist, was explicit in regarding language as a mental reality (Palmer 1917: 29–30). Even Bloomfield in his early 'mentalist' phase, before he had come under the influence of the behaviourist Albert Weiss, wrote about the need for pronunciation drill and the building up of 'associative habits' in the language learner (Bloomfield 1914: 294).

And on the other side of the fence, François Gouin, Diller's archetypal advocate of 'rationalist' teaching methods, ridiculed the idea that the child has a gift or instinct for language (Gouin 1892: 6).

We must conclude therefore that neither empiricism nor rationalism has been shown to dictate a choice of pedagogy, even in the most general terms. Thus, the implicational strategy for the application of linguistic competence is as problematic as the mechanical and the terminological.

As we have seen, then, the history of the attempts to apply the generativist conception of competence to language teaching is one of extreme diversity of opinion and uncertain results. There is little reason to think that this situation is a consequence of either a flawed grammatical theory or of a lack of ingenuity on the part of the teacher. Rather, it may lie in the curious idea that a theory of the representation of knowledge invites a strategy for the imparting of that knowledge.

I fear that I have painted a rather gloomy picture of the relevance of linguistic theory to second language teaching. A study of the history of the interaction of the two fields, however, does not support the extreme conclusion that there are no useful points of contact between the two fields. For example, many would agree that linguistics provides the teacher with an *attitude* towards language and helps to break down the prejudices that are so deeply ingrained in our society. And it encourages a *feel* for language – an appreciation of its subtleties, complexities, and internal logic – that any sympathetic teacher will find of value.

Furthermore, interaction between theoretical linguists and language teachers has led to the new field of second language learning *research*, which addresses, not teaching methodology *per se*, but the *processes* by which second languages are learned. This field has already achieved some modest successes in predicting, entirely on the basis of theory-internal considerations, the types of error that learners are more likely or less likely to make (for an important collection of papers in this vein, see Flynn and O'Neil 1988). It goes without saying that such knowledge is of potential value to the teacher.

At the same time, linguistic theory stands to benefit from research in the field of second language learning. Given the assumption that our biological endowment for language acquisition remains active throughout our lives (contra Lenneberg 1967), it follows that data gleaned from second language learning research are as potentially useful to the theorist as those arising from observations of first language acquisition, speech errors, the speech of aphasic patients, and those obtained from psycholinguistic experimentation. If notions posited by theoretical linguistics such as 'markedness', 'the sonority hierarchy', 'parameterized grammars', and so on can be shown to be necessitated by the facts of second language acquisition, then their incorporation into the theory of universal grammar is *ipso facto* supported.

In conclusion, the recent history of the attempt to apply linguistic theory to the teaching of foreign languages is one of false starts and unfulfilled promises. Nevertheless, there appears to be hope that theoretical linguists and language teachers can meet with a less ambitious agenda, though one that is not without intellectual and (possibly) practical interest.

Notes

2 BLOOMFIELD, JAKOBSON, CHOMSKY, AND THE ROOTS OF GENERATIVE GRAMMAR

1 I am indebted to Noam Chomsky, Herbert Coats, Robert Fradkin, and Morris Halle for answering my queries on the subject matter of this paper.
2 Goddard (1987) suggests that Bloomfield adopted this device as a result of discussions with Morris Swadesh.
3 Shapiro explicitly identified Jakobson's paper as representing 'the beginnings of generative grammar' (Shapiro 1974: 29; see also Shapiro 1973).
4 In a letter to Hockett (see Hockett 1970: 375).

3 THE STRUCTURE OF THE FIELD OF LINGUISTICS AND ITS CONSEQUENCES FOR WOMEN

1 I would like to thank Alice Davison, Joseph Emonds, Randy Harris, Laurence Horn, Ellen Kaisse, Patricia Keating, Joan Maling, Craige Roberts, and Sol Saporta for their input into this chapter.

4 HAS THERE BEEN A 'CHOMSKYAN REVOLUTION' IN LINGUISTICS?

1 I would like to thank William Bright, Noam Chomsky, Joseph Emonds, Patricia Keating, David Lightfoot, James McCawley, Richard Ogle, Keith Percival, Geoffrey Pullum, and Sol Saporta for commenting on an earlier draft of this chapter. It goes without saying that they bear no responsibility for errors of either fact or interpretation.
2 Throughout this chapter, the terms 'generative grammarian' and 'generativist' will be used to refer to any individual whose published work has been devoted largely to the elaboration or defence of the conception of language outlined in Chomsky's *Syntactic Structures* and *Aspects of the Theory of Syntax*. That is, the terms will be applied to those who are committed to the programme of characterizing the human linguistic capability in terms of grammars whose essential properties are universal and which consist of a set of formal, discrete, and interacting rules. By such a criterion, individuals who might agree with Chomsky's conception, yet have published little or nothing in generative grammar, will not be classed as 'generativists'. Likewise, the

term as thus defined excludes those whose approach to grammar challenges the competence/performance dichotomy by abandoning the discrete rule, as in the 'fuzzy grammar' theory of G. Lakoff (1973) or in models embodying 'variable rules' (see, for example, Labov 1972a). Needless to say, a person could be a 'generativist' at one stage of his or her career, but not at another.

3 Many European structuralists, including Saussure, have explicitly regarded themselves as doing 'scientific' linguistics, though it is fairly clear that they have not seen themselves as paralleling natural scientists in their goals and methodology. For many, the term 'scientific' seems to have meant little more than 'objective' or 'nonprescriptive'. Note the following passage from Martinet (1960: 9): 'Une étude est dite scientifique lorsqu'elle se fonde sur l'observation des faits et s'abstient de proposer un choix parmi ces faits au nom de certains principes esthétiques ou moraux. "Scientifique" s'oppose donc à "prescriptif".'

4 The 'structuralism' issue is confused by the fact that in the early 1960s, Chomsky and his followers began to reserve the label 'structuralist' for those synchronic approaches in the Saussurean tradition that do not share their views on theory construction. The result is that now within linguistics, when one speaks of a 'structuralist', it is normally understood that one is referring to a pre-Chomskyan or an anti-Chomskyan. Interestingly, commentators from outside the field have always labelled Chomsky a 'structuralist', and we find his ideas discussed in most overviews of twentieth-century structuralism (see, for example, Lane 1970: 28–9 and De George and De George 1972: xx).

5 Chomsky's 1949 undergraduate thesis and his 1951 master's thesis (now published as Chomsky 1979b), which propose a generative account of Hebrew, predate the Harris and Hockett papers by several years. Koerner (1984), apparently unaware of Chomsky's earlier work, cites these latter papers to bolster his charge that Chomsky's ideas were not revolutionary. In fact, Harris and Hockett present a far more rudimentary theory than that of Chomsky's 1949 thesis, in that the rule system they point to does not assign a full structural description to every linguistic expression generated.

6 McCawley (1985) interprets Kuhn's universal assent claim to demand only the appearance of consensus, rather than actual consensus, i.e., normal science exists when adherents of the dominant approach do not bother to reply to critics of that approach. Even if McCawley is correct, however, I do not believe that there has ever existed an approach in linguistics whose partisans have felt secure enough to ignore their critics. In particular, many of Chomsky's publications devote close to half of their pages to rebuttals of and replies to critics of generative grammar (see especially Chomsky 1972a, 1975c).

7 The Chomskyan revolution failed to meet Kuhnian conditions in another respect. For Kuhn, a revolution is in part a response to 'crisis', to a situation in which, in the 'typical' case, there is 'a pronounced failure in the normal problem-solving activity' (Kuhn 1970: 74–5). Yet far from being in a state of crisis, post-Bloomfieldian structuralism in 1957 was enjoying a period of unprecedented optimism, in which it was believed that the fundamental questions of linguistic analysis had all been solved (see Newmeyer 1980: 1–3). It is rather puzzling, then, that so many commentators, generativist and nongenerativist alike, have taken the Chomskyan revolution to exemplify Kuhn's conception of a scientific revolution (see, for example, Katz and Bever 1976: 11; Koerner 1976: 709; Maclay 1971: 163; Searle 1972: 16; Sklar 1968: 213; Thorne 1965: 74).

It should be pointed out that Percival maintains a critical stance with respect to Kuhn throughout his article and is careful not to suggest that the failure of the latter's criteria to apply to linguistics should lead to the conclusion that the transition from pre-Chomskyan to post-Chomskyan linguistics should not be characterized as 'revolutionary'.

8 However, Chomsky's opponents typically exaggerate his ease of acceptance by the field. Murray, for example, writes that 'two publishers were interested in publishing [Chomsky's MS] *LSLT* [*Logical Structure of Linguistic Theory*] in 1957' (Murray 1980: 78), and that, in this period, Chomsky 'had many chances to move. Indiana tried to get him about 1957–8' (*ibid.*: 82). Murray provides no documentary evidence to support these claims, and, as far as I have been able to determine, none has ever existed.

9 Two coincidences, however, played a role in Chomsky's being named a speaker: Zellig Harris's turning down his own invitation and the holding of the meeting in Cambridge, Massachusetts. (See Newmeyer 1980: 51 for further discussion.)

10 See Newmeyer (1980: 47–8) and Murray (1980). However, Hall (1981: 182) implies that Bloch did *not* aid Chomsky.

11 Kuhn writes elsewhere that 'some' scientists cling to older views (1970: 19) and points out that 'only a few of the older chemists' (*ibid.*: 134) rejected Dalton's chemical theory. The major study of the resistance of established scientists to new theories, Barber (1962), warns against exaggerating the commonness and importance of this resistance. And Hymes and Fought (1981: 48) point out that many major pre-structuralist linguists commented quite favourably on the classic of early American structuralism, Bloomfield's *Language* (1933).

12 I cited only the final clause of the Voegelin quotation in Newmeyer (1980) and was accused by Koerner (1983) of thus giving a distorted impression of Voegelin's intent. The full sentence shows clearly that Voegelin regarded the abandonment of the structuralist phoneme as revolutionary, though he was careful throughout his review to maintain a critical stance with respect to the desirability of such an abandonment. Koerner is correct that Voegelin saw transformations as a natural outgrowth of earlier work by Zellig Harris; however, Koerner's observation is irrelevant, given that Voegelin's quote was directed to the implications of generativist theory for phonology, not syntax. In fact, Voegelin saw at least revolutionary *potential* in generative syntax as well, suggesting that transformations might lead to 'a palace revolution, perhaps, in contrast to the interdisciplinary revolutions plotted by David Bidney, *Six Copernican Revolutions* . . .' (1958: 230). By 'palace revolution', Voegelin had in mind a revolution within the structuralist tradition. The 'interdisciplinary revolution', needless to say, began with Chomsky's review of Skinner's *Verbal Behavior* (Chomsky 1959) in the following year.

13 Koerner (1983) claims that far from characterizing the publication of *Syntactic Structures* as one of the four linguistic breakthroughs (as seems quite explicit in the above quote), Hockett intended 'more the opposite' (1965: 162). Koerner's only support for such an idea is based on the following quotation, also from Hockett's article:

> We are currently living in the period of what I believe is our fourth major breakthrough; it is therefore difficult to see the forest for the trees, and requires a measure of derecthesis on my part to say anything not wholly vague. Instead of a long list of names, I shall venture only the two of which I am sure; and since the two are rarely linked I shall carefully put them almost a sentence apart. I mean Noam Chomsky on the one hand and, on the other, Sydney M. Lamb. The order is intentional; Chomsky is un-questionably the prime mover.
>
> (Hockett 1965: 196)

Why Koerner feels the above quote represents the 'opposite' from the one cited in the main text (and why the latter rather than the former should be taken as representing Hockett's true views) is never revealed.

14 I take it as uncontroversial that the question does not even arise in any other country.

15 Paul Chapin, the National Science Foundation Program Director for linguistics, has a doctorate in linguistics from MIT. However, his 1983 advisory panel consisted of only one generativist, namely Susumo Kuno (the other members were Melissa Bowerman, Michael Krauss, Peter McNeilage, Brian McWhinney, and Gillian Sankoff). Kuno himself is better known for his functionalist alternatives to generative principles than for his contributions to generative grammar *per se*.

16 While both Labov and Ladefoged have adopted conceptions from generative grammar in their work, they have also been highly critical of certain central generativist notions, in particular the competence/performance dichotomy (see Labov 1972b, Ladefoged 1988). In any event, little of their funded research is devoted to questions of grammatical analysis.

17 I have not checked with each of these individuals to find out their reason for not belonging to the LSA.

18 I do not wish to imply that the editor of *Language*, William Bright, is anything but scrupulously fair in his handling of submissions to the journal. I know from personal experience that he is a model of impartiality.

19 Though Koerner (regrettably) errs when he writes that I 'was appointed to teach the History of Linguistics at the Linguistic Institute held in summer 1983 at the University of California, Los Angeles' (1983: 165).

20 Chomsky feels that '*if* the kind of linguistics [he is] interested in survives in the United States, it may very likely be in [cognitive science programmes] rather than in linguistics departments' (Chomsky 1982a: 8; emphasis added).

5 RULES AND PRINCIPLES IN THE HISTORICAL DEVELOPMENT OF GENERATIVE SYNTAX

1 I would like to thank David Gil, John Goldsmith, Randy Harris, Geoffrey Huck, and James McCawley for their helpful (albeit critical) comments on an early version of this chapter.

2 Dingwall (1965) lists no fewer than 962 items in its bibliography. However, despite its title, *Transformational Generative Grammar: A Bibliography*, many of these works are in Zellig Harris's framework and others are in tagmemics. Additionally, a number deal with transformational generative grammar only to criticize it. Nevertheless, when all of the latter are filtered out, well over 100 works remain that are written wholly within the *Syntactic Structures* framework.

3 Chomsky had proposed each of these in a series of lectures at the Linguistic Institute of the Linguistic Society of America, held at Indiana University in the summer of 1964. The lectures were later published as Chomsky (1966). The principle of cyclic application drew on work by Fillmore (1963).

4 Ross's dissertation was finally published in 1985 under the title *Infinite Syntax*!

5 Generative semanticists joked in print about the hopelessness of writing formal rules. For example, Rogers (1972) stated that the derivation of constructions involving psychological predicates from the complex underlying structure he proposed 'will probably have to be a modern miracle' (*ibid.*: 312).

6 Geoffrey Huck has suggested to me (personal communication) that *Aspects*, not Katz and Postal's book, should be regarded as the primary inspiration of

generative semantics. As he points out, *Aspects* was the first work that thoroughly challenged the fundamental assumptions of *Syntactic Structures* on the basis of problems that had surfaced in the execution of its research programme. Some of the innovations of *Aspects*, such as the centrality of syntactic deep structure and the pairing of the Katz–Postal hypothesis with Fillmore's proposal for the cyclic application of transformational rules, were adopted unchallenged by generative semantics.

However, for the most part, what was new in *Aspects* was *reacted against* by generative semantics, in particular, the possibility of lexical rules; the approach advocated there for lexical insertion; and ultimately, the rationalist underpinnings of the theory. While it is true that the pairing of Katz–Postal with the cycle became architecturally central to generative semantics, after 1969 or so rules and rule orderings played such a small role in generative semantics that the cycle was never given more than lip service.

7 The common generative semantic practice of hinting at rules rather than stating them explicitly is presaged in Katz and Postal (1964), as for example in the discussion on pages 141–2.

8 David Perlmutter's work prior to relational grammar was not for the most part 'hard-core' generative semantics, since many of his most important contributions dealt with close-to-the-surface phenomena about which generative semantics had little to say (see, for example, Perlmutter 1970). He did, however, take the essential generative semantic position that syntax and semantics are inseparable (Perlmutter 1969).

9 See, for example, Cole (1977); Frantz (1976); Jacobson (1975); Pullum (1977).

10 'Lexicalism', the position that derivational processes are lexical rather than transformational, and 'interpretivism', the position that rules of semantic interpretation apply to superficial levels of syntactic structure, are logically independent. However, since in the 1970s it was extremely rare for a linguist to adopt one of these positions but not both, for purposes of exposition I will characterize them jointly as 'lexicalism'.

11 Chomsky (1980c, 1982a) has argued that the Peters–Ritchie results have been 'seriously misinterpreted' (1980c: 122), and that they became quite irrelevant as the conception of transformational grammar developed that had sprung from the 'Conditions on transformations' paper of 1973 (discussed below, pp. 61–65).

12 The thematic hierarchy condition is criticized in Gee (1974) and Hust and Brame (1976). To be fair to Freidin, he explicitly considered the possibility that certain ungrammatical passives might result from some independent principle interacting with the passive rule (1975: 391).

13 Two of the descendants of 1970s lexicalism, lexical-functional grammar and generalized phrase structure grammar, will be discussed in the next section.

14 The journals are *Journal of Linguistics*, 22; *Language*, 62; *Linguistic Analysis*, 16 (1–2); *Linguistic Inquiry*, 17 (articles only); *Linguistic Review*, 5 (1–2); *Linguistics and Philosophy*, 9; and *Natural Language and Linguistic Theory*, 4. The conferences are annual meetings of the Chicago Linguistic Society, the Linguistic Society of America, the North Eastern Linguistic Society, and the West Coast Conference on Formal Linguistics.

6 CHOMSKY'S 1962 PROGRAMME FOR LINGUISTICS

1 One rhetorical change that one notes in Chomsky's writing between 'LBLT' and the present is increasingly less emphasis on pointing to the theory's historical

antecedents. This is of course natural, since the theory has had thirty years to mature. Given that 'LBLT' is remembered first and foremost for its attacks on post-Bloomfieldian phonology, it needs to be stressed that Chomsky goes overboard there to acknowledge the antecedents of many of his ideas in prior work. Pages are devoted to defending the idea that the roots of trans-formational generative grammar lie squarely within traditional grammar, and that its goals are to a large extent congruent. Chomsky writes in the first footnote to 'LBLT' that its account of linguistic structure in part incorporates and in part responds to 'many stimulating ideas of Zellig Harris and Roman Jakobson' (1964c: 914). The first reference in the paper is an approving one to Hermann Paul and the copious acknowledgements to von Humboldt are noted above. Furthermore, Chomsky attributes to Saussure the competence-performance distinction and throughout 'LBLT' gives later 'structuralists' credit for careful formulation of their ideas, where credit is due. The picture we get of Chomsky from a reading of 'LBLT' is miles away from the image of the wanton destroyer of all that linguists of the early 1960s held dear, an image that he neither sought nor merited.

2 It is well known that Chomsky has of late tended to downplay any intrinsic interest in weak generative capacity and has attributed the considerable atten-tion that *Syntactic Structures* devotes to that issue to the fact that the book was based on lecture notes for MIT students, who were familiar with automata theory (see Chomsky 1982a: 63). Sceptics have tended to relate his professed lack of interest in such matters to a latter-day desire to deflect the criticism of such linguists as Gerald Gazdar, Joan Bresnan, and others, who have attempted to capitalize on the apparent greater restrictiveness of their models in so far as weak generation is concerned. But, in fact, in 'LBLT' he dismissed the idea that the question of what sets of strings are generable is a particularly important one (916–17).

3 As Chomsky has noted (Chomsky 1991a: 20–4), this conceptual shift has re-sulted in the theory manifesting to a much smaller degree the flavour of traditional grammar. In 'LBLT', as in traditional grammar, grammatical con-structions are paralleled in most cases by construction-particular grammatical rules. But in the current conception, constructions are simply artifacts, 'perhaps useful for descriptive taxonomy, but nothing more' (*ibid.*: 24).

4 An idea that (rhetorically, at least) is central to the 'LBLT' theory is that speakers have 'the ability to . . . impose an interpretation on [deviant sen-tences]' (1964c: 914), an idea that was approached by the grammar's assigning varying 'degrees of grammaticalness' to less than well-formed sentences. There have been a number of recent attempts to correlate the degree of ill-formedness with the number and nature of constraints that have been violated, as in the discussion of subjacency and ECP violations in Chomsky (1986a: Ch. 7). More recently, however, Chomsky has remarked that the automatic assignment of a particular degree of grammaticalness to a deviant string is really a feature of an E-language, rather than an I-language and that, in any event, the 'dimensions of deviance' are far more varied than can be captured in terms of structural distance from some particular well-formed sentence (Chomsky 1991a: 10).

5 In 'LBLT', as in all his earliest work, Chomsky hoped that the theory might provide an evaluation (or simplicity) measure, by which the grammars which would be most highly valued according to some theory-internal criterion (e.g., in phonology, those minimizing distinctive feature specifications) would be those chosen by an explanatorily adequate theory. By the late 1960s, Chomsky had dropped discussion of such measures, only to revive it again in the 1990s,

when he notes that such principles as 'full interpretation', which holds that representations should contain no superfluous elements, and the 'last resort' theory of movement, which reduces the length of derivations, have the effect of the evaluation measures that were sought after 'in the earliest work in contemporary generative grammar forty years ago' (Chomsky 1991b: 43).

6 Chomsky's 1962 opinion has evolved only slightly to become his *Knowledge of Language* view that 'the shift toward a computational theory of mind encompasses a substantial part of what has been called "semantics" as well . . .' (Chomsky 1986b: 45). Such is particularly apparent in his current approach to co-reference and quantification (for remarks on the latter see Chomsky 1991b: 38), but somewhat less so in those aspects of meaning related to the thematic structure of the sentence. Indeed, he would surely reject today the analysis in 'LBLT' which in part motivated the opinion stated above, namely positing that the derivation of the sentence *It was an intriguing plan* involves the string underlying *The plan intrigued one*. Furthermore, as is well known, he resisted vigorously the generative semantic attempt to provide a syntactic analysis of word-internal semantic relations (for discussion, see Newmeyer 1986a: Ch. 5). And his recent ideas on deriving subcategorization from thematic role (Chomsky 1986b) seem a dramatic departure from the conception of a deepening syntax ever further encompassing what has been traditionally considered to be semantics. The current approach of Emonds (1991) seems much more 'Chomskyan' in this regard.

7 LINGUISTIC DIVERSITY AND UNIVERSAL GRAMMAR

1 Fifteen years earlier Emmon Bach had made the same point, endorsing the physicist P. A. M. Dirac's (only slightly tongue-in-cheek) statement that 'it is more important to have beauty in one's equations than to have them fit experiment' (see Bach 1965: 113–14).

2 For discussion of the slide of generative semantics into descriptivism, see Newmeyer (1986a, 1991). Interestingly, Chomsky has been called an 'empiricist' in turn by the generative semanticist George Lakoff (G. Lakoff 1974a: 172) and a 'logical positivist' by Pike (1975: 20) and Anttila (1975: 60), presumably for his advocacy of formalism and his programme for capturing the distribution of linguistic forms independently of their meanings.

3 Chomsky (1977: 311, 1982a: 83) notes, in defence of the idea that explanatory gains often entail descriptive losses, the fact that Galilean physics had a more restricted domain of explanation than did Aristotelian and scholastic physics (and was criticized for it).

8 THE STEPS TO GENERATIVE SEMANTICS

1 George Lakoff had actually proposed as early as 1963 that the rules of the base might generate semantic structures. However, the not very widely circulated mimeographed paper in which he proposed this (now published as G. Lakoff 1976) was largely forgotten during the later years of the decade.

2 Lakoff and Ross's specific example of post-transformational lexical insertion involved idioms, not causatives.

9 THE END OF GENERATIVE SEMANTICS

1 For later work directly addressing the question of the mismatch between syntactic and semantic regularity, see Akmajian (1984); Grimshaw (1979); Newmeyer (1983: 5–11); and Williams (1980).

2 There have also been objections to grammatical approaches to performatives from a philosophical standpoint. See, for example, Pelletier (1977) and Searle (1976).

3 Apparently Ross's mid-1970s squishes lacked significance even when evaluated on their own terms. Gazdar and Klein point out that 'it is crucial to Ross's argument [for squishes] in this paper [i.e., Ross 1975], as in his others, that the matrices exhibit statistically significant scalar properties that would not typically show up on an arbitrary matrix. He does not subject his matrices to any kind of significance test, nor does he seem to be aware that any such testing is necessary' (1978: 666). After applying the appropriate statistical technique (Guttman scaling) to Ross's major clausematiness 'squishoid', they conclude from the results that 'Ross's squishoid provides no backing whatever for his claim that grammars require a quantifiable predicate of clausematiness' (*ibid.*: 666).

  For arguments that fuzzy logic is formally unsuitable for the linguistic goals to which Lakoff and Ross wish to apply it, see Morgan and Pelletier (1977).

4 R. Lakoff (1974) has attempted to provide the generative semantic rejection of formalism with explicit political motivation, arguing that 'undue obeisance to formalism' (xiv–23) discourages women from the field. While she did not state whether mathematics and the sciences should also abandon formalism as a step towards sexual equality, she did, astonishingly, explicitly leave open the possibility that the 'indisposition toward formalism among women' might be 'inherent'!

5 I am indebted to Ann Banfield and Joseph Emonds for first making me aware of the issue discussed in this section. For remarks in a similar vein, see Hagège (1976); Percival (1971); and Sampson (1976).

10 REVIEW OF GEOFFREY J. HUCK AND JOHN A. GOLDSMITH, *IDEOLOGY AND LINGUISTIC THEORY: NOAM CHOMSKY AND THE DEEP STRUCTURE DEBATES*

1 *ILT* claims:

> First, it was incorrect to suggest that no restrictions in principle were imposed, or could be imposed, on the form and function of global rules. The global mechanisms proposed by generative semanticists were no less subject to constraint than were local mechanisms (transformations) (see Parret 1974: 177, 268).
>
> (Huck and Goldsmith 1995: 37)

But on page 177 of the Parret book of interviews, Lakoff says that 'the real problem with global rules is not that they are too powerful, but that they are too *weak*' (G. Lakoff 1974a: 177; emphasis in original), and on page 268, McCawley does not propose a single constraint on their operation.

  At first it was suggested that any particular global rule could refer to at most two nodes (G. Lakoff 1971a: 234). This was later increased to 'hopefully no more than three or four' (G. Lakoff 1972a: 87). The fact that restrictions 'could be' imposed on global rules is quite beside the point. They were not so imposed and that is all that matters. The fact that a theory 'could' have been patched up hardly counts as a justifiable defence of it *vis-à-vis* its rivals.

2 A global rule solution mimicking the trace theory approach was unavailable to generative semanticists, since, given their core principles, the parallelism between the antecedent–anaphor relation and the antecedent–trace relation that formed the cornerstone of trace theory was unformulable.

3 *ILT* denies that 'late interpretivism' (i.e., the EST model of the early 1970s) was a distributional theory, since it left so many distributional facts about language to be handled by systems outside grammar proper. They suggest that the perception of the danger of 'becoming a theory without any concrete linguistic phenomena for it to be a theory of' is what led 'late interpretivists to try to recast the principal core propositions of the moribund generative semantics movement in terms they could accept' (Huck and Goldsmith 1995: 43). My reaction to this statement is more one of perplexity than anything else. Surely Chomsky's increased appeal to 'modularity' has led him to place even *greater* stock in extragrammatical factors interacting with grammatical ones today than he did twenty years ago.

4 The Appendix contains interviews with Ray Jackendoff, John R. Ross, and Paul Postal, as well as with George Lakoff.

5 Interestingly, *ILT* includes part of a 1972 letter from Chomsky to Searle making the same point (Huck and Goldsmith 1995: 34), though they do not comment on it. Randy Harris, another analyst of the debates, also endorses the idea that the core conception of generative semantics was the nonexistence of a level of deep structure:

> The kernel of generative semantics was an obliteration of the syntax–semantics boundary at the deepest level of grammar – the axiom that the true deep structure *was* the semantic representation, not a syntactic input to the semantic component – and everyone in the community held this tenet.
>   (R.A. Harris 1993b: 409–10; emphasis in original)

6 In a somewhat personal aside, I attempted a have-your-cake-and-eat-it-too reconciliation of generative and interpretive semantics (Newmeyer 1971, 1976), suggesting that lexical insertion applied before the classical cyclic rules (passive, *wh*-movement, etc.) but after such generative semantics-inspired rules as predicate raising and nominalization. I was told by the leading advocates of this model that my proposal 'wasn't generative semantics', i.e., by allowing the equivalent of a level of deep structure, I had abandoned a core proposition of generative semantics.

7 *ILT* endorses the claim in McCawley (1988) that a generative semantic equivalent of Emonds' (1970) theory of structure preservation is to be found in 'the idea that there are target structures that the derivational constraints applying to semantic representations conspire to make surface structure conform to' (Huck and Goldsmith 1995: 50; see also p. 154). Huck and Goldsmith and McCawley are mistaken, however. As Oehrle (1976, 1977) noted, such target structures could not be properties of the grammar as a whole, but only of the subpart relevant to a particular construction subject to it. Hence, each rule in the grammar would have to be marked with a feature of some sort to indicate whether or not it was subject to a particular conspiracy/target structure. A theory that has a level of deep structure as *input* to the syntactic rules suffers no such problem.

8 The lexicalist models developed in the late 1970s also rejected a level of deep structure, of course. However, the generalizations stateable at that level were

handled in a greatly enriched lexicon in ways that would have been wholly uncongenial to generative semantics.

9 Newmeyer (1980, 1986a) stresses generative semantic *methodology* as a major contributing factor leading to its demise, i.e., the a priori assumption that any linguistic fact is *ipso facto* to be incorporated into a theory of grammar. In fact, Huck and Goldsmith maintain that 'the most significant of the differences between the generative semanticists and the interpretive semanticists lay in the methodological values they each held' (Huck and Goldsmith 1995: 93–4), though they are neither very critical of the values of the latter nor point to them as a significant factor in leading to the demise of that model.

11 REVIEW OF *THE BEST OF CLS: A SELECTION OF OUT-OF-PRINT PAPERS FROM 1968 TO 1975*, EDITED BY ERIC SCHILLER, BARBARA NEED, DOUGLAS VARLEY, AND WILLIAM H. EILFORT

1 This review has benefited from discussion with Ellen Kaisse, who is, however, absolved from any responsibility for its content.

2 The editors, in the first line of the Preface, mistakenly refer to their organization as the 'Chicago Linguistics Society'. And curiously, despite the book's subtitle, two of the papers (Lloyd Anderson's and James McCawley's) date from 1967. The McCawley paper is given a different title in the Table of Contents from the one that is printed on its title page. Two other serious typographical errors are the misspelling of contributor Robert Bley-Vroman's name in two places as 'Bley-Vronman', and the appearance of the word 'synthetic' instead of 'syntactic' on page 313.

3 Such an approach (at least so far as syntax is concerned) was far and away the dominant one in American linguistics in the period covered by *BCLS*. If one were queried in, say, 1970, as to who were the five most prominent syntacticians in that country, in addition to Chomsky's name one would surely have replied: 'George Lakoff, James McCawley, John R. Ross, and Paul Postal'. George Lakoff, McCawley, and Ross were frequent contributors to CLS, and Postal contributed a seminal paper on anaphora (reprinted in *BCLS*). Thus I find very misleading the editors' remarks in the Preface that 'many *CLS* contributions . . . challenged prevailing linguistic scripture. Heretical ideas have always been welcomed by the Society, and its conferences are well known to permit discussion of views which would not get an airing in more orthodox environments'. While the above is qualified by the additional remark that 'important contributions to established theories are an annual event at [CLS]', the editors' implication is clearly that CLS at the time approached being a subversive underground organization, struggling against all odds to air openly the ideas of the persecuted. Nothing could be farther from the truth. CLS meetings were – and were seen as – a forum for prominent American linguists, and their students, to extend a set of ideas that were already widely accepted.

4 For accounts of the decline of generative semantics and natural phonology, see Newmeyer (1986a) and Anderson (1985) respectively. It should be pointed out that virtually all phonologists agree that there will be no returning to the degree of abstractness of underlying phonological representations countenanced by *SPE*. The Zwicky contribution to *BCLS* made a modest contribution to shaping this current consensus.

5 It is important to point out that two contributions to *BCLS*, the under-appreciated papers by LeGrand and Weiser, do point to the existence of principles distinct to each of the three domains.

6 There is no indication in the book itself of the date of publication of any of the contributions. *BCLS* is accompanied by a loose addendum sheet that lists the author, title, and CLS volume of each paper, but not its original date of publication. The addendum also contains postscripts to the papers by Anderson and J. McCawley and calls attention to a few of the book's errata (though not the ones mentioned in n.1 above).

7 In some cases, of course, alphabetical order leads by chance to the correct order of presentation. Hence, Lawler's 1973 paper on presupposition, which appeals to 'fuzzy' quantifiers, follows Horn's 1969 study, written before fuzzy grammar was introduced.

8 Certain frequent contributors were overlooked as well. For example, between 1968 and 1975, Robert Binnick gave six CLS papers and Robin Lakoff gave five, yet neither is represented in *BCLS*.

12 THE ONTOGENESIS OF THE FIELD OF SECOND LANGUAGE LEARNING RESEARCH

1 We would like to thank Robert Bley-Vroman and Georgette Ioup for their helpful discussions with us on the subject matter of this paper.

13 THE CURRENT CONVERGENCE IN LINGUISTIC THEORY

1 I would like to thank Steven Weinberger for his helpful comments on an earlier version of this chapter.

2 See Chomsky (1970a). To be accurate, Chomsky was directing his remarks to the relevance of linguistic theory to second language *teaching*, though they carry over *a fortiori* to second language *learning*.

3 Some care needs to be taken, however, in defining 'the field'. Just as linguistics proper contains a significant contingent that denies the need for abstract specifically grammatical principles, so there are second language learning researchers who attempt to bypass formal grammar and ground learning entirely in discourse, cognition, or whatever. For example, as recently as 1980 an article could appear entitled 'Theory and research in second language learning: an emerging paradigm' with hardly a mention of research directed towards the acquisition of grammatical principles (McLaughlin 1980). Thus, the locution 'the field of second language learning research' in this chapter must be understood as referring to the work of those who reject such reductionist approaches to grammar.

4 For representative work that assumes or defends the idea that UG drives second language acquisition, see Adjémian and Liceras (1984), Finer and Broselow (1986), Flynn (1983), Schmidt (1980), and White (1985b). This idea runs counter to the long accepted premise, stated most forcefully in Lenneberg (1967), that the 'language acquisition device' shuts off at puberty. Indeed, some investigators have cited instances where second language acquisition does not appear to obey the principles of UG (see, for example, Clahsen 1982 and Felix 1985). For a general discussion of the problem, see Cook (1985).

5 For discussion of concrete cases, see Newmeyer (1983, 1988a).

6 For interesting remarks on how the learner's structural competence is differ-

entially reflected in production and comprehension, see Flynn (1986) and Sharwood Smith (1986).

7 It is important not to exaggerate the degree of convergence among the frameworks with respect to their treatment of the interface between syntax and semantics. The GPSG accounts of scope assignment and anaphora, for example, make only minimal use of syntactic principles, while GB attempts to assimilate these phenomena to such wholly syntactic constructs as the binding theory and the ECP (for discussion, see Enç 1988). Furthermore, Chomsky has always steadfastly opposed the model theoretic approaches to semantics that are central to GPSG and LFG; it is not clear that he sees a role in linguistic theory for any semantic notions beyond thematic relations (for a statement of his position, see Chomsky 1979a: 141–4). Yet it is clear that there is nothing intrinsic to GB that prevents its syntactic conceptions from being linked to a model theoretical semantics; indeed, Enç (1983) and Heim (1988) have done just that.

8 Zwicky (1986) discusses the GPSG move away from rule-construction homomorphism.

9 In the development of GPSG called 'head-driven phrase structure grammar' (HPSG) (C. Pollard 1984, 1985) lexical ID rules are eliminated, and subcategorization is stated as a property of lexical heads. Thus, the idea that syntactic structure is projected from the lexicon is captured directly.

10 If movement is abandoned in favour of base-generation, then the subjacency principle (see below) would have to be reinterpreted as a condition on representations containing trace-antecedent pairings. There seems to be no insuperable difficulty to this step. Another obstacle to the base-generation of S-structures has been removed as a result of the abandonment of the contextual definition of empty categories (Chomsky 1982b) on the basis of arguments put forward in Brody (1984). Since contextual definition allowed 'the same' empty category to have distinct properties at D-structure and S-structure, it was incompatible with base-generation of the latter level.

Even if S-structures are base-generated, GB and GPSG would still differ on *where* traces are posited. GPSG allows them only for A-bar binding, and rejects a trace solution for the analogue of 'NP movements'. Here the issue revolves around the empirical question of whether the distribution of passive and raising subjects is parallel to that of the antecedents of anaphors, rather than on any principled difference between GB and GPSG. Along the same lines, a framework as restrictive as GPSG could posit empty NPs in 'PRO' positions; that GPSG does not do so is a point of analysis, not metatheory.

It is worth pointing out that GB has increasingly distinguished between the properties of 'NP movements' and '*wh*-movements', which in the 1970s EST were assumed to be governed by identical principles. Thus they are now treated differently by the binding theory (Chomsky 1981) and perhaps also by the ECP (Chomsky 1986a; Lasnik and Saito 1984). This fact also represents a convergence between GB and GPSG and LFG, the latter two treating the analogues of these phenomena in completely distinct ways.

14 COMPETENCE VS. PERFORMANCE; THEORETICAL VS. APPLIED

1 I would like to thank Steven Weinberger and Vivian Cook for their helpful comments on this chapter and for their suggestions on how it could be improved.

2 The material in the following paragraphs is treated in greater detail in Newmeyer (1991) (reprinted in this volume).

3 Two other current frameworks, generalized phrase structure grammar and lexical-functional grammar, have also evolved in a principle-orientated direction. For discussion, see Newmeyer (1987) (reprinted in this volume).

4 Newmeyer (1983) endorses, I now feel incorrectly, the views of Newmark and Reibel, and Spolsky.

References

Adjémian, Christian (1976) 'On the nature of interlanguage systems', *Language Learning* 26: 297–320.

—— and Liceras, Juana (1984) 'Accounting for adult acquisition of relative clauses: Universal grammar, L1, and structuring the intake' in F. Eckman, L. Bell and D. Nelson (eds) *Universals of Second Language Acquisition*, Rowley, MA: Newbury House, 101–18.

Aissen, Judith (1992) 'Varieties of *wh*-movement in Tzotzil', Paper presented at the Workshop on Specifiers, University of California Santa Cruz, March.

Akhmanova, Olga and Berezin, F. M. (eds) (1980) *Transformacionno-Generativnaja Grammatika v svete sovremennoj naučnoi Kritiki: Referativnyj sbornik*, Moscow: Institut Nauchnoi Informatsii po Obschestvennym Naukam.

Akmajian, Adrian (1984) 'Sentence types and the form-function fit', *Natural Language and Linguistic Theory* 2: 1–24.

—— and Heny, Frank (1975) *An Introduction to the Principles of Tranformational Syntax*, Cambridge, MA: MIT Press.

Alatis, James E. (1968) 'Introductory remarks' in James E. Alatis (ed.) *Report of the Nineteenth Annual Round Table Meeting on Linguistics and Language Studies*, Washington: Georgetown University Press, 1–5.

Anderson, Stephen R. (1971) *On the Linguistic Status of the Performative/Constative Distinction*, Bloomington: Indiana University Linguistics Club.

—— (1974) *The Organization of Phonology*, New York: Academic Press.

—— (1977) 'Comments on the paper by Wasow' in Peter Culicover, Thomas Wasow, and Adrian Akmajian (eds) *Formal Syntax*, New York: Academic Press, 361–77.

—— (1981) 'Why phonology isn't natural', *Linguistic Inquiry* 12: 493–540.

—— (1985) *Phonology in the Twentieth Century*, Chicago: University of Chicago Press.

Andrews, Avery (1982) 'The representation of case in modern Icelandic' in Joan Bresnan (ed.) *The Mental Representation of Grammatical Relations*, Cambridge, MA: MIT Press, 427–503.

Anttila, Raimo (1975) 'Comments on K. L. Pike's and W. P. Lehmann's papers' in Robert Austerlitz (ed.) *The Scope of American Linguistics*, Lisse: Peter de Ridder Press, 59–62.

Bach, Emmon (1962) 'The order of elements in a transformational grammar of German', *Language* 38: 263–9.

—— (1965) 'Structural linguistics and the philosophy of science', *Diogenes* 51: 111–28.

—— (1968) 'Nouns and noun phrases' in Emmon Bach and R. Harms (eds) *Universals in Linguistic Theory*, New York: Holt, Rinehart & Winston, 91–124.

—— (1977) 'Comments on the paper by Chomsky' in Peter Culicover, Thomas Wasow, and Adrian Akmajian (eds) *Formal Syntax*, New York: Academic Press, 133–56.

Bailey, Nathalie, Madden, Carolyn, and Krashen, Stephen (1974) 'Is there a "natural sequence" in adult second language learning?', *Language Learning* 24: 235–43.

Baker, C. Leroy and Brame, Michael K. (1972) 'Global rules: A rejoinder', *Language* 48: 51–77.

Baker, Mark (1988) *Incorporation: A Theory of Grammatical Function Changing*, Chicago: University of Chicago Press.

Banathy, Bela, Trager, Edith, and Waddle, Carl (1966) 'The use of contrastive data in foreign language course development' in Albert Valdman (ed.) *Trends in Language Teaching*, New York: McGraw-Hill, 35–56.

Banfield, Ann (1973) 'Narrative style and the grammar of direct and indirect speech', *Foundations of Language* 10: 1–40.

Bar-Hillel, Yehoshua (1962) 'Some recent results in theoretical linguistics' in E. Nagel, P. Suppes, and A. Tarski (eds) *Logic, Methodology, and the Philosophy of Science*, Stanford: Stanford University Press, 551–7.

Barber, Bernard (1962) 'Resistance by scientists to scientific discovery' in B. Barber and W. Hirsch (eds) *Sociology of Science*, New York: Free Press of Glencoe, 539–56.

Battistella, Edwin (1990) *Markedness: The Evaluative Superstructure of Language*, Albany, NY: State University of New York Press.

Belasco, Simon (1985) 'Toward the identification of a core grammar in L2 acquisition', *Studies in Second Language Acquisition* 7: 91–8.

Bennis, Hans and Koster, Jan (1984) 'GLOW Colloquium 1984, call for papers: Parametric typology', *GLOW Newsletter* 12: 6–7.

Berent, Gerald B. (1985) 'Markedness considerations in the acquisition of conditional sentences', *Language Learning* 35: 337–72.

Berman, Stephen (1991) 'On the semantics and logical form of *wh*-clauses', Ph.D. dissertation, University of Massachusetts.

Bloomfield, Leonard (1914) *Introduction to the Study of Language*, New York: Henry Holt & Co. (New edn, with an introduction by Joseph F. Kess, Amsterdam: John Benjamins, 1983.)

—— (1933) *Language*, New York: Holt.

—— (1939) 'Menomini morphophonemics', *Travaux du Cercle Linguistique de Prague* 8: 105–15.

Bolinger, Dwight (1960) 'Linguistic science and linguistic engineering', *Word* 16: 374–91.

—— (1961) 'Syntactic blends and other matters', *Language* 37: 366–81.

Borer, Hagit (1980) 'Empty subjects in Modern Hebrew and constraints on thematic relations', *North Eastern Linguistics Society* 10: 25–38.

Borkin, Ann (1972) *Where the Rules Fail: A Student's Guide. An Unauthorized Appendix to M. K. Burt's From Deep to Surface Structure*, Bloomington, IN: Indiana University Linguistics Club.

Bowers, John (1970) 'A note on "remind"', *Linguistic Inquiry* 1: 559–60.

—— (1973) 'Grammatical relations', Ph.D. dissertation, MIT.

Brame, Michael K. (1976) *Conjectures and Refutations in Syntax and Semantics*, New York: North Holland.

—— (1978) *Base Generated Syntax*, Seattle, WA: Noit Amrofer.

—— (1979) *Essays toward Realistic Syntax*, Seattle, WA: Noit Amrofer.

—— (1981) 'Trace theory with filters vs. lexically based syntax without', *Linguistic Inquiry* 12: 275–93.

Bresnan, Joan W. (1970) 'On complementizers: Toward a syntactic theory of complement types', *Foundations of Language* 6: 297–321.

—— (1972) 'Theory of complementation in English syntax', Ph.D. dissertation, MIT.

—— (1978) 'A realistic transformational grammar' in Morris Halle, Joan Bresnan, and George Miller (eds) *Linguistic Theory and Psychological Reality*, Cambridge, MA: MIT Press, 1–59.

—— (ed.) (1982a) *The Mental Representation of Grammatical Relations*, Cambridge, MA: MIT Press.

—— (1982b) 'Control and complementation', *Linguistic Inquiry* 13: 343–434.

Brody, Michael (1984) 'On contextual definitions and the role of chains', *Linguistic Inquiry* 15: 355–80.

Broselow, Ellen I. (1984) 'An investigation of transfer in second language phonology', *International Review of Applied Linguistics* 22: 253–69.

Brown, H. Douglas (1972a) 'The next twenty-five years: Shaping the revolution', *TESOL Quarterly* 6: 80–5.

—— (1972b) 'The psychological reality of "grammar" in the ESL classroom', *TESOL Quarterly* 6: 263–9.

Brown, Roger (1970) *Psycholinguistics*, New York: Free Press.

—— (1973) *A First Language*, Cambridge, MA: Harvard University Press.

Brown, T. Grant (1971) 'Pedagogical implications of a case grammar of French', *International Review of Applied Linguistics* 9: 229–44.

Burt, Marina K. (1971) *From Deep to Surface Structure*, New York: Harper & Row.

Buyssens, Eric (1969) 'La grammaire générative selon Chomsky', *Revue Belge de Philologie et d'Histoire* 47: 840–57.

Cameron, Deborah (1985) *Feminism and Linguistic Theory*, London: Macmillan.

Cantrall, William (1970), 'If you hiss or anything, I'll do it back', *Chicago Linguistic Society* 6: 168–77.

Carden, Guy (1968) 'English quantifiers' in *The Computation Laboratory of Harvard University, Mathematical Linguistics and Automatic Translation, Report no. NSF-20 to the National Science Foundation*, IX-1–IX-45.

Carlson, Greg (1983) 'Review of J. Bresnan, *The Mental Representation of Grammatical Relations*', *Natural Language and Linguistic Theory* 1: 261–80.

Carnap, Rudolf (1928) *Der logische Aufbau der Welt*, Berlin-Schlachtensee: Weltkreis-Verlag.

—— (1937) *The Logical Syntax of Language*, New York: Harcourt, Brace.

Carroll, John B. (1953) *The Study of Language*, Cambridge, MA: Harvard University Press.

Chomsky, Noam (1949) 'Morphophonemics of Modern Hebrew', undergraduate honors essay, University of Pennsylvania.

—— (1951) 'Morphophonemics of Modern Hebrew', MA thesis, University of Pennsylvania.

—— (1955) 'The logical structure of linguistic theory', unpublished manuscript.

—— (1957) *Syntactic Structures*, Janua Linguarum Series Minor, 4, The Hague: Mouton.

—— (1959) 'Review of B. F. Skinner, *Verbal Behavior*', *Language* 35: 26–57. Reprinted in Jerry A. Fodor and Jerrold J. Katz (eds) (1964) *The Structure of Language: Readings in the Philosophy of Language*, Englewood-Cliffs, NJ: Prentice-Hall, 119–36.

—— (1962a) 'Explanatory models in linguistics' in Ernst Nagel, P. Suppes, and A. Tarski (eds) *Logic, Methodology, and Philosophy of Science*, Stanford, CA: Stanford University Press, 528–50.

—— (1962b) 'A transformational approach to syntax' in Archibald A. Hill (ed.) *Proceedings of the Third Texas Conference on Problems of Linguistic Analysis in English*, Austin: University of Texas Press, 124–58.

—— (1964a) *Current Issues in Linguistic Theory*, Janua Linguarum Series Minor, 38, The Hague: Mouton.

—— (1964b) 'Current issues in linguistic theory' in Jerry A. Fodor and Jerrold J. Katz (eds) *The Structure of Language: Readings in the Philosophy of Language*, Englewood Cliffs, NJ: Prentice-Hall, 50–118.

—— (1964c) 'The logical basis of linguistic theory' in Horace G. Lunt (ed.) *Proceedings of the Ninth International Congress of Linguists*, The Hague: Mouton, 914–77.

—— (1965) *Aspects of the Theory of Syntax*, Cambridge, MA: MIT Press.

—— (1966) 'Topics in the theory of generative grammar' in Thomas A. Sebeok (ed.) *Current Trends in Linguistics, Vol. 3: Theoretical Foundations*, The Hague: Mouton, 1–60.

—— (1967) 'The formal nature of language', appendix in E. Lenneberg, *Biological Foundations of Language* (Appendix A), New York: Wiley, 397–442.

—— (1968) *Language and Mind*, New York: Harcourt, Brace & World.

—— (1970a) 'Linguistic theory' in Mark Lester (ed.) *Readings in Applied Transformational Grammar*, New York: Holt, Rinehart & Winston, 51–60.

—— (1970b) 'Noam Chomsky's view of language' in Mark Lester (ed.) *Readings in Applied Transformational Grammar* [Interview with Stuart Hampshire, edited with an introduction by Alasdair McIntyre], New York: Holt, Rinehart & Winston, 96–113.

—— (1970c) 'Remarks on nominalization' in Roderick Jacobs and Peter Rosenbaum (eds) *Readings in English Transformational Grammar*, Waltham, MA: Ginn, 184–221. Reprinted in Noam Chomsky (1972) *Studies on Semantics in Generative Grammar*, The Hague: Mouton, 11–61.

—— (1971) 'Deep structure, surface structure, and semantic interpretation' in Danny Steinberg and Leon Jakobovits (eds) *Semantics: An Interdisciplinary Reader in Philosophy, Linguistics, and Psychology*, Cambridge: Cambridge University Press, 183–216. Reprinted in Noam Chomsky (1972) *Studies on Semantics in Generative Grammar*, The Hague: Mouton, 62–119.

—— (1972a) *Language and Mind: Enlarged Edition*, New York: Harcourt Brace Jovanovich.

—— (1972b) 'Some empirical issues in the theory of transformational grammar' in P. S. Peters (ed.) *Goals of Linguistic Theory*, Englewood Cliffs, NJ: Prentice-Hall, 63–130. Reprinted in Noam Chomsky (1972c) *Studies on Semantics in Generative Grammar*, The Hague: Mouton, 120–202.

—— (1973) 'Conditions on transformations' in Steven Anderson and Paul Kiparsky (eds) *A Festschrift for Morris Halle*, New York: Holt Rinehart & Winston, 232–86.

—— (1975a) 'Introduction' to *The Logical Structure of Linguistic Theory* Chicago: University of Chicago Press, 1–53.

—— (1975b) *The Logical Structure of Linguistic Theory*, Chicago: University of Chicago Press.

—— (1975c) *Reflections on Language*, New York: Pantheon.

—— (1977) 'An interview with Noam Chomsky', *Linguistic Analysis* 4: 301–20.

—— (1979a) *Language and Responsibility: Based on Conversations with Mitsou Ronat*, New York: Pantheon.

—— (1979b) *Morphophonemics of Modern Hebrew*, New York: Garland.

—— (1980a) 'On binding', *Linguistic Inquiry* 11: 1–46.

—— (1980b) 'On cognitive structures and their development: A reply to Piaget' in Massimo Piattelli-Palmarini (ed.) *Language and Learning: The Debate Between Jean Piaget and Noam Chomsky*, Cambridge, MA: Harvard, 35–54.

—— (1980c) *Rules and Representations*, New York: Columbia University Press.

—— (1981) *Lectures on Government and Binding*, Studies in Generative Grammar, 9, Dordrecht: Foris.

—— (1982a) *The Generative Enterprise: A Discussion with Riny Huybregts and Henk van Riemsdijk*, Dordrecht: Foris.

—— (1982b) *Some Concepts and Consequences of the Theory of Government and Binding*, Cambridge, MA: MIT Press.

—— (1986a) *Barriers*, Cambridge, MA: MIT Press.

—— (1986b) *Knowledge of Language: Its Nature, Origin, and Use*, New York: Praeger.

—— (1991a) 'Linguistics and adjacent fields: A personal view' in Asa Kasher (ed.) *The Chomskyan Turn: Generative Linguistics, Philosophy, Mathematics, and Psychology*, Oxford: Blackwell, 3–25.

—— (1991b) 'Linguistics and cognitive science: Problems and mysteries' in Asa Kasher (ed.) *The Chomskyan Turn: Generative Linguistics, Philosophy, Mathematics, and Psychology*, Oxford: Blackwell, 26–55.

—— (1993) 'A minimalist program for linguistic theory' in Kenneth Hale and Samuel Jay Keyser (eds) *The View from Building 20: Essays in honor of Sylvain Bromberger*, Cambridge, MA: MIT Press, 1–52.

—— and Halle, Morris (1965) 'Some controversial questions in phonological theory', *Journal of Linguistics* 1: 97–138.

—— and Halle, Morris (1968) *Sound Pattern of English*, New York: Harper & Row.

—— and Lasnik, Howard (1977) 'Filters and control', *Linguistic Inquiry* 8: 425–504.

—— and Miller, George (1963) 'Introduction to the formal analysis of natural languages' in Philip Luce, R. Bush, and E. Galanter (eds) *Handbook of Mathematical Psychology*, vol. 2, New York: Wiley, 269–322.

Clahsen, Harald (1982) *Spracherwerb in der Kindheit*, Tübingen: G. Narr.

Cole, Peter and Sadock, Jerry (eds) (1977) *Syntax and Semantics, vol. 8: Grammatical Relations*, New York: Academic Press.

Collinder, Björn (1970) *Noam Chomsky und die generative Grammatik: eine kritische Betrachtung*, Acta Universitatis Upsaliensis NS. 2: 1, Uppsala: Almqvist & Wiksell.

Comrie, Bernard (1981) *Language Universals and Linguistic Typology*, Chicago: University of Chicago Press.

—— (1988) 'Linguistic typology' in Frederick J. Newmeyer (ed.) *Linguistics: The Cambridge Survey*, vol. 1, Cambridge: Cambridge University Press, 447–61.

Cook, Vivian (1985) 'Universal grammar and second language learning', *Applied Linguistics* 6: 2–18.

Coopmans, Peter (1983) 'Review of B. Comrie, *Language universals and linguistic typology*', *Journal of Linguistics* 19: 455–74.

Corder, Stephen Pit (1967) 'The significance of learners' errors', *International Review of Applied Linguistics* 4: 161–70.

Corum, Claudia, Smith-Stark, C. Cedric, and Weiser, Ann (eds) (1973) *You Take the High Node and I'll Take the Low Node*, Chicago: Chicago Linguistic Society.

Culicover, Peter (1977) 'An invalid evaluation metric', *Linguistic Analysis* 3: 65–100.

—— (1981) *Negative Curiosities*, Bloomington, IN: Indiana University Linguistics Club.

d'Anglejan, Alison and Tucker, G. Richard (1975) 'The acquisition of complex structures by language learners', *Language Learning* 25: 245–58.

Daneš, František. (1964) 'A three-level approach to syntax', *Travaux Linguistiques de Prague* 1: 225–40.

Darden, Bill J. (1974) 'Introduction' in A. Bruck, R. Fox, and M. LeGaly (eds) *Papers from the Parasession on Natural Phonology*, Chicago: Chicago Linguistic Society, n.p.

De George, Richard and De George, Fernande (eds) (1972) *The Structuralists: From Marx to Lévi-Strauss*, Garden City, NY: Doubleday.

De Villiers, Jill G. and De Villiers, Peter A. (1973) 'A cross-sectional study of the acquisition of grammatical morphemes', *Journal of Psycholinguistic Research* 2: 267–78.

Di Pietro, Robert J. (1968) 'Contrastive analysis and the notions of deep and surface grammar' in James E. Alatis (ed.) *Report of the Nineteenth Annual Round Table Meeting on Linguistics and Language Studies*, Washington: Georgetown University Press, 65–82.

Dijk, Teun van (1972) *Some Aspects of Text Grammars: A Study in Theoretical Linguistics and Poetics*, The Hague: Mouton.

Dik, Simon C. (1981) *Functional Grammar*, Dordrecht: Foris.

Diller, Karl (1971) *Generative Grammar, Structural Linguistics, and Language Teaching*, Rowley, MA: Newbury House.

Dingwall, William O. (1964) 'Transformational generative grammar and contrastive analysis', *Language Learning* 14: 147–60.

—— (1965) *Transformational Generative Grammar: A Bibliography*, Washington: Center for Applied Linguistics.

Dirven, René (1974) 'The relevance of generative semantics for language teaching' in Stephen Pit Corder and Eddy Roulet (eds) *Linguistic Insights in Applied Linguistics*, Brussels: AIMAV, 27–44.

Dougherty, Ray (1974) 'Generative semantic methods: A Bloomfieldian counter-revolution', *International Journal of Dravidian Linguistics* 3: 255–86.

Dowty, David (1979) *Word Meaning and Montague Grammar*, Dordrecht: Reidel.

Dulay, Heidi and Burt, Marina K. (1974) 'Natural sequences in child second language acquisition', *Language Learning* 24: 37–53.

Ebeling, Carl L. (1960) *Linguistic Units*, Janua Linguarum Series Minor, 12, The Hague: Mouton.

Eckman, Fred R. (1977) 'Markedness and the contrastive analysis hypothesis', *Language Learning* 27: 315–30.

—— (1981) 'On the naturalness of interlanguage phonological rules', *Language Learning* 31: 195–216.

—— (1985) 'The markedness differential hypothesis: theory and applications' in Barbara Wheatley, Ashley Hastings, Fred R. Eckman, Lawrence Ball, Gary Krukar, and Rita Ruthowski (eds) *Current Approaches to Second Language Acquisition: Proceedings of the 1984 University of Wisconsin–Milwaukee Linguistics Symposium*, Bloomington, IN: Indiana University Linguistics Club, 3–21.

Emonds, Joseph E. (1970) 'Root and structure-preserving transformations', Ph.D. dissertation, MIT.

—— (1973) 'Alternatives to global constraints', *Glossa* 7: 39–62.

—— (1976) *A Transformational Approach to English Syntax*, New York: Academic Press.

—— (1991) 'Subcategorization and syntax-based theta-role assignment', *Natural Language and Linguistic Theory* 9: 369–430.

Enç, Murvet (1983) 'Anchored expressions', *West Coast Conference on Formal Linguistics* 2: 79–88.

—— (1988) 'The syntax–semantics interface' in Frederick J. Newmeyer (ed.) *Linguistics: The Cambridge Survey*, vol. 1, Cambridge: Cambridge University Press, 239–54.

Felix, Sasha (1985) 'More evidence on competing cognitive systems', *Second Language Research* 1: 47–72.

Ferguson, Charles A. (1963) 'Linguistic theory and language learning' in Robert J. Di Pietro (ed.) *Report of the Fourteenth Annual Round Table Meeting on Linguistics and Language Studies*, Washington: Georgetown University Press, 115–24.

Fillmore, Charles (1963) 'The position of embedding transformations in a grammar', *Word* 19: 208–31.

—— (1972) 'On generativity' in P. S. Peters (ed.) *Goals of Linguistic Theory*, Englewood Cliffs, NJ: Prentice-Hall, 1–20.

—— (1985) 'Syntactic intrusions and the notion of grammatical construction', *Berkeley Linguistics Society* 11: 73–86.

——, Kay, Paul, and O'Connor, Mary Catherine (1988) 'Regularity and idiomaticity in grammatical constructions', *Language* 64: 501–38.

Finer, Daniel L. and Broselow, Ellen I. (1986) 'Second language acquisition of reflexive binding', *North Eastern Linguistic Society* 16: 154–68.

Fisiak, Jacek (1980) 'Introduction' in Jacek Fisiak (ed.) *Theoretical Issues in Contrastive Linguistics*, Amsterdam: John Benjamins.

Flege, James E. and Hillenbrand, James (1984) 'Limits on the phonetic accuracy in foreign language speech production', *Journal of the Acoustical Society of America* 76: 708–21.

Flickinger, Daniel (1983) 'Lexical heads and phrasal gaps', *West Coast Conference on Formal Linguistics* 2: 89–101.

Flynn, Suzanne (1983) 'Similarities and differences between first and second language acquisition: Setting the parameters of universal grammar' in D. Rogers and J. Sloboda (eds) *Acquisition of Symbolic Skills*, New York: Plenum, 485–500.

—— (1984) 'A universal in L2 acquisition based on a PBD typology' in Fred R. Eckman, Lawrence Bell, and Diane Nelson (eds) *Universals of Second Language Acquisition*, Rowley, MA: Newbury House, 75–87.

—— (1986) 'Production vs. comprehension: Differences in underlying competences', *Studies in Second Language Acquisition* 8: 17–46.

—— (1987) *Adult L2 Acquisition: Resetting the Parameters of Universal Grammar*, Dordrecht: Reidel.

—— and O'Neil, Wayne (eds) (1988) *Linguistic Theory in Second Language Acquisition*, Dordrecht: Kluwer.

Fodor, Jerry A. (1970) 'Three reasons for not deriving "kill" from "cause to die"', *Linguistic Inquiry* 1: 429–38.

—— and Katz, Jerrold J. (eds) (1964) *The Structure of Language: Readings in the Philosophy of Language*, Englewood Cliffs, NJ: Prentice-Hall.

Foley, William and Van Valin, Robert (1984) *Functional Syntax and Universal Grammar*, Cambridge: Cambridge University Press.

Fox, Melvin J. and Skolnick, Betty P. (1975) *Language in Education: Problems and Prospects in Research and Teaching*, New York: The Ford Foundation.

Frantz, Donald (1974) *Generative Semantics: An Introduction, with Bibliography*, Bloomington, IN: Indiana University Linguistics Club.

—— (1976) 'Equi-subject clause union', *Berkeley Linguistics Society* 2: 179–87.

Fraser, Bruce (1974) 'An examination of the performative analysis', *Papers in Linguistics* 7: 1–40.

Freidin, Robert (1975) 'The analysis of passives', *Language* 51: 384–405.

—— (1978) 'Cyclicity and the theory of grammar', *Linguistic Inquiry* 9: 519–50.

Fries, Charles C. (1945) *Teaching and Learning English as a Foreign Language*, Ann Arbor, MI: University of Michigan Press.

Gass, Susan (1979) 'Language transfer and universal grammatical relations', *Language Learning* 29: 327–44.

—— (1984) 'A review of interlanguage syntax: Language transfer and language universals', *Language Learning* 34: 115–32.

—— and Selinker, Larry (eds) (1983) *Language Transfer in Language Learning*, Rowley, MA: Newbury House.

Gazdar, Gerald (1979) *Pragmatics: Implicature, Presupposition, and Logical Form*, New York: Academic Press.

—— (1981) 'Phrase structure grammar' in P. Jacobson and G. Pullum (eds) *The Nature of Syntactic Representation*, Dordrecht: Reidel, 131–86.

—— (1982) 'Review of M. K. Brame, *Base Generated Syntax*', *Journal of Linguistics* 18: 464–73.

—— and Klein, Ewan (1978) 'Review of E. L. Keenan (ed.), *Formal Semantics of Natural Language*', *Language* 54: 661–7.

——, Klein, Ewan, Pullum, Geoffrey K., and Sag, Ivan (1985) *Generalized Phrase Structure Grammar*, Cambridge, MA: Harvard University Press.

Gee, James (1974) 'Jackendoff's thematic hierarchy condition and the passive construction', *Linguistic Inquiry* 5: 304–8.

Gefen, Raphael (1966) 'Theoretical prerequisites for second-language teaching', *International Review of Applied Linguistics* 4: 227–43.

—— (1967) '"Sentence patterns" in the light of language theories and classroom needs', *International Review of Applied Linguistics* 5: 185–92.

Georgopoulos, Carol (1991) 'Canonical government and the specifier parameter: An ECP account of weak crossover', *Natural Language and Linguistic Theory* 9: 1–46.

Gildin, Bonny (1978) 'Concerning radios in performative clauses', *Pragmatics Microfiche* 3: 4.

Givón, Talmy (1979) *On Understanding Grammar*, New York: Academic Press.

Goddard, Ives (1987) 'Leonard Bloomfield's descriptive and comparative studies of Algonquian', *Historiographia Linguistica* 14: 179–217.

Godel, Robert (1957) *Les sources manuscrites du Cours de linguistique générale de F. de Saussure*, Paris: Minard.

Goodman, Nelson (1951) *The Structure of Appearance*, Cambridge, MA: Harvard University Press.

Gouin, François (1892) *The Art of Teaching and Studying Languages*, London: Philip.

Gray, Bennison (1976) 'Counter-revolution in the hierarchy', *Forum Linguisticum* 1: 38–50.

Green, Georgia M. (1972) 'Some observations on the syntax and semantics of instrumental verbs', *Chicago Linguistic Society* 8: 83–97.

—— (1974) *Semantics and Syntactic Regularity*, Bloomington, IN: Indiana University Press.

Greenberg, Joseph H. (1963) 'Some universals of language with special reference to the order of meaningful elements' in Joseph Greenberg (ed.) *Universals of Language*, Cambridge, MA: MIT Press, 73–113.

—— (1973) 'Linguistics as a pilot science' in Eric Hamp (ed.) *Themes in Linguistics: The 1970s*, The Hague: Mouton, 45–60.

Greene, Judith (1972) *Psycholinguistics: Chomsky and Psychology*, Harmondsworth: Penguin.

Grimshaw, Jane (1979) 'Complement selection and the lexicon', *Linguistic Inquiry* 10: 279–326.

Gross, Maurice (1979) 'On the failure of generative grammar', *Language* 55: 859–85.

Guillaume, Gustave (1964) *Langage et science de langage*, Paris: Nizet.

Hagège, Claude (1976) *La grammaire générative: réflexions critiques*, Paris: Presses Universitaires de France.

Hakuta, Kenji and Cancino, Herlinda (1977) 'Trends in second language acquisition research', *Harvard Educational Review* 47: 294–316.

Hall, Robert A. (1965) 'Fact and fiction in grammatical analysis', *Foundations of Language* 1: 337–45.

—— (1969) 'Some recent developments in American linguistics', *Neuphilologische Mitteilungen* 70: 192–227.

—— (1977) 'Review of Claude Hagège, *La grammaire générative: réflexions critiques'*, *Forum Linguisticum* 2: 75–9.

—— (1981) 'Review of F. Newmeyer, *Linguistic Theory in America'*, *Forum Linguisticum* 6: 177–83.

Halle, Morris (1988) 'The Bloomfield–Jakobson correspondence, 1944–46', *Language* 64: 737–54.

Halliday, M. A. K. (1985) *An Introduction to Functional Grammar*, London: Edward Arnold.

Hammer, John H. and Rice, Frank A. (eds) (1965) *A Bibliography of Contrastive Linguistics*, Washington: Center for Applied Linguistics.

Hamp, Eric P. (1968) 'What contrastive grammar is not, if it is' in James E. Alatis (ed.) *Report of the Nineteenth Annual Round Table Meeting on Linguistics and Language Studies*, Washington: Georgetown University Press, 137–50.

Harris, James (1973) 'Linguistics and language teaching: Applications versus implications' in Kurt R. Jankowsky (ed.) *Georgetown University Round Table on Languages and Linguistics 1973*, Washington: Georgetown University Press, 11–18.

Harris, Randy A. (1993a) *The Linguistics Wars*, Oxford: Oxford University Press.

—— (1993b) 'The origin and development of generative semantics', *Historiographia Linguistica* 20: 399–440.

Harris, Zellig S. (1941) 'Review of N. Trubetzkoy, *Grundzüge der Phonologie'*, *Language* 17: 345–9.

—— (1942) 'Morpheme alternants in linguistic analysis', *Language* 18: 169–80. Reprinted in Martin Joos (ed.) (1957) *Readings in Linguistics*, New York: American Council of Learned Societies, 109–15.

—— (1951) *Methods in Structural Linguistics*, Chicago: University of Chicago Press.

—— (1954) 'Transfer grammar', *International Journal of American Linguistics* 20: 259–70.

—— (1957) 'Co-occurrence and transformation in linguistic structure', *Language* 33: 283–340.

Heal, Jane (1977) 'Ross and Lakoff on declarative sentences', *Studies in Language* 1: 337–62.

Heim, Irene (1988) *The Semantics of Definite and Indefinite Noun Phrases*, New York: Garland.

Higgins, F. R. (1973) 'The pseudo-cleft construction in English', Ph.D. dissertation, MIT.

Hill, Archibald A. (1980) 'How many revolutions can a linguist live through?' in Boyd Davis and Raymond O' Cain (eds) *First Person Singular: Papers from the Conference on an Oral Archive for the History of American Linguistics*, Amsterdam: John Benjamins, 69–76.

Hintikka, Jaakko (1974) *Knowledge and Known*, Dordrecht: Reidel.

Hintikka, Merrill and Hintikka, Jaakko (1983) 'How can language be sexist?' in Susan Harding and Merrill Hintikka (eds) *Discovering Reality*, Dordrecht: Reidel, 139–48.

Hiż, Henry (1967) 'Methodological aspects of the theory of syntax', *Journal of Philosophy* 64: 67–74.

Hockett, Charles F. (1948) 'Implications of Bloomfield's Algonquian studies', *Language* 24: 117–31.

—— (1952) 'Review of *Travaux du Cercle Linguistique de Copenhague, vol. 5: Recherches structurales'*, *International Journal of American Linguistics* 18: 86–99.

—— (1954) 'Two models of grammatical description', *Word* 10: 210–31.

—— (1965) 'Sound change', *Language* 41: 185–204.

—— (1966) *Language, Mathematics, and Linguistics*, The Hague: Mouton. [Also published in Thomas A. Sebeok (ed.) (1966) *Current Trends in Linguistics, vol 3: Theoretical Foundations*, The Hague: Mouton, 155–304.]

—— (1968) *The State of the Art*, Janua Linguarum Series Minor, 73, Mouton: The Hague.

—— (ed.) (1970) *A Leonard Bloomfield Anthology*, Bloomington, IN: Indiana University Press.

Horn, Laurence R. (1970) 'Ain't it hard (anymore)?', *Chicago Linguistic Society* 6: 318–27.

Hornstein, Norbert (1984) *Logic as Grammar*, Cambridge, MA: MIT Press.

Householder, Fred (1965) 'On some recent claims in phonological theory', *Journal of Linguistics* 1: 13–34.

Huang, James (1984) 'On the distribution and reference of empty pronouns', *Linguistic Inquiry* 15: 531–74.

Huck, Geoffrey J. and Goldsmith, John A. (1995) *Ideology and Linguistic Theory: Noam Chomsky and the Deep Structure Debates*, London: Routledge.

Hunt, Kellogg W. (1970) 'How little sentences grow into big ones' in Mark Lester (ed.) *Readings in Applied Transformational Grammar*, New York: Holt, Rinehart & Winston, 170–86.

Hust, Joel (1977) 'The syntax of the unpassive construction in English', *Linguistic Analysis* 3: 31–64.

—— and Brame, Michael K. (1976) 'Jackendoff on interpretive semantics', *Linguistic Analysis* 2: 243–78.

Hymes, Dell (1964) 'Directions in (ethno-)linguistic theory' in A. K. Romney and R. G. D'Andrade (eds) *Transcultural Studies in Cognition* (*American Anthropologist* 66: 3, part 2), Washington: American Anthropological Association, 6–56.

—— and Fought, John (1981) *American Structuralism*, The Hague: Mouton.

Ioup, Georgette and Kruse, Anna (1977) 'Interference vs. structural complexity in second language acquisition' in Douglas Brown, Carlos A. Yorio, and Ruth A. Crymes (eds) *Teaching and Learning English as a Second Language: Trends in Research and Practice*, Washington: Teachers of English to Speakers of Other Languages, 159–71.

—— and Weinberger, Stephen H. (eds) (1987) *Interlanguage Phonology*, Rowley, MA: Newbury House.

Itkonen, Esa (1991) *Universal History of Linguistics: India, China, Arabia, Europe*, Amsterdam Studies in the Theory and History of Linguistic Science: Series III – Studies in the History of the Language Sciences, 65, Amsterdam: John Benjamins.

—— (1992) 'Remarks on the language universals research II' in Maria Vilkuna (ed.) *SKY 1992* (*Suomen Kielitieteellisen Yhdistyksen Vuosikirja 1992*), Helsinki: Suomen Kielitieteellinen Yhdistyks, 53–82.

Jackendoff, Ray (1969) 'Some rules of semantic interpretation for English', Ph.D. dissertation, MIT.

—— (1972) *Semantic Interpretation in Generative Grammar*, Cambridge, MA: Cambridge University Press.

—— (1977) *X-bar Syntax: A Study of Phrase Structure*, Cambridge, MA: MIT Press.

—— (1983) *Semantics and Cognition*, Cambridge, MA: MIT Press.

Jacobson, Pauline (1975) 'Crossover and *about*-movement in a relational grammar', *Berkeley Linguistics Society* 1: 233–45.

Jacobson, Rudolfo (1966) 'The role of deep structure in language teaching', *Language Learning* 16: 153–60.

Jakobovits, Leon (1970) 'Implications of recent psycholinguistic developments for the teaching of a second language' in Mark Lester (ed.) *Readings in Applied Transformational Grammar*, New York: Holt, 253–75.

Jakobson, Roman (1948) 'Russian conjugation', *Word* 4: 155–67. Reprinted in Roman Jakobson (1971) *Selected Writings, vol. 2: Word and Language*, The Hauge: Mouton, 119–29.

—— (1957) 'Notes on Gilyak', *Studies Presented to Yuen Ren Chao (Bulletin of the Institute of History and Philology, Academia Sinica* 29: 255–81). Reprinted in R. Jakobson (1971) *Selected Writings, vol. 2: Word and Language*, The Hague: Mouton, 72–97.

James, Carl (1969) 'Deeper contrastive study', *International Review of Applied Linguistics* 7: 83–95.

Jenkins, Lyle (1972) 'Modality in English syntax', Ph.D. dissertation, MIT.

Jespersen, Otto (1924) *The Philosophy of Grammar*, London: Allen & Unwin.

Joos, Martin (ed.) (1957) *Readings in Linguistics: The Development of Descriptive Linguistics in America since 1925*, New York: American Council of Learned Societies.

—— (1961) 'Linguistic prospects in the United States' in C. Mohrmann, A. Sommerfelt and J. Whatmough (eds) *Trends in European and American Linguistics 1930–1960*, Utrecht: Spectrum, 11–20.

—— (1986) *Notes on the Development of the Linguistic Society of America 1924 to 1950*, Ithaca: Privately printed by J. M. Cowan and C. Hockett.

Kac, Michael (1972) 'Action and result: Two aspects of predication in English' in John Kimball (ed.) *Syntax and Semantics*, vol. 1, New York: Seminar Press, 117–24.

—— (1980) 'Review of M. K. Brame, *Base Generated Syntax*', *Language* 56: 855–62.

Katz, Jerrold J. and Bever, Thomas G. (1976) 'The fall and rise of empiricism' in Thomas G. Bever, Jerrold J. Katz, and D. Terence Langendoen (eds) *An Integrated Theory of Linguistic Ability*, New York: Crowell, 11–64.

—— and Fodor, Jerry A. (1963) 'The structure of a semantic theory', *Language* 39: 170–210. Reprinted in Jerry A. Fodor and Jerrold J. Katz (eds) (1964) *The Structure of Language: Readings in the Philosophy of Language*, Englewood Cliffs, NJ: Prentice-Hall, 479–518.

—— and Postal, Paul (1964) *An Integrated Theory of Linguistic Descriptions*, Cambridge, MA: MIT Press.

Kayne, Richard S. (1984) *Connectedness and Binary Branching*, Studies in Generative Grammar, 16, Dordrecht: Foris.

Keenan, Edward L. and Comrie, Bernard (1977) 'Noun phrase accessibility and universal grammar', *Linguistic Inquiry* 8: 63–99.

Kempson, Ruth (1975) *Presupposition and the Delimitation of Semantics*, Cambridge: Cambridge University Press.

Kiparsky, Paul and Menn, Lise (1977) 'On the acquisition of phonology' in John MacNamara (ed.) *Language Learning and Thought*, New York: Academic Press, 47–78.

Koerner, E. F. Konrad (1976) 'Towards a historiography of linguistics: Nineteenth- and twentieth-century paradigms' in Herman Parret (ed.) *History of Linguistic Thought and Contemporary Linguistics*, Berlin: Walter de Gruyter, 685–718. Reprinted in E. F. Konrad Koerner (ed.) (1978) *Toward a Historiography of Linguistics*, Amsterdam: John Benjamins, 21–54. An earlier version appeared in *Anthropological Linguistics* 14: 255–80.

—— (1983) 'The "Chomskyan revolution" and its historiography: A few critical remarks', *Language and Communication* 3: 147–69.

—— (1984) 'Remarques critiques sur la linguistique américaine et son historiographie', *Linguisticae Investigationes* 8: 87–103.

—— and Tajima, Matsuju (1986) *Noam Chomsky: A Personal Bibliography*, Amsterdam Studies in the Theory and History of Linguistic Science, 11, Amsterdam: John Benjamins.

Koopman, Hilda and Sportiche, Dominique (1991) 'The position of subjects', *Lingua* 75: 211–58.

Koster, Jan (1978) *Locality Principles in Syntax*, Dordrecht: Foris.

—— (1986) *Domains and Dynasties: The Radical Autonomy of Syntax*, Studies in Generative Grammar, 30, Dordrecht: Foris.

—— and May, Robert (1982) 'On the constituency of infinitives', *Language* 58: 116–43.

Krashen, Stephen D. (1973) 'Lateralization, language learning, and the critical period: Some new evidence', *Language Learning* 23: 63–74.

—— (1978a) 'Individual variation in the use of the monitor' in William C. Ritchie (ed.) *Second Language Acquisition Research*, New York: Academic Press, 175–84.

—— (1978b) 'The monitor model for second language acquisition' in R. Gingras (ed.) *Second Language Acquisition and Foreign Language Teaching*, Arlington, VA: Center for Applied Linguistics, 1–26.

—— (1982) *Principles and Practice in Second Language Acquisition*, Oxford: Pergamon Press.

Kuhn, Thomas S. (1970) *The Structure of Scientific Revolutions*, 2nd edn, Chicago: University of Chicago Press.

Kuipers, A. H. (1968) 'Unique types and typological universals' in J. C. Heesterman, G. H. Schoecker, and V. I. Subramoniam (eds) *Pratidānam: Indian, Iranian, and Indo-European Studies Presented to F. B. J. Kuiper on his Sixtieth Birthday*, The Hague: Mouton, 68–88.

Kuno, Susumu (1987) *Functional Syntax: Anaphora, Discourse, and Empathy*, Chicago: University of Chicago Press.

Labov, William (1972a) *Sociolinguistic Patterns*, Philadelphia: University of Pennsylvania Press.

—— (1972b) 'Some principles of linguistic methodology', *Language in Society* 1: 97–120.

Ladefoged, Peter (1988) 'Redefining the scope of phonology' in Caroline Duncan-Rose and Theo Vennemann (eds) *On Language: Rhetorica, Phonologica, Syntactica: A Festschrift for Robert P. Stockwell from his Friends and Colleagues*, London: Routledge, 212–20.

Lado, Robert (1957) *Linguistics Across Cultures*, Ann Arbor, MI: University of Michigan Press.

—— (1968) 'Contrastive linguistics in a mentalistic theory of language learning' in James E. Alatis (ed.) *Report of the Nineteenth Annual Round Table Meeting on Linguistics and Language Studies*, Washington: Georgetown University Press, 123–35.

Lakatos, Imre (1970) 'Falsification and the methodology of scientific research programmes' in Imre Lakatos and Alan Musgrave (eds) *Criticism and the Growth of Knowledge*, Cambridge: Cambridge University Press, 91–196.

Lakoff, George (1968a) *Deep and Surface Grammar*, Bloomington, IN: Indiana University Linguistics Club.

—— (1968b) 'Instrumental adverbs and the concept of deep structure', *Foundations of Language* 4: 4–29.

—— (1970a) 'Global rules', *Language* 46: 627–39.

—— (1970b) *Irregularity in Syntax*, New York: Holt, Rinehart & Winston.

—— (1971a) 'On generative semantics' in Danny Steinberg and Leon Jakobovits (eds) *Semantics: An Interdisciplinary Reader in Philosophy, Linguistics, and Psychology*, New York: Cambridge University Press, 232–96.

—— (1971b) 'Presupposition and relative well-formedness' in Danny Steinberg and Leon Jakobovits (eds) *Semantics: An Interdisciplinary Reader in Philosophy, Linguistics, and Psychology*, New York: Cambridge University Press, 329–40.

—— (1972a) 'The arbitrary basis of transformational grammar', *Language* 48: 76–87.

—— (1972b) 'Foreword' to A. Borkin, *Where the Rules Fail: A Student's Guide. An Unauthorized Appendix to M. K. Burt's From Deep to Surface Structure*, Bloomington: Indiana University Linguistics Club, i–v.

—— (1972c) From an article in the *New York Times*, September 10.

—— (1972d) 'Linguistics and natural logic' in Donald Davidson and Gilbert Harmon (eds) *The Semantics of Natural Language*, Dordrecht: Reidel, 545–665.

—— (1973) 'Fuzzy grammar and the performance/competence terminology game', *Chicago Linguistic Society* 9: 271–91.

—— (1974a) 'Interview' in Herman Parret (ed.) *Discussing Language: Dialogues with [various linguists]*, The Hague: Mouton, 151–78.

—— (1974b) 'Notes toward a theory of global transderivational well-formedness grammar', unpublished manuscript, University of California.

—— (1975) 'Dual-hierarchy grammar', unpublished manuscript, University of California.

—— (1976) 'Toward generative semantics' in James D. McCawley (ed.) *Syntax and Semantics, vol. 7: Notes from the Linguistic Underground*, New York: Academic Press, 43–62.

—— (1977) 'Linguistic gestalts', *Chicago Linguistic Society* 13: 236–87.

—— and Peters, P. Stanley (1969) 'Phrasal conjunction and symmetric predicates' in David Reibel and Sanford Schane (eds) *Modern Studies in English*, Englewood Cliffs, NJ: Prentice-Hall, 113–42.

—— and Ross, John R. (1976) 'Is deep structure necessary?' in James D. McCawley (ed.) *Syntax and Semantics, vol. 7: Notes from the Linguistic Underground*, New York: Academic Press, 159–64.

—— and Thompson, Henry (1975) 'Introducing cognitive grammar', *Berkeley Linguistics Society* 1: 295–313.

Lakoff, Robin T. (1969) 'Transformational grammar and language teaching', *Language Learning* 19: 117–40.

—— (1971) 'If's, and's and but's about conjunction' in Charles H. Fillmore and D. Terence Langendoen (eds) *Studies in Linguistic Semantics*, New York: Holt, Rinehart & Winston, 115–50.

—— (1973) 'The logic of politeness; or minding your p's and q's', *Chicago Linguistic Society* 9: 292–305.

—— (1974) 'Pluralism in linguistics', *Berkeley Studies in Syntax and Semantics* 1: XIV-1–XIV-36.

—— (1975a) *Language and Woman's Place*, New York: Harper.

—— (1975b) 'Linguistic theory and the real world', *Language Learning* 25: 309–39.

—— (1989) 'The way we were: Or, the real actual truth about generative semantics: A memoir', *Journal of Pragmatics* 13: 939–88.

Lamb, Sydney (1966) 'Prolegomena to a theory of phonology', *Language* 42: 536–73.

Lamendella, John (1969) 'On the irrelevance of transformational grammar to second language pedagogy', *Language Learning* 19: 255–70.

Lane, Michael (1970) *Introduction to Structuralism*, New York: Basic Books.

Langacker, Ronald (1982) 'Space grammar, analysability, and the English passive', *Language* 58: 22–80.

—— (1987) *Foundations of Cognitive Grammar: vol.1: Theoretical Prerequisites*, Stanford, CT: Stanford University Press.

Lasnik, Howard (1972) 'Analyses of negation in English', Ph.D. dissertation, MIT.
—— and Saito, Mamoru (1984) 'On the nature of proper government', *Linguistic Inquiry* 15: 235–90.
Laudan, Larry (1977) *Progress and its Problems: Toward a Theory of Scientific Growth*, Berkeley and Los Angeles: University of California Press.
Lawler, John (1973) 'Tracking the generic toad', *Chicago Linguistic Society* 9: 320–31.
Lees, Robert B. (1960) *The Grammar of English Nominalizations*, The Hague: Mouton.
—— (1965) 'Two views of linguistic research', *Linguistics* 11: 21–9.
Lenneberg, Eric (1967) *Biological Foundations of Language*, New York: Wiley.
Lesnin, I. M., Petrova, Luba, and Bloomfield, Leonard (1945) *Spoken Russian, Basic Course*, Madison: Published for the United States Armed Forces Institute by the Linguistic Society of America.
Levin, Samuel R. (1965) 'Langue and parole in American linguistics', *Foundations of Language* 1: 83–94.
Li, Y.-H. Audrey (1992) 'Indefinite *wh* in Mandarin Chinese', *Journal of East Asian Linguistics* 1: 125–56.
Liceras, Juana (1987) 'L2 learnability: Delimiting the domain of core grammar as distinct from the marked periphery' in Suzanne Flynn and Wayne O'Neil (eds) *Linguistic Theory in Second Language Acquisition*, Dordrecht: Reidel, 199–224.
Lightfoot, David (1979) 'Review of C. Li, *Mechanisms of Syntactic Change*', *Language* 55: 381–95.
—— (1991) *How to Set Parameters: Arguments from Language Change*, Cambridge, MA: MIT Press.
Longacre, Robert E. (1964) *Grammar Discovery Procedures*, Janua Linguarum Series Minor, 33, The Hague: Mouton.
—— (1967) 'Reply to Postal's review of *Grammar Discovery Procedures*', *International Journal of American Linguistics* 33: 323–8.
—— (1979) 'Why we need a vertical revolution in linguistics' in W. Wölck and P. Garvin (eds) *The Fifth LACUS Forum*, Columbia, SC: Hornbeam Press, 247–70.
McCawley, James D. (1967) 'Meaning and the description of languages', *Kotoba no uchû* 2, no. 9–11. Reprinted in James D. McCawley (1976) *Grammar and Meaning*, New York: Academic Press, 99–120.
—— (1968a) 'Lexical insertion in a transformational grammar without deep structure', *Chicago Linguistic Society* 4: 71-80. Reprinted in James D. McCawley (1976) *Grammar and Meaning*, New York: Academic Press, 155–66.
—— (1968b) 'The role of semantics in grammar' in Emmon Bach and Robert Harms (eds) *Universals in Linguistic Theory*, New York: Holt, Rinehart & Winston, 125–70. Reprinted in James D. McCawley (1976) *Grammar and Meaning*, New York: Academic Press, 59–98.
—— (1970) 'Where do noun phrases come from?' in Roderick Jacobs and Peter Rosenbaum (eds) *Readings in English Transformational Grammar*, Waltham, MA: Ginn, 166–83. Reprinted in James D. McCawley (1976) *Grammar and Meaning*, New York: Academic Press, 133–54.
—— (1973a) 'External NPs versus annotated deep structures', *Linguistic Inquiry* 4: 221–40.
—— (1973b) 'Syntactic and logical arguments for semantic structures' in Osamu Fujimura (ed.) *Three Dimensions of Linguistic Theory*, Tokyo TEC Company, Ltd, 259–376.
—— (1977) 'The nonexistence of syntactic categories', *Second Annual Linguistic Metatheory Conference Proceedings*, 212–22. Reprinted in James D. McCawley, *Thirty Million Theories of Grammar*, Chicago: University of Chicago Press, 176–203.

—— (1979) 'Preface' in James D. McCawley (ed.) *Adverbs, Vowels, and Other Objects of Wonder*, Chicago: University of Chicago Press, vii–ix.

—— (1985) 'Kuhnian paradigms as markedness conventions' in Adam Makkai and Alan K. Melby (eds) *Linguistics and Philosophy: Essays in Honour of Rulon S. Wells*, Amsterdam: John Benjamins, 23–44.

—— (1988) *The Syntactic Phenomena of English*, Chicago: University of Chicago Press.

McCloskey, James (1988) 'Syntactic theory' in Frederick J. Newmeyer (ed.) *Linguistics: The Cambridge Survey*, vol. 1, Cambridge: Cambridge University Press, 18–59.

Macedo, Donaldo B. (1986) 'The role of core grammar in pidgin development', *Language Learning* 36: 65–75.

Mackey, William (1973) 'Language didactics and applied linguistics' in John W. Oller and Jack C. Richards (eds) *Focus on the Learner*, Rowley, MA: Newbury House, 4–15.

McLaughlin, Barry (1980) 'Theory and research in second language learning: An emerging paradigm', *Language Learning* 30: 331–50.

Maclay, Howard (1971) 'Linguistics: Overview' in Danny Steinberg and Leon Jakobovits (eds) *Semantics: An Interdisciplinary Reader in Philosophy, Linguistics, and Psychology*, Cambridge: Cambridge University Press, 157–82.

Maher, J. Peter (1980) 'The transformational–generative paradigm: A silver anniversary polemic', *Forum Linguisticum* 5: 1–35.

Martinet, André (1960) *Éléments de linguistique générale*, Paris: Librairie Armand Colin.

May, Robert (1977) 'The grammar of quantification', Ph.D. dissertation, MIT.

—— (1985) *Logical Form: Its Structure and Derivation*, Cambridge, MA: MIT Press.

Mazurkewich, Irene (1984) 'The acquisition of the dative alternation by second language learners and linguistic theory', *Language Learning* 34: 91–110.

Miller, George A., Galanter, E., and Pribram, K. (1960) *Plans and the Structure of Behavior*, New York: Holt, Rinehart & Winston.

Montague, Richard (1970) 'Universal grammar', *Theoria* 36: 373–98.

Moore, Terence and Carling, Christine (1982) *Language Understanding: Towards a Post-Chomskyan Linguistics*, New York: St Martin's Press.

Morgan, Charles G. and Pelletier, Francis Jeffry (1977) 'Some notes concerning fuzzy logics', *Linguistics and Philosophy* 1: 79–98.

Morgan, Jerry L. (1977) 'Conversational postulates revisited', *Language* 53: 277–84.

Murray, Stephen O. (1980) 'Gatekeepers and the "Chomskyan revolution"', *Journal of the History of the Behavioral Sciences* 16: 73–88.

—— (1983) *Group Formation in Social Science*, Edmonton: Linguistic Research, Inc.

Newmark, Leonard (1966) 'How not to interfere with language learning', *International Journal of American Linguistics* 32: 77–83.

—— and Reibel, David (1970) 'Necessity and sufficiency in language learning' in Mark Lester (ed.) *Readings in Applied Transformational Grammar*, New York: Holt, Rinehart & Winston, 228–52.

Newmeyer, Frederick J. (1971) 'The source of derived nominals in English', *Language* 47: 786–96.

—— (1974) 'The regularity of idiom behavior', *Lingua* 34: 327–42.

—— (1975) *English Aspectual Verbs*, The Hague: Mouton.

—— (1976) 'The precyclic nature of predicate raising' in Mayayoshi Shibatani (ed.) *Syntax and Semantics, vol. 6: The Grammar of Causative Constructions*, New York: Academic Press, 131–64.

—— (1980) *Linguistic Theory in America*, New York: Academic Press.

—— (1983) *Grammatical Theory: Its Limits and its Possibilities*, Chicago: University of Chicago Press.

—— (1986a) *Linguistic Theory in America: Second Edition*, New York: Academic Press.

—— (1986b) *The Politics of Linguistics*, Chicago: University of Chicago Press.

—— (1987) 'Current convergences in grammatical theory: Some implications for second language acquisition research', *Second Language Research* 3: 1–19.

—— (1988a) 'Extensions and implications of linguistic theory: An overview' in Frederick J. Newmeyer (ed.) *Linguistics: The Cambridge Survey*, vol. 2, Cambridge: Cambridge University Press, 1–14.

—— (1988b) 'Minor movement rules' in Caroline Duncan-Rose and Theo Vennemann (eds) *On Language: Rhetorica, Phonologica, Syntactica: A Festschrift for Robert P. Stockwell from his Friends and Colleagues*, London: Routledge, 402–12.

—— (1990) 'The structure of the field of linguistics and its consequences for women' in Alice Davidson and Penelope Eckert (eds) *The Cornell Lectures: Women in the Linguistics Profession*, Washington: Linguistic Society of America, 43–54.

—— (1991) 'Rules and principles in the historical development of generative syntax' in Asa Kasher (ed.) *The Chomskyan Turn: Generative Linguistics, Philosophy, Mathematics, and Psychology*, Oxford: Blackwell, 200–30.

—— and Joseph E. Emonds (1971) 'The linguist in American society', *Chicago Linguistic Society* 7: 285–306.

Nida, Eugene A. (1948) 'The analysis of grammatical constituents', *Language* 24: 168–77.

Nilsen, Don (1971) 'The use of case grammar in teaching English as a foreign language', *TESOL Quarterly* 5: 293–300.

Nishigauchi, Taisuke (1990) *Quantification in the Theory of Grammar*, Dordrecht: Kluwer.

Oehrle, Richard (1976) 'The grammatical status of the English dative alternation', Ph.D. dissertation, MIT.

—— (1977) 'Review of G. Green, *Semantics and Syntactic Regularity*', *Language* 53: 198–208.

Ohmann, Richard (1964) 'Generative grammars and the concept of literary style', *Word* 20: 423–39.

Oller, John W. (1973) 'Some psycholinguistic controversies' in John W. Oller and J. Richards (eds) *Focus on the Learner*, Rowley, MA: Newbury House, 36–49.

—— (1979) 'The psychology of language and contrastive linguistics: The research and the debate', *Foreign Language Annals* 12: 299–309.

Osgood, Charles and Sebeok, Thomas A. (eds) (1954) *Psycholinguistics*, Bloomington: Indiana University Press.

Palmer, Harold E. (1917) *The Scientific Teaching and Study of Languages*, Yonkers, NY: World.

Parret, Herman (ed.) (1974) *Discussing Language; Interviews with [various linguists]*, The Hague: Mouton.

Pelletier, Francis Jeffry (1977) 'How/why does linguistics matter to philosophy?', *Southern Journal of Philosophy* 15: 393–426.

Penfield, Wilder and Roberts, Lamar (1959) *Speech and Brain Mechanisms*, Princeton: Princeton University Press.

Percival, W. Keith (1971) 'Review of P. Salus, *Linguistics*', *Language* 47: 181–5.

—— (1976) 'The applicability of Kuhn's paradigm to the history of linguistics', *Language* 52: 285–94.

Perkins, Kyle, Brutten, Sheila R., and Angelis, Paul J. (1986) 'Derivational complexity and item difficulty in a sentence repetition task', *Language Learning* 36: 125–42.

Perlmutter, David (1969) 'On the separability of syntax and semantics', Paper presented to the forty-fourth annual meeting of the Linguistic Society of America.

—— (1970) 'Surface structure constraints in syntax', *Linguistic Inquiry* 1: 187–256.

Peters, P. Stanley and Ritchie, Robert (1969) 'A note on the universal base hypothesis', *Journal of Linguistics* 5: 150–2.

—— and Ritchie, Robert (1971) 'On restricting the base component of transformational grammars', *Information and Control* 18: 483–501.

—— and Ritchie, Robert (1973) 'On the generative power of transformational grammars', *Information Sciences* 6: 49–83.

Pike, Kenneth L. (1943) 'Taxemes and immediate constituents', *Language* 19: 65–82.

—— (1947) *Phonemics: A Technique for Reducing Languages to Writing*, Ann Arbor, MI: University of Michigan Press.

—— (1975) 'On describing languages' in Robert Austerlitz (ed.) *The Scope of American Linguistics*, Lisse: Peter de Ridder Press, 9–40.

Pollard, Carl (1984) 'Generalized phrase structure grammars, head grammars, and natural language', Ph.D. dissertation, Stanford University.

—— (1985) 'Phrase structure grammar without metarules', *West Coast Conference on Formal Linguistics* 3: 246–61.

Pollard, Lucille (1977) *Women on College and University Faculties*, New York: Arno Press.

Pollock, Jean-Yves (1989) 'Verb movement, universal grammar, and the structure of IP', *Linguistic Inquiry* 20: 365–424.

Postal, Paul M. (1968) *Aspects of Phonological Theory*, New York: Harper & Row.

—— (1969) 'Anaphoric islands', *Chicago Linguistic Society* 5: 205–39.

—— (1970) 'On the surface verb "remind"', *Linguistic Inquiry* 1: 37–120.

—— (1971) *Cross-over Phenomena*, New York: Holt, Rinehart & Winston.

—— (1972) 'The best theory' in P. Stanley Peters (ed.) *Goals of Linguistic Theory*, Englewood Cliffs, NJ: Prentice-Hall, 131–70.

—— (1976) 'Linguistic anarchy notes' in James D. McCawley (ed.) *Syntax and Semantics, vol. 7: Notes from the Linguistic Underground*, New York: Academic Press, 201–26.

Prideaux, Gary D., Derwing, Bruce, and Baker, William (eds) (1980) *Experimental Linguistics*, Ghent: Story-Scientia.

Pullum, Geoffrey K. (1977) 'Word order relations and grammatical relations' in Peter Cole and Jerrold Sadock (eds) *Syntax and Semantics, vol. 8: Grammatical Relations*, New York: Academic Press, 249–77.

—— and Wilson, Deirdre (1977) 'Autonomous syntax and analysis of auxiliaries', *Language* 53: 741–88.

—— and Zwicky, Arnold M. (1991) 'Condition duplication, paradigm homonymy, and transconstructional constraints', *Berkeley Linguistics Society* 17: 252–66.

Putnam, Hilary (1961) 'Some issues in the theory of grammar' in *Structure of Language and its Mathematical Aspects* (Proceedings of Symposia in Applied Mathematics, 12), Providence: American Mathematical Society, 25–42.

Quicoli, A. Carlos (1972) 'Aspects of Portuguese complementation', Ph.D. dissertation, State University of New York at Buffalo.

—— (1982) *The Structure of Complementation*, Ghent: Story-Scientia.

Riemsdijk, Henk van and Williams, Edwin (1986) *Introduction to the Theory of Grammar*, Cambridge, MA: MIT Press.

Ritchie, William C. (1978) 'The right roof constraint in an adult acquired language' in William C. Ritchie (ed.) *Second Language Acquisition Research*, New York: Academic Press, 33–64.

Rizzi, Luigi (1978) 'Violations of the *wh*-island constraint in Italian and the subjacency condition' in C. Dubuisson, David Lightfoot, and Y. C. Morin (eds) *Montreal Working Papers in Linguistics*, no. 11. Reprinted in Luigi Rizzi (1982) *Issues in Italian Syntax*, Dordrecht: Foris, 49–76.

—— (1982) *Issues in Italian Syntax*, Studies in Generative Grammar, 11, Dordrecht: Foris.

—— (1991) *Relativized Minimality*, Cambridge, MA: MIT Press.

Robins, Robert H. (1971) 'Malinowski, Firth, and context of situation' in Edwin Ardener (ed.) *Social Anthropology and Language*, London: Tavistock, 33–46.

—— (1973) 'Theory-orientation versus data-orientation: A recurrent theme in linguistics', *Historiographia Linguistica* 1: 11–26.

Robinson, Ian (1975) *The New Grammarian's Funeral: A Critique of Noam Chomsky's Linguistics*, Cambridge: Cambridge University Press.

Rogers, Andy (1972) 'Another look at flip perception verbs', *Chicago Linguistic Society* 8: 303–15.

—— (1974) 'A transderivational constraint on Richard?', *Chicago Linguistic Society* 10: 551–8.

Ronat, Mitsou (1972) *A propos du verbe 'remind' selon P. M. Postal, La sémantique générative: Une réminiscence du structuralisme?*, Padova: Liviana Editrice.

Rosansky, Ellen J. (1976) 'Methods and morphemes in second language acquisition research', *Language Learning* 26: 409–25.

Rosenbaum, Peter (1967) *The Grammar of English Predicate Complement Constructions*, Cambridge, MA: MIT Press.

Ross, John R. (1967) 'Constraints on variables in syntax', Ph.D. dissertation, MIT.

—— (1969a) 'Adjectives as noun phrases' in David Reibel and Sanford Schane (eds) *Modern Studies in English*, Englewood Cliffs, NJ: Prentice-Hall, 352–60.

—— (1969b) 'Auxiliaries as main verbs' in W. Todd (ed.) *Studies in Philosophical Linguistics* I, Evanston, IL: Great Expectations Press, 77–102.

—— (1970) 'On declarative sentences' in Roderick Jacobs and Peter Rosenbaum (eds) *Readings in English Transformational Grammar*, Waltham, MA: Ginn, 222–72.

—— (1972a) 'Act' in Donald Davidson and Gilbert Harman (eds) *Semantics of Natural Language*, Dordrecht: Reidel, 70–126.

—— (1972b) 'Doubl-ing', *Linguistic Inquiry* 3: 61–86. Reprinted in J. Kimball (ed.) (1972) *Syntax and Semantics, vol. 1*, New York: Academic Press, 157–86.

—— (1973a) 'A fake NP squish' in C.-J. N. Bailey and R. Shuy (eds) *New Ways of Analyzing Variation in English*, Washington: Georgetown, 96–140.

—— (1973b) 'Slifting' in Maurice Gross, Morris Halle, and M. Schützenberger (eds) *The Formal Analysis of Natural Language*, The Hague: Mouton, 133–72.

—— (1975) 'Clausematiness' in Edward L. Keenan (ed.) *Formal Semantics of Natural Language*, London: Cambridge University Press, 422–75.

—— (1985) *Infinite Syntax!*, Norwood, NJ: Ablex.

Rouveret, Alain and Vergnaud, Jean-Roger (1980) 'Specifying reference to the subject: French causatives and conditions on representations', *Linguistic Inquiry* 11: 97–202.

Rubach, Jerzy (1984) 'Rule typology and phonological interference' in Stig Eliasson (ed.) *Theoretical Issues in Contrastive Phonology*. Heidelberg: Julius Groos Verlag.

Rutherford, William E. (1968) *Modern English*, New York: Harcourt, Brace & World.

—— (1982) 'Markedness in second language acquisition', *Language Learning* 32: 85–108.

—— (1987) *Second Language Grammar: Learning and Teaching*, London: Longman.

—— and Sharwood Smith, Michael (eds) (1988) *Grammar and Second Language Teaching*, Rowley, MA: Newbury House.

Sadock, Jerrold M. (1974) *Toward a Linguistic Theory of Speech Acts*, New York: Academic Press.

Sampson, Geoffrey (1976) 'Review of D. Cohen, *Explaining Linguistic Phenomena*', *Journal of Linguistics* 12: 177–81.

—— (1980) *Schools of Linguistics*, Stanford, CT: Stanford University Press.

Sapir, Edward (1963 [1933]) 'The psychological realities of phonemes' in D. G. Mandelbaum (ed.) *Selected Writings of Edward Sapir*, Berkeley, CA: University of California Press, 46–60.

Saporta, Sol, Blumenthal, Arthur, and Reiff, Donald (1963) 'Grammatical models and language learning' in Robert Di Pietro (ed.) *Report of the Fourteenth Annual Round Table Meeting on Linguistics and Language Studies*, Washington: Georgetown University Press, 133–42.

Saussure, Ferdinand de (1966) *Course in General Linguistics*, New York: McGraw-Hill. [Translation of *Cours de linguistique générale*, Paris: Payot, 1916.]

Scheffler, Israel (1963) *The Anatomy of Inquiry*, New York: Knopf.

Schiller, Eric, Need, Barbara, Varley, Douglas, and Eilfort, William H. (eds) (1988) *The Best of CLS: A Selection of Out-of-Print Papers from 1968 to 1975*, Chicago: Chicago Linguistics Society.

Schmidt, Maxime (1980) 'Coordinate structures and language universals in interlanguage', *Language Learning* 30: 396–416.

Scovel, Tom (1969) 'Foreign accents, language acquisition and cerebral dominance', *Language Learning* 19: 245–53.

Searle, John (1972) 'Chomsky's revolution in linguistics', *New York Review of Books*, 29 June: 16–24. Reprinted in G. Harman (ed.) (1974) *On Noam Chomsky: Critical Essays*, Garden City, NY: Anchor Books, 2–33.

—— (1976) 'Review of J. Sadock, *Toward a Linguistic Theory of Speech Acts*', *Language* 52: 966–71.

Sebeok, Thomas A. (1969) 'Foreword' to Robert Godel (ed.) *A Geneva School Reader in Linguistics*, Bloomington: Indiana University Press, vii–viii.

Selinker, Larry (1972) 'Interlanguage', *International Review of Applied Linguistics* 10: 201–31.

Selkirk, Elisabeth (1972) 'The phrase phonology of English and French', Ph.D. dissertation, MIT.

—— (1982) *The Syntax of Words*, Cambridge, MA: MIT Press.

Sells, Peter (1985) *Lectures on Contemporary Syntactic Theories*, Chicago: University of Chicago Press.

Shapiro, Michael (1973) 'Review of R. Jakobson, *Selected Writings*, vol. 2', *Indogermanische Forschungen* 78: 193–201.

—— (1974) 'Morphophonemics as semiotic', *Acta Linguistica Hafniensia* 15: 29–49.

Sharwood Smith, Michael (1982) 'Learnability and second language acquisition', unpublished manuscript, University of Utrecht.

—— (1986) 'Comprehension vs. acquisition: Two ways of processing input', *Applied Linguistics* 7: 239–56.

Sklar, Robert (1968) 'Chomsky's revolution in linguistics', *The Nation*, 9 September: 213–17.

Spolsky, Bernard (1970) 'Linguistics and language pedagogy – applications or implications?' in James E. Alatis (ed.) *Georgetown University Round Table on Languages and Linguistics 1969*, Washington: Georgetown University Press, 143–55.

Stockwell, Robert P., Bowen, J. Donald, and Martin, John W. (1965) *The Grammatical Structures of English and Spanish*, Chicago: The University of Chicago Press.

Stowell, Timothy (1981) 'Origins of phrase structure', Ph.D. dissertation, MIT.

Tarone, Elaine (1980) 'Some influences on the syllable structure of interlanguage phonology', *International Review of Applied Linguistics* 18: 139–52.

Tesnière, Lucien (1959) *Elements de syntaxe structurale*, Paris: C. Klincksieck.

Thorne, James P. (1965) 'Review of P. Postal, *Constituent Structure*', *Journal of Linguistics* 1: 73–6.

Travis, Lisa (1984) 'Parameters and effects of word order variation', Ph.D. dissertation, MIT.

Uhlenbeck, E. M. (1975) *Critical Comments on Transformational Generative Grammar, 1962–1972*, The Hague: Smits.

Voegelin, C. F. (1958) 'Review of N. Chomsky, *Syntactic Structures*', *International Journal of American Linguistics* 24: 229–31.

Wasow, Thomas (1972) 'Anaphoric relations in English', Ph.D. dissertation, MIT.

—— (1976) 'McCawley on generative semantics', *Linguistic Analysis* 2: 279–301.

Wasserman, Elga, Lewin, Arie, and Bleiweis, Linda (eds) (1975) *Women in Academia*, New York: Praeger.

Weinreich, Uriel (1966) 'Explorations in semantic theory' in Thomas A. Sebeok (ed.) *Current Trends in Linguistics*, vol. 3, The Hague: Mouton, 395–478.

Wells, Rulon S. (1947) 'Immediate constituents', *Language* 23: 81–117, 169–80. Reprinted in Martin Joos (ed.) (1957) *Readings in Linguistics*, New York: American Council of Learned Societies, 186–207.

Wexler, Kenneth and Culicover, Peter (1980) *Formal Principles of Language Acquisition*, Cambridge, MA: MIT Press.

Weydt, Harald (1976) *Noam Chomskys Werk: Kritik, Kommentar, Bibliographie*, Tübingen: Narr.

Wheatley, Barbara, Hastings, Ashley, Eckman, Fred R., Bell, Lawrence, Krukar, Gary, and Rutkowski, Rita (eds) (1985) *Current Approaches to Second Language Acquisition: Proceedings of the 1984 University of Wisconsin–Milwaukee Linguistics Symposium*, Bloomington, IN: Indiana University Linguistics Club.

White, Lydia (1985a) 'The "pro-drop" parameter in adult second language acquisition', *Language Learning* 35: 47–63.

—— (1985b) 'Universal grammar as a source of explanation in second language acquisition' in Barbara Wheatley, Ashley Hastings, Fred R. Eckman, Lawrence Bell, Gary Krukar, and Rita Rutkowski (eds) *Current Approaches to Second Language Acquisition: Proceedings of the 1984 University of Wisconsin–Milwaukee Linguistics Symposium*, Bloomington: Indiana University Linguistics Club, 43–69.

Williams, Edwin (1980) 'Abstract triggers', *Journal of Linguistic Research* 1: 71–82.

—— (1981) 'Argument structure and morphology', *Linguistic Review* 1: 81–114.

—— (1986) 'A reassignment of the functions of LF', *Linguistic Inquiry* 17: 265–300.

Zobl, Helmut (1986) 'Word order typology, lexical government, and the prediction of multiple graded effects in L2 word order', *Language Learning* 36: 159–83.

Zwicky, Arnold M. (1968) 'Naturalness arguments in syntax', *Chicago Linguistic Society* 4: 94–102.

—— (1986) 'What's become of construction types?', *Ohio State University Working Papers in Linguistics* 32: 157–62.

—— (1987) 'Constructions in monostratal syntax', *Chicago Linguistic Society* 23: 389–401.

Name index

Subject index

A-over-A principle 39, 46
abstractness in syntax 101–12
adequacy (explanatory-descriptive-
    observational) 67, 69
affix-hopping 44
anaphora 53, 57, 114, 129
applied linguistics 19, 145–54, 169–77;
    see also second language learning
audio-lingual method 146, 173–5
autonomy hypothesis 158–9
auxiliaries 48–9, 85, 161

Berkeley Linguistics Society 126

category membership 49–50, 102, 114–15
Center for Applied Linguistics 35, 146
Chicago Linguistic Society 138–42,
    187–8
Chomskyan revolution 23–38;
    sociology of 28–34
competence and performance 25, 169–70
complementation 46–7
constraints *see* principles, syntactic;
    structure preservation; etc.
constructions, grammatical 44–5, 86,
    161
contrastive analysis 145–8, 152, 167
conversational implicature 118–19
critical period hypothesis 149–50, 153
cross-over 47

D-structure 74, 163
data base of generative grammar
    81–5, 120–1
dative movement 57–8
deep structure 68, 74, 101–12, 115–17,
    135–7; debate over 115–17, 129, 173
deletion rules 165–6

derivation vs. representation 165–8
description vs. explanation 80–5, 87–8

empiricism in linguistics 24–5, 173–5
empty category principles (ECP)
    89–90, 130, 166
English-orientation 91–7
equi-NP-deletion 46, 60
error analysis 148–9
evaluation metric 76–9, 183
extraposition 46

filters 165–6
formalization 121
fuzzy grammar 121, 179, 185

gender 20–1; *see also* women in
    linguistics
generalized phrase structure
    grammar (GPSG) 19, 63–4, 156–7,
    160–7, 189
generative capacity 55–6, 183
generative grammar: convergences in
    157–68; organizational success of
    34–8; roots of 11–16, 27–8
generative semantics 42, 47–57, 62,
    83–4, 101–41, 156, 170–3, 181–2;
    birth of 101–12; compared to its
    interpretivist rival 129–37; decline
    of 113–28; legacy of 126;
    organizational problems 125–8,
    137; and second language learning
    149, 170–3; style 124–5, 141
global rules 53, 62, 117–18, 131, 134, 141,
    185–6
government 167
government-binding theory (GB) 19,
    42, 63–5, 72–5, 85–9, 156–68, 171, 189